S0-BAC-999

KARL SHAW was a journalist for several years before working in the advertising industry and in marketing – at one time for the country's largest manufacturer of stool sample jars. He currently lives in North Staffordshire, England, where he has channelled a misdirected education into several bestselling books including *Royal Babylon: The Alarming History of European Royalty* and *10 Ways to Recycle a Corpse*.

JAMES NUNN is an illustrator. Born in Bradford during the 3-day week, he learned to draw almost entirely in the dark, finally reaping the rewards 40 years later when illustrating Alex Quick's *At Night: A Guide for the Wakeful*. With *The Corbyn Colouring Book* he turned Jeremy Corbyn briefly from a mere man into a living legend before Brexit turned him back into a man again. His book *Colouring the Tour de France* restored credibility to that tarnished event. Following his 2016 flop, *What the Hygge!* (Old Street) he is wanted in Denmark for crimes against cosiness. He also designs quite nice book covers and sells his illustrations from his website: jamesnunn.co.uk. If you like his work you should get in touch. He really, really needs the money.

ABJECT QUIZZERY

ABJECT QUIZZERY

KARL SHAW

THE UTTERLY DEPRESSING QUIZ BOOK

INTRODUCTION

We're living in dark, depressing times. Wars and famines, Covid variants Alpha through Omega, racism and food banks, Brexit, Boris, billionaires flying big-boy rockets into space instead of paying taxes... Every day, a parade of awfulness. The planet is locked in a global-warming death spiral and we're knee-deep in the shit we've casually dumped in the air and the sea and all around us, on the grounds that it will probably be fine, or someone will work out a way of making it not matter in the long run, or we can always move to Mars. Experts say that watching the news can make us depressed. Tell us something we don't know.

But does it really matter in the long run? We are all doomed anyway from the moment of conception, merely sacks of chemicals drifting blindly towards the sudden abyss of death. Nothing matters. Everything we've ever done, as individuals or as a species, will eventually become ashes and count for nothing. There's no meaning in the universe, it's all just one big existential bummer. We might as well just shrivel into a ball of *ennui* and hide in the corner until it's all over.

In the meantime, here's a little quiz to help take your mind off it all. Enjoy!

Karl Shaw, 2021

QUIZ ROUNDS

KEY – ANGST RATING

These quizzes may have an effect on your mood. Please use this helpful key to ensure that you are emotionally robust enough to see it through. (Needless to say, neither donkey nor publisher accept the smallest liability for any temporary or lasting distress caused by this publication.)

1

MILDLY ENERVATED
Accompanying noise: *Hmm*
Cultural Comparison: Mark E. Smith

2

LISTLESS
Accompanying noise: *Sigh*
Cultural Comparison: Leonard Cohen

3

DEPRESSED
Accompanying noise: *Uuugh*
Cultural Comparison: Thomas Hardy

4

BREAKDOWN
Accompanying noise: *Aaaargh!*
Cultural Comparison: Edvard Munch

5

DO NOT RESUSCITATE
Accompanying noise: *Beeeeeeeep*
Cultural Comparison: Gulag Tales by Varlam Shalamov

First published in 'Great' Britain by
Old Street Publishing Ltd
Notaries House, Exeter EX1 1AJ

This paperback edition published in 2021.

www.oldstreetpublishing.co.uk*

*This website is permanently out of date. Independent publishers
simply have no time for activities that don't contribute directly to basic
survival, feeding offspring, etc.

ISBN 978-1-913083-03-8

The right of Karl Shaw to be identified as the author of this work
has been asserted by him in accordance with the Copyright, Designs
and Patents Act 1988. Not that it'll do him any good. It's a *book*.
Nobody reads any more.

Copyright © 2021 Karl Shaw

Copyright in the illustrations © 2019 James Nunn

All rights reserved. No part of this publication may be reproduced,
stored in or introduced into a retrieval system, or transmitted, in
any form, or by any means (electronic, mechanical, photocopying,
recording or otherwise) without the prior written permission of the
publisher. (Good luck getting the publisher to actually reply to any
correspondence within, like, an aeon.)

10 9 8 7 6 5 4 3 2 1

A CIP catalogue record for this title is available from
the British Library (or the British Information Hub,
as no doubt it will soon be rebranded).

Page design, illustration and typeset by James Nunn, whose blind faith
that he will one day receive adequate remuneration for his services is
both touching and pitiful.

Printed and bound in 'Great' Britain.
In the last factory with the lights still on.

What links these animals, and which is the odd one out?

ANSWERS
p.
222

Spoiler alert! Do not attempt the bonus questions overleaf until you have completed this round!

I. During training for the Mercury 5 mission in November 1961, what aspect of chimp-cosmonaut Enos' behaviour caused concerns to his NASA handlers?

    A. The noise of rocket engines made him defecate.

    B. Weightlessness sent him to sleep.

    C. He was a keen masturbator.

    D. He was fond of chewing wires.

2. Why was Laika chosen for the mission just a few days before the flight?

    A. The previous contender, Bobik, fell ill.

    B. A senior official saw the stray lurking near the barracks and felt she was a more 'Soviet' looking dog than Bobik.

    C. Bobik vanished.

    D. Bobik's flatulence caused safety concerns, and Laika was far less windy.

3. And – for a bonus bonus point – why was Laika known by the acronym ZIB?

"If it's true that our species is alone in the universe, then I'd have to say that the universe aimed rather low and settled for very little." George Carlin

TRUE OR FALSE?

1. You are more likely to be hit on the head by a part of a plane falling from the sky or crushed by a falling meteor than win the UK lottery jackpot.

2. You are more likely to be killed in an accident at work than in a road accident.

3. You are twice as likely to die from a heart attack or stroke than die from cancer.

4. You are more likely to drown in the bath than be killed in a train crash.

5. You are more likely to die by falling out of bed than by falling off a ladder.

6. If you live in the USA, you are more likely to die in a lawnmower accident than a terrorist attack.

7. You are more likely to be killed by a bee sting than by a lion, bear or snake.

8. You are more likely to die of food poisoning than choke to death while eating.

9. You are more likely to die on your birthday than on any other day.

10. You are more likely to be killed by a falling coconut than a shark attack.

ANSWERS
p.
224

"He was just a coward and that was the worst luck any man could have." Ernest Hemingway, *For Whom the Bell Tolls*

NAMED & SHAMED

Monarchs – they don't half like a monicker. But which of these regal epithets are real, and which are made up?

1. CONSTANTINE 'THE COPRONYMOUS' – thus named because he was alleged to have shat in the baptismal font at his christening.

2. LOUIS 'THE NEEDLESS' – the title refers to the man's untimely death from a fall which occurred six hours into his Coronation Feast in Liechtenstein, in 1272.

3. ALFONSO 'THE SLOBBERER' – so called due to the 12th-century Galician ruler's habit of foaming at the mouth when he lost it.

4. CHARLES 'THE PUNGENT' – due to the ambiguity of the original Occitan term, historians aren't sure whether Chaz exuded an aura of manliness, or just body odour.

5. JOHN, CHARLES, MARIA, LUDWIG AND IBRAHIM 'THE MAD' – unrelated rulers who have shared the occupational hazard of absolute power. And interbreeding.

6. HENRY 'THE IMPOTENT' – this 16th-century Castilian ruler claimed he'd been unable to consummate his first marriage due to a curse.

7. SELIM 'THE GRIM' – a draconian Ottoman Sultan, who ironically threatened to remove the testicles and tongue of anyone who called him 'the Grim'.

8. ANNE 'THE HAIRY' – today we know that the 17th-century Serbian Queen suffered from polycystic ovarian syndrome, resulting in excessive body and facial hair, as well as infertility. In her own time, she was just 'hairy'.

9. WILLIAM 'THE BASTARD' – we call him 'the Conqueror', but 11th century people were more direct..

10. ALBERT 'WITH THE PIGTAIL' – portraits of Albert III of Austria (1349-1395) emphasise the auburn plait he proudly sported. Going your own way was a family tradition: his son was called 'Albert the Peculiar'.

ANSWERS p. 225

"Sometimes I wish we could hear of a country that's out of kings." Mark Twain

What do these jobs have in common, and which is the odd one out?

A. TELEMARKETER

B. HAND SEWER

C. ORDER CLERK

D. INSURANCE UNDERWRITER

E. LOAN OFFICER

G. GIG WORKER

F. WATCH REPAIRER

H. MACHINE SETTER

I. COBBLER

ANSWERS p. 226

"I was looking for a job and then I found a job and Heaven knows, I'm miserable now." Morrissey

INGRATITUDE JOURNAL NO. 1

20 BODY PARTS YOU WISH YOU HAD
THE MONEY TO GET FIXED

BODY PART	REASON FOR INGRATITUDE
Thighs	Mottled, hairy

INGRATITUDE JOURNAL NO. 2

20 LIKEABLE CELEBRITIES YOU LOATHE FOR SOME ENTIRELY SUPERFICIAL REASON

CELEBRITY	REASON FOR LOATHING
Tom Hanks	He's definitely hiding something

1. **Why was Shakespeare's play 'King Lear' banned in Britain from 1788 to 1820?**

    A. The Archbishop of Canterbury declared the play off-limits, taking exception to the 'jokes' about illegitimate children and venereal disease.

    B. Given the bouts of insanity suffered by King George III, it was thought offensive to stage a play about a mad king.

    C. It wasn't. William Kenrick's awful satire 'King Leer' was banned, because disappointed audiences kept smashing up theatres when they couldn't get a refund.

    D. The play was blamed for a rash of fathers disowning and banishing their daughters in the early 1780s. Changes in the inheritance laws were the real cause, but 'King Lear' took the rap.

2. **Who was the last British author to have their works removed from UK libraries and destroyed?**

    A. James Joyce   **B.** D.H. Lawrence

    C. Aleister Crowley   **D.** P.G. Wodehouse

3. **Under General Franco, Spanish censors were kept busy banning pop songs, for assorted moral, patriotic and simply barking mad reasons. Are the following censors' verdicts *cierto* or *falso*?**

    A. 'Good Vibrations', Beach Boys, 1966 – the 'vibrations' were clearly a reference to orgasm.

    B. 'Just Like A Woman', Bob Dylan, 1966 – if you are 'just like a woman', but not, then you must be a homosexual.

    C. 'Donna' from the 1967 musical 'Hair' – the reference to a '16-year-old virgin' implies that 16-year-old virgins are rare.

    D. 'The Ballad of John and Yoko', The Beatles, 1969 – the song refers to John and Yoko's recent marriage in Gibraltar, a disputed territory.

ANSWERS
p.
227

E. 'Heroin', The Velvet Underground, 1967 – no probs with the brown powder, but the phrase 'for the kingdom' was misheard as 'foiking', which sounded rude.

F. 'Theme for a Dream', Cliff Richard, 1961 – Richard's suggestion that an 'angel' might make his 'dreams come true' implied an inappropriate relationship between the singer and the heavenly host.

4. Which book was banned in the Soviet Union, Nazi Germany, Yugoslavia, Greece, the US state of Tennessee and from the library of Trinity College, Cambridge, where the author was once a student?

    A. Lord Byron's *The Letters and Journals*
    B. E. M. Forster's *Maurice*
    C. Charles Darwin's *On the Origin of Species*
    D. Voltaire's *Candide*

5. Which of these much-loved children's books has NOT been banned?

    A. *Where The Wild Things Are*
    B. *Alice in Wonderland*
    C. *The Wizard of Oz*
    D. *Just William*

6 (i) In what year did James Joyce's 1922 epic *Ulysses* finally become available in the British Isles, after being banned due to its graphic depictions of defecation, masturbation and sexual intercourse?

    A. It's still banned in the Isle of Man. **B.** 1927
    C. 1963 **D.** 1936

(ii) In which other English-speaking country did it remain banned (on and off) until the mid-1950s?

    A. The USA   **B.** Ireland   **C.** Canada
    D. Australia   **E.** New Zealand

(iii) And where couldn't you buy a copy until the middle of the 1960s?

CENSOR SENSIBILITY

"Wherever they burn books they will also, in the end, burn human beings."
Heinrich Heine

7. **Which, if any, of the following are porky pies? George Orwell's** *Animal Farm* **(1943) has been banned/rejected/withdrawn in:**

A. The USA as it might expose readers to communist ideas.

B. North Korea (and other communist states) because it is critical of totalitarian regimes.

C. The UAE, because it contains references to pigs.

D. Israel, because giving the name 'Moses' to a ritually-impure raven was offensive to the ultra-Orthodox community.

E. Britain, because even Orwell's publishers feared it could jeopardise the wartime pact between Britain and the USSR.

8. **Which word, according to the famous** *Lady Chatterley* **obscenity trial of 1960, features no less than 14 times in the novel?**

A. cock   B. cunt   C. prick   D. pussy   E. balls
F. come   G. quim   H. tit   I. crack   J. clit   K. shit

9. **Which of these countries/principalities has NOT banned Dan Brown's** *Da Vinci Code*?

A. Egypt   B. Jordan   C. China
D. The Faroe Islands   E. Samoa   F. Serbia
G. The Solomon Islands   H. Sri Lanka   I. Lebanon

10. **At the end of 2001, a church in Alamogordo, New Mexico, invited the community to...**

A. a public burning of Harry Potter books.

B. join them in smashing the 'obscene' mural painted by Diego Rivera in the municipal park in 1953.

C. hang an effigy of Attorney-General Hector Balderas, who was prosecuting them for violating Freedom of Speech laws.

D. tear down the Christmas decorations made by local schoolchildren, as they were 'idolatrous' and 'pagan'.

Since 1991 the Ig Nobel Prizes have highlighted the best 'improbable research' the past year had to offer. Which of these are genuine prize-winners?

1. Welsh doctors for their cautionary medical report *'A Man Who Pricked His Finger and Smelled Putrid for Five Years'* (1998).

2. A study by Sweden's National Board for Fisheries which shows that herring use flatulence to communicate (2004).

3. An algorithm developed by Scottish programmers predicts with 96.7% accuracy whether the *Daily Mail*'s front-page headline on any given day will feature the Royal Family, immigrants, or a celebrity's dramatic weight loss (2005).

4. Australian scientists calculate the minimum number of photographs that should be taken to ensure that nobody in a group photo will have their eyes shut (2006).

5. Researchers from Brazil prove that most of the 'vandalism' done to archaeological sites is committed by armadillos (2008).

6. Researchers from the Czech Republic discover that dogs align their bodies with the earth's magnetic axis when they defecate (2014).

7. An historic collaboration between Israeli and Egyptian mathematicians answers the question 'How long is a piece of string?' (2017).

8. A team from Portugal measures to what degree human saliva is a good cleaning agent for dirty surfaces (2018).

9. French duo Roger Guisset and Bourras Bengoudifa examine scrotal temperature assymetry in groups of clothed and unclothed lab technicians (2019).

10. A global study involving researchers from Scotland, Poland, France, Brazil, Chile, Colombia and elsewhere assesses the relationship between income disparity and mouth-to-mouth kissing (2020).

ANSWERS
p.
228

"Science is a wonderful thing if one does not have to earn one's living at it."
Albert Einstein

1. **Which country has the highest murder rate?**

   A. Honduras   **B.** South Africa
   C. El Salvador   **D.** Mexico
   E. Colombia   **F.** Jamaica

2. **Which country is the world's biggest CO2 polluter?**

   A. China   **B.** USA   **C.** Russia
   D. Indonesia **E.** India   **F.** Australia

3. **In 2020, which U.S. city reported the most homicides?**

   A. Los Angeles, California
   B. Philadelphia, Pennsylvania
   C. Chicago, Illinois
   D. St. Louis, Missouri

4. **In 2020 was the England and Wales homicide rate, per million:**

   A. 14.6   **B.** 17.9
   C. 12.4   **D.** 11.7

5. **Roughly how many people in the world are currently in prison?**

   A. 500,000 or less **B.** 1 million   **C.** 2.5 million
   D. 3-4 million   **E.** 9 million

6. **In which three countries are most of those people imprisoned?**

   A. China **B.** Russia **C.** Egypt **D.** India   **E.** Australia
   F. Brazil **G.** USA   **H.** Iran   **I.** Bangladesh

7. **Which country is the biggest consumer of Class A narcotics?**

   A. USA   **B.** Brazil   **C.** Iran   **D.** Colombia,
   E. Ireland **F.** Russia   **G.** Indonesia **H.** Netherlands

ANSWERS
p.
230

8. **Which of these countries, according to UN data in 2020, has the highest infant mortality rate?**

   A. Sierra Leone **B.** Chad   **C.** Nepal   **D.** Nigeria

   E. South Sudan   **F.** Yemen   **G.** Mali   **H.** Bangladesh

---

"The better I get to know men, the more I find myself loving dogs."
Charles De Gaulle

9. And is it, per 1,000 live births:

    A. 117   **B.** 96   **C.** 77   **D.** 61   **E.** 44

10. This pile of cheeseburgers – 263 calories each – represents the average daily calorie intake for a citizen of the USA. How many cheeseburgers would represent the daily calorie intake of the countries below?

ETHIOPIA	**SURINAME**
ARGENTINA	**LIBYA**
NORTH KOREA	**BAHAMAS**
CUBA	**ERITREA**

THE KIDS' MENU

1. Which solitary carnivore often leaves single offspring to die because it prefers multiple offspring in a litter?

2. Why might you suddenly go off your cuddly female hamster?

   A. In oestrus, females spray copious amounts of eye-wateringly ammoniac urine.

   B. They sometimes eat their babies.

   C. They experience a hamster version of Pre-Menstrual Tension, making them extremely aggressive.

   D. In order to have ample reserves for their young, females gorge before hibernation – and then fart roughly once every ten minutes. For three months.

3. In order to remain the main man, which male African carnivore kills and eats the young in its social group?

4. Everyone wants to swim with dolphins. But is it really such a good idea? Only one of the below is untrue. Which one?

   A. Randy males sometimes make a play for humans.

   B. If a male spies a female with a calf, he will kill her offspring before mating with her.

   C. Groups of males will sometimes harass, then effectively gang-rape, lone female dolphins.

   D. The male initiates coitus by voiding his bowels – the resulting cloud of floating dolphin doo-doo screens him and his chosen mate from unwanted attention.

5. Which omnivorous farmyard animal performs auto-fellatio?

6. Dolphins are renowned for their inventiveness when it comes to self-pleasure, and will sometimes use dead fish as a compliant receptacle. But the use of which cetaceous sex toy truly shocked researchers when they first observed it?

   A. The eye sockets of a human skull in a shipwreck.

   B. The wake of passing freighter ships.

   C. A wriggling eel.

   D. The lower gills of the hump-backed wrasse fish.

ANSWERS p. **231**

7. **For which romantic habit is the sea otter renowned?**

   A. Drowning his mate and copulating with her corpse.

   B. Vomiting at the point of orgasm.

   C. Knocking females unconscious with his tail before mating with them.

   D. Courting her with 'gifts' of fossilized guano and the secretions of his own anal glands.

8. **Why did naturalist George Murray Levick censor his own study of the Adélie penguin?**

   A. Despite mating for life, males and females were rampantly promiscuous, a fact which Levick felt the penguin-loving Edwardian public couldn't handle.

   B. Female Adélies showed no concern for their offspring.

   C. Owing to the outrageous and revolting behaviour of the so-called 'hooligan cocks'.

   D. During a 1910-13 polar expedition, Levick was stranded for months on the Bluff Peninsula, and was forced to kill and eat large quantities of the tame and friendly penguins in order to survive.

9. **What regular spectacle can visitors to the Bear Sanctuary at Kutarevo in Croatia expect to witness?**

   A. Peter, the black bear, is in love with Ludmilla, a rare-breed goat quartered next door, and flings his dung at her whenever she appears.

   B. Alyosha – donated to the zoo by President Putin – experiences regular erections.

   C. A pair of male brown bears engages in regular acts of fellatio, accompanied by loud humming.

   D. Stepan, a male grizzly, gazes intently at an advertising hoarding visible from his den, rubbing himself and groaning.

THE KIDS' MENU

10. The females of which carnivorous species only have two nipples – meaning that the least aggressive cub of a litter of three often starves?

11. To what extraordinary lengths does the black lace weaver spider go in order to ensure that her hatchlings are well-fed? (N.B. There are two correct answers.)

   A. She lays a second round of eggs, solely as a first dinner for her babies.
   B. She feeds them the preserved and fermented remains of their father.
   C. She kills the weakest-looking babies and feeds them to the stronger ones.
   D. Three days after hatching, she feeds herself to her children.

12. What do rabbits eat as a digestive aid?

   A. Grass   **B.** Cardboard/wood/wallpaper
   C. Litter   **D.** Their own faeces

13. What is the most dangerous creature that ever lived?

   A. The sea snake   **B.** The trapdoor spider
   C. The common flea   **D.** The mosquito
   E. Tyrannosaurus Rex

14. What does the Spanish Dancer Sea Cucumber do when it feels threatened?

   A. It drops dead.
   B. It jettisons its lungs through its anus.
   C. It pretends to be dead, not just by sinking to the ocean floor but by emitting the scent of putrefying sea cucumber.
   D. It mimics the clicking of the tiny splinter fish, attracting shoals of hungry marlin and thus scaring away the threat.

15. **Why are scientists interested in the defecatory habits of the wombat?**

   A. They rarely poo. In fact some might never do so.

   B. Wombats trade their nutrient-rich poo for a type of thorny seed that collects in the scales of goanna lizards. The denser the wombat poo, the more seeds the goannas let them eat.

   C. Its cube-shaped turds – specifically, the method of their production within the wombat anus – are a puzzle to engineers.

   D. The bi-monthly (on average) wombat dump causes so much fluid loss and bleeding, it isn't clear how the species has survived.

16. **Which animal changed the course of human history by having a nasty cough?**

   A. The wolf   **B.** The Mongolian marmot

   C. The ape   **D.** The cow

THE KIDS' MENU

"You know what 'meow' means? It mean 'woof' in Cat." George Carlin

15

TYRANTS ON TOUR #1

What links these leaders and who is the odd one out?

A
Hastings Banda,
President of Malawi

B
The Shah of Persia

C
King Zog of Albania

D
King Fahd,
Saudi Arabia

E
Idi Amin,
Uganda

F
Nicolae Ceaucescu,
Romania

G
Leopold II,
King of the Belgians

H
Joseph Mobutu,
Zaire

I
Robert Mugabe,
Zimbabwe

ANSWERS p.
233

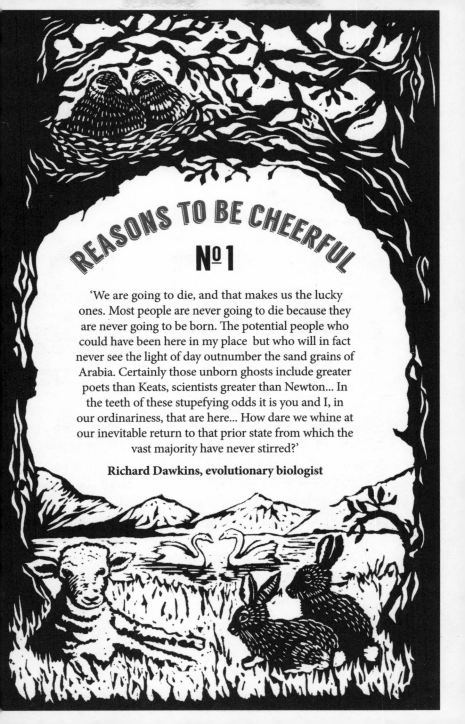

REASONS TO BE CHEERFUL

№ 1

'We are going to die, and that makes us the lucky ones. Most people are never going to die because they are never going to be born. The potential people who could have been here in my place but who will in fact never see the light of day outnumber the sand grains of Arabia. Certainly those unborn ghosts include greater poets than Keats, scientists greater than Newton... In the teeth of these stupefying odds it is you and I, in our ordinariness, that are here... How dare we whine at our inevitable return to that prior state from which the vast majority have never stirred?'

Richard Dawkins, evolutionary biologist

GENERALISSIMO KNOWLEDGE

PART ONE. Can you match the leader with their despotic foible? (One point for the correct picture, another if you can also supply the name.)

1. Dubbed 'The Chief', this island despot and former U.S. Marine tested the loyalty of his functionaries by sleeping with their wives and daughters and asking them to join in.

2. This intellectual with royal connections returned from his scholarship at the Sorbonne to orchestrate the deaths of 1.6-1.8 million of his fellow citizens.

3. The first dictator of the colour TV era, this former army cook had several political opponents beheaded live on television, specifying that the victims must wear white 'to make it easy to see the blood'.

4. This lover of Swiss cheese made a fondue of his enemies by blasting them with rocket grenades, then grilling them with flamethrowers.

5. This charmer banned all jokes under a new catch-all offence: 'speaking weird words'. Under the new decree, anything from satire to simple wisecracks could have you arrested.

6. This decorated army captain forgot to dispose of the contents of his fridge before fleeing the country he'd controlled, leaving behind the body of a school teacher hanging on a freezer hook.

7. Whilst keeping his population in thrall with magic and myths, this fatherly former physician had people stoned and burned alive, their corpses hung in trees for everyone to see.

8. Due to this leader's mission to double his country's population within a generation, women were forced to undergo monthly body searches by a 'menstrual police unit' to ensure that they weren't secretly using contraceptive devices.

ANSWERS
p. **235**

"Death is the solution to all problems. No man, no problem." Joseph Stalin

A

B

C

D

E

F

G

H

PART TWO. Every self-respecting despot needs a prop or two. Can you identify the dictator from the selection below?

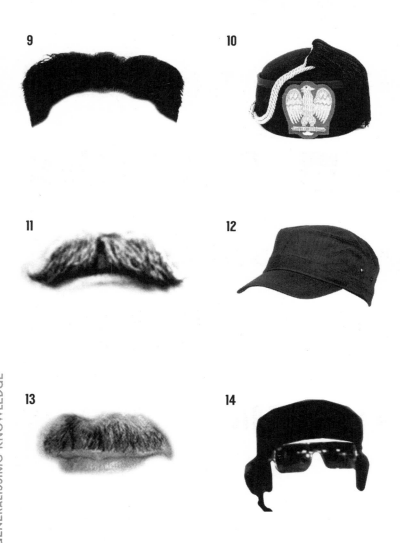

9

10

11

12

13

14

GENERALISSIMO KNOWLEDGE

20

PART THREE. Identify the psychopathic statesman from these anagrams.

15. ONe TOP US CIA THuG

16. StERNeR SoRe aDOLFS

17. HaNOVeR HeX

18. DiSUsed ShaMan

19. OH tAR Us

20. Dr AFRiCAN deMoNS

"If you want a picture of the future, imagine a boot stamping on a human face — forever." O'Brien in George Orwell's *1984*

GENERALISSIMO KNOWLEDGE

PART ONE. What do the numbers 1, 11 and 5 below represent?

100g of chocolate: **1**

100g of cinnamon: **11**

623g (22oz) jar of peanut butter: **5**

A. Nanometres of polar ice lost due to the manufacture, transportation and sale of that quantity of the product.

B. The number of marine species that could be removed from the endangered list in five years – if we all reduced our monthly consumption of the product by that quantity.

C. The number of cows that would not be slaughtered if each person replaced calories from meat with calories from that quantity of the product.

D. The maximum permissible quantity of rat hairs in that quantity of the product, according to US food safety standards.

ANSWERS
p.
236

"The early bird catches the worm. But it's the second mouse that gets the cheese." Willie Nelson

PART TWO. What is the link between these creatures and which is the odd one out?

A

B

C

D

E

F

G

H

I

MONUMENTAL **CK-UPS

1. After it had been rebuilt following a flood, the Temple of Artemis – regarded as one of the seven wonders of the ancient world – was destroyed by Herostratus. Why did he do it?

   A. An early act of terrorism – he was a local lad who hated the Greek overlords.
   B. He just wanted to be famous, for something.
   C. The goddess Artemis told him to do it because its opulence displeased her.
   D. He was just doing his job: sacking it, and the city of Ephesus, that being what Goth generals generally did.

2. The 6th-century Buddhas of Bamiyan were famously dynamited by Afghanistan's Taliban rulers in 2001. What had the Taliban suggested doing to them first?

   A. Preserving them, because there were no Buddhists left to worship them, and they might attract tourists.
   B. Removing them in sections – with expert advice – and selling them to UNESCO.
   C. Pouring concrete over them.
   D. Praying for their destruction by earthquake.

3. After the destruction, the Taliban's leader Mullah Omar said he hadn't wanted to do it, but...

   A. they were ugly to look at, and definitely not as old as people said they were.
   B. the fact that the West had protested about some old statues, and not the famine ravaging the country made him angry.
   C. the people responsible had slipped across the border, – and were CIA agents.
   D. it was the will of God.

ANSWERS
p.
237

"Here lies one who meant well, tried a little, failed much."
Robert Louis Stevenson's gravestone

4. In 2013, what happened to the 2,300-year-old pyramid, Noh Mul, one of the most important Mayan sites in Belize?

A. Short answer: floods and landslip. More accurately, the Minister of Heritage diverted flood defence funds to an offshore account before slipping the country.

B. A technician at the US Geological Service's Earthquake Hazard Unit forgot to forward a quake warning, just as pyramid repairs were at a crucial stage.

C. A construction crew smashed the complex to smithereens in order to build a road.

D. US satellite Dove 2 smashed into the building.

5. What helpful act by a pair of Utah scout leaders resulted in irreparable damage, a court case and hefty fines?

A. They gave a hefty push to a motorist stranded in the national park, whose vehicle plunged into Scrimshaw's Canyon, causing a forest fire that raged for six days.

B. They toppled a hoodoo (a unique 170-million-year-old rock formation) because it posed a health and safety risk.

C. They rescued and then dumped an unconscious cougar outside a public hospital. When it awoke it caused $1.5 million in damages to people and property.

D. They towed a caravan down Interstate Highway 70 before their reef knot gave way, causing a huge pile-up.

6 What landmark in Niger's Sahara desert was obliterated by a tipsy Libyan driver in 1973?

A. The Ténéré Tree. It was the only tree for 250 miles, its mere existence a near-miracle in such a hostile environment.

B. The Megalith of Maradi – a 22-foot basalt standing stone carved with undeciphered pictograms.

C. The Boys of Bouza – a 2,800-year-old rock painting of small male figures dancing around a larger female.

D. The Temple of Timia – a Neolithic structure, cleverly repurposed by nomads for shade and shelter.

7 In what month and year did Islamic State blow up the Triumphal Arch of Palmyra along with other monuments in the city?

    A. October 2016   **B.** October 2015

    C. September 2017   **D.** November 2014

8 Who is to blame for the ruination of the Singapore Stone – a monument covered in undeciphered script, possibly commemorating the accession of a Hindu king?

    A. The British in 1843

    B. The Japanese in 1944

    C. A self-funded French 'archaeologist' in 1902

    D. Prime Minister Lee Kuan Yew in 1964

9 Who was responsible for destroying the Great Library of Alexandria?

    A. Julius Caesar in 48 BCE

    B. Aurelian in 272 AD

    C. Diocletian in 297 AD

    D. Theophilus, Bishop of Alexandria in 392 AD

    E. Caliph Omar in 642 AD

10 What rash act, in 1759, meant that the Revd. William Gastrell had to flee New Place, the home he'd bought in a Warwickshire town just six years earlier?

    A. After dismissing talk of curses and hauntings as 'folkish dribble-drabble', the Revd. eventually set light to his medieval house and fled it in terror.

    B. After he declared the 'Kissing Well' in the grounds to be a 'heathen fancy' and bricked it up, his parishioners simply stopped coming to church.

    C. He moved the church organ into his house, ignoring warnings that the Norman timbers couldn't take the weight.

    D. Sick of tourists besieging the house, which had once been Shakespeare's, the Reverend pulled it down, and was then chased away by irate locals.

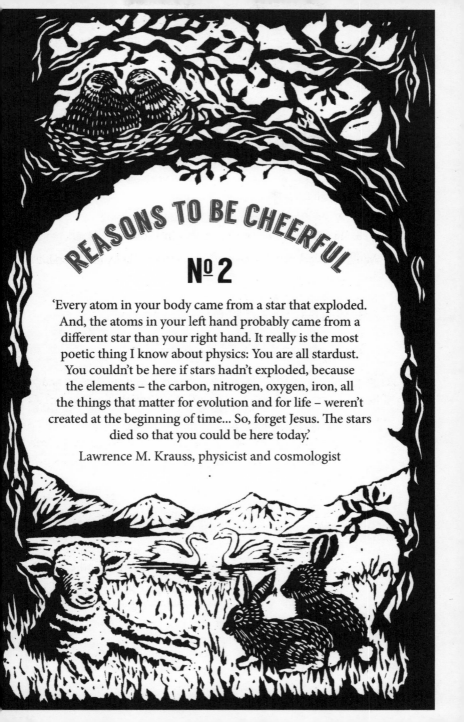

REASONS TO BE CHEERFUL

№ 2

'Every atom in your body came from a star that exploded. And, the atoms in your left hand probably came from a different star than your right hand. It really is the most poetic thing I know about physics: You are all stardust. You couldn't be here if stars hadn't exploded, because the elements – the carbon, nitrogen, oxygen, iron, all the things that matter for evolution and for life – weren't created at the beginning of time... So, forget Jesus. The stars died so that you could be here today.'

Lawrence M. Krauss, physicist and cosmologist

1. **What did Samuel Pepys do at the public execution of convicted burglar James Turner?**

    A. Wept, due to 'the wretch's pathetic countenance and the pitiful sobbing of his little daughter'.

    B. Fell asleep: it was hot and his friend Bosanquet had 'stood [him] a quart of Canary wine at luncheon'.

    C. Paid a shilling for a better view.

    D. Held a neighbour's five-year-old child on his shoulders, so that 'the little Master should see the Dead Man's Dance'.

2. **What was Lord Byron's reaction to seeing the beheading of three robbers in Rome?**

    A. Laughing hysterically.

    B. He vomited upon a Cardinal.

    C. He suffered a lifetime of nightmares.

    D. He was troubled by the first decapitation but announced himself unaffected by the lopping-off of heads two and three.

3. **Which novel was inspired by its author witnessing the public hanging of murderess Elizabeth Martha Browne in 1856, especially 'her writhing body in the tight dress'?**

    A. *Tess of the D'Urbevilles* by Thomas Hardy

    B. *The Woman In White* by Wilkie Collins

    C. *Great Expectations* by Charles Dickens

    D. *Can You Forgive Her?* by Anthony Trollope

4. **What were the last words of Marie-Antoinette at her execution in 1793?**

    A. 'Such a crowd. For me.'

    B. 'Pardon me, sir, I meant not to do it.'

    C. 'I should never have mentioned cake.'

    D. '*Ave Maria, gratia plena, Dominus tecum…*'

ANSWERS p. **238**

5. In which decade was the last person sentenced to death in the British Isles?

6. Hanged at Wandsworth Prison in 1949 for killing six young women and dissolving them in vats of industrial acid, what unusual bequest did John George Haigh make?

7 What unusual contribution did William 'Deacon' Brodie make to his own execution?

8 In the US, apart from their last meal, what do all prisoners awaiting their execution on Death Row also get?

   A. A Bible, crucifix or other religious item to hold.
   B. A phone call.
   C. An uncensored newspaper.
   D. A medical to ensure they are fit enough to die.

9. Which country still conducts public executions by stoning?

   A. Saudi Arabia
   B. Mauritania
   C. Somalia
   D. Nigeria (Sokoto state)

10 Which country executes the most people today?

"Capital punishment is the most premeditated of all murders." Albert Camus

l. One in five American millennials has never heard of...

   A. Wales **B.** The Holocaust **C.** Vinyl **D.** Woodstock

2. Mark Antony was one of the very first people to employ a

   A. personal bottom-wiper **B.** shoe-wearer
   C. food taster **D.** funeral director

3. The 19th-century Fijian chief Ratu Udre Udre holds the Guinness world record for what?

   A. Most prolific cannibal
   B. Most prolific rapist
   C. Heaviest royal person
   D. Shortest ever reign

4. In his quest to rid the world of sexual ignorance, the American academic Alfred Kinsey did what?

   A. He photographed and sketched some ten thousand penises, and three thousand vaginas.
   B. He inserted a toothbrush, bristles first, into his penis.
   C. He took detailed timings and measurements each time he masturbated (which was thrice daily).
   D. He slept with more than 1,000 men and women.

5. During World War One, what did Harrods promote as 'a useful present for friends at the front'?

   A. Soft ply toilet paper
   B. A Colt .45 revolver
   C. Morphine and syringe kits
   D. A gentleman's tongue scraping kit

ANSWERS
p.
240

6. Which country has the highest suicide rate?

   A. Guyana **B.** North Korea **C.** Japan **D.** Russia

7. **How did John Tiptoft, Earl of Worcester, earn the nickname 'the Butcher of England'?**

   A. Before he was ennobled, he was a master butcher.

   B. Having quelled a rebellion he used stakes sharpened at both ends to attach the rebels' severed heads to their rectums.

   C. During the Wars of the Roses, he fed victims to his dogs.

   D. He kept his enemies alive and had their children killed.

8. **What was unique about Elizabeth I's chief torturer Richard Topcliffe?**

   A. He liked to take his work home with him.

   B. He kept very regular hours, broke for lunch at midday and 'clocked off' every day at precisely 5pm.

   C. He couldn't stand the sight of blood.

   D. He was ordained as a priest.

9. **Concerned about sexually transmitted diseases picked up from prostitutes of inferior races, how did Himmler protect his Nazi troops?**

   A. He gave them super-strength 'Nazi condoms' (and yep, they had swastikas on them).

   B. He provided 'racially clean' female camp followers.

   C. He gave them free pornographic literature.

   D. He provided them with blow-up sex dolls.

10. **In 2005, how did Kenneth Pinyan from Seattle, Washington, effect a change in the law?**

    A. He ate his mother-in-law. Until that time there was no statute in Washington State forbidding cannibalism.

    B. He died of acute peritonitis after receiving anal intercourse from a stallion. The case lead to the criminalisation of bestiality in Washington State.

    C. He was convicted of charging customers in his bar for his performances of one-armed piano playing. Previously, one-armed players in Washington had to perform for free.

    D. He challenged a state law which stated that the harassment of Bigfoot, Sasquatch or other undiscovered subspecies is a crime punishable by a fine and/or imprisonment.

20 TOXIC PERSONALITY TRAITS YOU INHERITED FROM A PARENT AND WILL INEVITABLY PASS ON TO YOUR KIDS (IF YOU'RE FOOL ENOUGH TO HAVE THEM)

Crippling social anxiety, introversion, alcoholism...

INGRATITUDE JOURNAL NO. 4

20 APPALLING THINGS ABOUT BEING OLD/MIDDLE-AGED/YOUNG/ALIVE (DELETE AS APPROPRIATE)

Fungal infections

1. According to UNICEF estimates, how many children are combatants in the approx. 30 ongoing conflicts around the world?

    A. 55,000   **B.** 150,000   **C.** 300,000   **D.** 800,000

2. In addition to the existing billion, how many more of the world's children are estimated by UNICEF to be living in poverty due to the 2020 Pandemic?

    A. 5 million   **B.** 150 million
    C. 15 million   **D.** 1.5 million

3. What does the figure 10,000 represent?

    A. The number of children who won't go to school today, due to poverty, war, famine and climate change.
    B. The number of children leaving a UK education each year unable to meet basic standards of literacy.
    C. The number of new doctors needed, per year, to provide the world's five poorest countries with basic healthcare.
    D. The number of children who will die today of hunger.

4. According to 2019-20 statistics, which of these UK areas were in the top five for obesity rates among 10 to 11 year-olds?

    A. Walsall   **B.** Rutland
    C. Islington   **D.** Greenwich
    E. Knowsley   **F.** Sandwell
    G. Barnet   **H.** Kingston-upon-Hull
    I. Tower Hamlets   **J.** Brighton and Hove

ANSWERS
p.
241

5. What factor, according to the same study, almost doubled the chances of a 4-5 or 10-11 year-old child being obese?

    A. Having a packed lunch instead of school dinners.
    B. Not eating as a family.
    C. Not walking to and from school.
    D. Low income.
    E. More than an hour a day's 'screen time'.

6. According to UNICEF's March 2019 statistics on percentages of children aged 5-14 in full-time work, which of these countries belong in the top ten?

    A. Afghanistan   **B.** Belize   **C.** Benin
    D. Guyana   **E.** Burundi   **F.** Burkina Faso
    G. Guinea-Bissau   **H.** Cambodia   **I.** Chad
    J. China   **K.** Democratic Rep. Congo
    L. Ethiopia   **M.** Niger   **N.** Honduras
    O. Laos   **P.** Mali   **Q.** Nepal
    R. Côte d'Ivoire   **S.** Central African Republic

7. There are nearly 210 million orphans in the world. 15% of them are expected to do what before they turn 18?

    A. Graduate
    B. Take part in an armed conflict
    C. Commit a serious criminal offence
    D. Commit suicide

8. What will cause the deaths of around 2 million children this year?

    A. Tuberculosis
    B. Climate change
    C. Health-poverty: in other words, not being able to afford treatment for a curable condition
    D. Pollution

9. According to a report published in December 2020, approximately 127,240 of the 0-17 year olds in the UK were:

    A. Unable to get a school, college or nursery place.
    B. Unable to be seen by an NHS doctor within 20 hours.
    C. Homeless and in temporary accommodation.
    D. Living in a household funded solely by benefits.

10. After pets, toys and gadgets, what is the most popular Christmas list request for children?

1. Name the delightful practice pictured below. For a bonus two points, when and where did it originate?

2. What was the Japanese punishment *kusuguri-zeme*?

   A. *Comb-stripping* – being slowly flayed with iron combs.
   B. *Liquor-drowning* – being forced to drink rice spirit until unconsciousness or death sets in.
   C. *Merciless tickling.*
   D. *Digging to the end.* In the Kamakura period (1185-1353) the punishment for banditry was to dig one's own grave before being buried alive in it.

3. In 16th-century England, why would court proceedings be interrupted for the procedure depicted below?

   A. If a defendant was suspected of lying under oath, 'pressing' was deployed until they changed their story.
   B. As above, but the procedure was deployed on anyone in the court room, including lawyers, who insulted or annoyed the presiding judge.

ANSWERS
p.
242

C. If anyone claimed they'd committed a crime due to demonic possession, 'pressing' forced the entity to make itself known (or the claimant to change his mind).

D. If anyone refused to enter a plea, pressure was applied in this manner, until they did. Or died.

4. Which dystopian novel included a torture sequence inspired by this mediaeval European method?

A. *Brave New World* – Aldous Huxley
B. *We* – Evgeny Zamyatin
C. *1984* – George Orwell
D. *V for Vendetta* – Alan Moore and David Lloyd
E. *The Lathe of Heaven* – Ursula K. LeGuin

5. This is the Brazen Bull, a melodic torture device whose valves, chimes and whistles converted the screams of the roasting victim into sweet music. What happened to its creator? (Multiple choice overleaf.)

A. The Brazen Bull was part of a school design project submitted in 1916 by a 15-year-old Walt Disney.

B. Phalaris, tyrannical ruler of Sicily, was so delighted when his slave presented this device to him that he set him free, with a sack of gold.

C. The sculptor Perillos of Athens unveiled his creation to Phalaris and was then tricked into becoming its first victim.

D. He swallowed a cyanide capsule while in British custody in 1945. The Bull was one of many designs and sketches commissioned by S.S. chief Heinrich Himmler for his proposed Nazi temple at Wewelsburg.

6. What links the device below to Bonfire Night?

A. Gunpowder Plot co-conspirator Thomas Percy was 'broken upon the wheel' to make him reveal the names of his colleagues, but he died without confessing.

B. The 3rd-century martyr Catherine of Alexandria was allegedly placed upon a spiked wheel by the pagan Emperor Maxentius when she refused to renounce her faith. As soon as she touched the wheel, it shattered. Both the later torture device and the spinning firework take their name from this episode.

C. The younger brother of Gunpowder Plot instigator Robert Catesby was killed by King James 1's gaolers using this horrific method.

D. For public punishments, gunpowder was sometimes applied to the rim of the wheel, so that the spectacle of someone being slowly murdered would be accompanied by a firework display.

7. What is this?

A. A skull crusher favoured by the Spanish Inquisition.

B. The back section of a garotte still being used in Spanish prisons in the 1970s.

C. A Spanish garlic crusher.

D. An bespoke knee-capping device found in the home of Mexican cartel boss Joaquin 'El Chapo' Guzman.

8. Liars, cheats and blasphemers in the Swiss cantons of Obwalden and Nidwalden were still being placed in the above device, an Iron Maiden, in the 1860s. True or false?

9. How could this vessel, made from a hollowed-out tree trunk, be a torture device?

    A. Among the Squamish tribes of America's northwest coast, the punishment for cowardice was to be strapped to a canoe, then pushed out to sea for a slow death.

    B. Faithless women of Turkey's Laz people were made to swim across Lake Van, pursued by the elders in a boat, throwing rocks.

    C. In ancient Persia, offenders were fed a purgative of milk and honey before being sealed into such a vessel and left to sit in their diarrhoea while insects descended on them.

    D. Sea-sickness – induced by a mildly toxic potion before a choppy journey – was used by the Vikings as a means of extracting confessions.

10. Name the device.

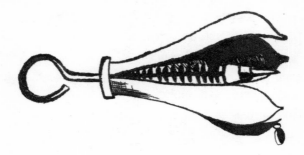

    A. The Devil's Onion
    B. The Pear of Anguish
    C. Tamerlaine's Tulip
    D. The Liar's Lily

BONUS QUESTIONS

11 Was the above device:

    A. Also known as the Pope's Pear, due to its use by the Inquisition?

    B. A fictional creation of the artist and erotic fiend Aubrey Beardsley?

    C. The final 'church instrument' shown to astronomer Galileo, thus forcing him to recant his heretical views?

    D. Part of a collection of sado-masochistic and downright ghastly equipment owned by Lord Byron and recently sold at auction in New York for $1.8 million?

12 Which Shakespeare play mentions the boat-based ordeal referenced in question 9?

"The basis of optimism is sheer terror." Oscar Wilde

THE UGLY TRUTH #2

Which of these comforting facts are TRUE and which are FALSE?

1. Britons are paragons of puritanism compared with the Russians, the booziest nation in the world.

2. Commercial flights are very safe.

3. Violence isn't rooted in our genes.

4. CPR (cardiopulmonary resuscitation) can mean the difference between life and death.

5. Nits are only attracted to clean hair.

6. You make your own luck in life.

7. Penis size doesn't matter.

8. The British monarchy more than pays for itself with the number of tourists it brings to the country.

9. Penguins mate for life, and when a male proposes he gifts his prospective mate a pebble as token of his love.

10. Several million miles away on a cold and distant Mars, a little robot is running around, collecting rock samples, testing the atmosphere and taking pictures. It is one small step in what could eventually lead to a brighter future, giving hope to us all.

ANSWERS
p.
244

What do these celebrities have in common?
And who is the odd one out?

A
B
C

D
E
F

G
H
I

ANSWERS
p.
247

1. Which alliterative judge earned unparalleled notoriety for brutal sentencing following the Monmouth Rebellion?

2. Why did he rush through his hearings at high speed?

   A. He couldn't bear to be parted from his pug dog, Hilda.

   B. He had what would today be diagnosed as a nasty case of Attention Deficit Disorder (ADD).

   C. He suffered from kidney stones, making frequent urination necessary.

   D. His wife, Hilda, beat him if he was late for dinner.

3. On what grounds did Texan judge and bar proprietor Roy Bean dismiss a murder charge against one of his regulars?

   A. In Judge Bean's view, 'it served [the victim] right for getting in front of a gun'.

   B. The saloon bar would lose considerable revenue if the accused was convicted.

   C. The victim was Californian.

   D. The accused had been drinking tequila (the so-called 'Tequila Defence' was valid in Texan courts until 1974).

4. During which famous 20th-century obscenity trial did Justice Michael Argyle pause from proceedings to tell a female detective 'you are much too attractive to be a policewoman'?

   A. The *Lady Chatterley's Lover* trial, aka Crown vs Penguin Books, 1960.

   B. The *Oz* magazine trial of 1970, sparked, amongst other things, by a cartoon of a sexually-aroused Rupert Bear.

   C. Crown vs Petrie (1978): Argyle absolved a pornographer, concluding 'depictions of males engaging in fellatio may no longer be considered any more likely to deprave than images of a man and woman engaged in the same, admittedly revolting act.'

ANSWERS
p.
247

"The more laws, the less justice." Cicero

D. Crown vs Blushes, Inc. (1978): the undercover detective had been invited to star in a spanking film in return for £11 and 'two tickets to [the première screening of] "Grease"', an offer which Argyle, famously, mistook to mean a foreign holiday.

5. **What name did the aforementioned Justice Michael Arygle give to his Nottinghamshire cottage?**

    A. The Clink   **B.** The Bench
    C. Scales   **D.** Truncheons

6. **What comment about televised cricket did Justice Argyle make to an Old Bailey jury during a trial in 1986?**

    A. Birching should be reintroduced for commentators who talked too much.

    B. Pundit Richie Benaud was 'a good argument for Australia remaining a penal colony'.

    C. It was 'just about the only thing those buggers and Bolsheviks at the BBC got right'.

    D. The scarcity of it was 'enough to make an Orthodox Jew join the Nazi Party'.

7. **What belief about childbirth was held by the 19th-century Scottish judge, Lord Monboddo, by repute 'the most learned of his day'?**

    A. Contrary to popular folk belief, babies were found under mulberry bushes.

    B. Most, if not all, were born male, but occasionally nudged in the female direction thanks to some judicious snipping by the midwife.

    C. Newborn babies all emerged with tails, which were immediately cut off by the midwives.

    D. The 'female faculty of reason' resided within the placenta, which explained why there were 'a few intelligent spinsters' but no mother 'could be considered capable of ordered thought'.

8. Why was Justice Argyle known as 'the domino judge'?

    A. He made a habit of visiting the cells to thrash the defendant at dominoes.

    B. He loved takeaway pizza.

    C. He had a habit of rubbing his hands with glee whenever a defence collapsed, exclaiming: 'One down, then the lot down, just like dominoes!'

    D. He typically passed sentences of five and seven years.

9. And what was unusual about his attitude to the death penalty?

    A. Despite being a hard-liner in many respects, he was utterly opposed to capital punishment.

    B. He thought it should be reinstated, but that the sentenced should be permitted, and equipped, to commit suicide.

    C. He thought it should be reinstated, but not, in most cases, for murder.

    D. He felt that public – and even televised – executions would be of value as a deterrent.

10. What was notable about Judge Jeffreys' treatment of the elderly Lady Alice Lisle?

    A. Brought before JJ for having offered shelter to fugitive Monmouth rebels, Lady Alice wept so bitterly that the Judge dismissed the case (and sent her a case of claret, yearly, on the anniversary of her arrest).

    B. He declared her actions to be as treasonable as any of the rebels' and ordered her to be burnt at the stake.

    C. The Judge had been minded to let Her Ladyship off with a fine until she pointed out that he was slurring his words, at which point, Jeffreys opted for death.

    D. He let her go as soon as Lady Lisle pointed out that she was a friend of the Judge's (formidable) second wife.

11. **What change did Justice Argyle's whimsical sentencing bring about?**

    A. After Argyle's retirement, all Judges were ordered to undergo psychiatric evaluation every two years.

    B. The stiff tariffs for minor offences led to a rise in more violent crimes like armed robbery.

    C. Phone box vandalism, a crime for which Argyle dished out mind-blowingly harsh sentences, all but vanished in the Birmingham area.

    D. The BBC did a U-turn on plans to move its Drama department to run-down Brum, with top BBC execs listing the proximity of Justice Argyle and his 'counter-liberal values' as a major factor.

12. **Why did Justice Rayner Goddard take two pairs of trousers with him for the final day of murder trials?**

    A. Being elderly – even by the standards of the British legal system – the Judge found it difficult to remain leak-free during the lengthy procedure.

    B. After passing sentence, he would don a tatty pair of tweed 'bags', and rush to his favourite fishing spot by the River Blackwater.

    C. He so hated imposing the death penalty that he would suffer stomach cramps and diarrhoea.

    D. He so enjoyed imposing the death penalty that he would ejaculate as he passed the sentence.

13. **How did 'Bloody Jeffreys' end up dying in the Tower of London?**

    A. When his protector King James II was ousted, Jeffreys fled London disguised as a sailor, but was unmasked in a Wapping pub by a man he'd previously sentenced, and hauled to the Tower, where he died of kidney problems.

    B. Prone to drunken outbursts, the Lord Chief Justice insulted the new monarchs at a State Banquet, and was convicted of treason.

C. Haunted by the ghosts of those he'd sentenced, Jeffreys lost his mind, and made an assassination attempt on the King.

D. King William stuck the hated JJ in the Tower for his own safety, but he died of kidney disease before better arrangements could be made.

14. What's the link between the pairs A and B, C and D, E and F?

A   B

C   D

E   F

15. The book *Town Without Pity* describes which miscarriage of justice?

A. Published in 1961, it relates events unfolding in a small German town after three American soldiers were accused of attacking a local woman.

B. Published in 1973 and shortlisted for a Pulitzer Prize, it pieces together the truth behind a series of attacks on black citizens in the town of Dothan, Alabama.

C. Published in Ireland and the UK just after the Good Friday Agreement, it investigates the 'execution' of suspected informer Paul Fintan McKee, by members of the INLA in the small town of Portrush.

D. Published in 2007, it describes the 27-year fight of Stephen Downing, unjustly imprisoned for the murder of legal secretary Wendy Sewell in the Derbyshire town of Bakewell.

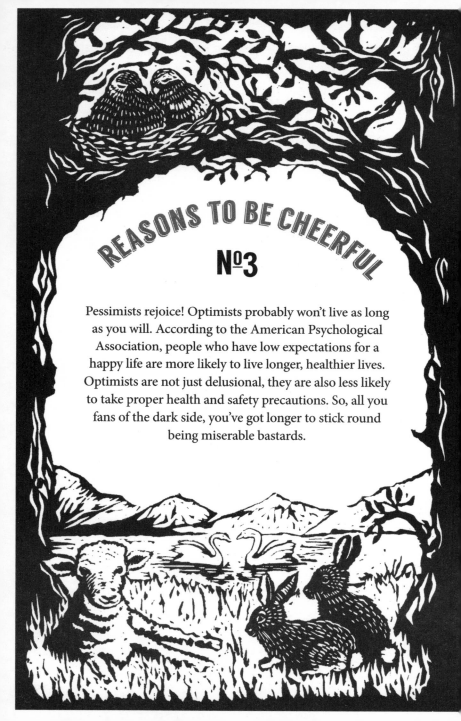

REASONS TO BE CHEERFUL

Nº3

Pessimists rejoice! Optimists probably won't live as long as you will. According to the American Psychological Association, people who have low expectations for a happy life are more likely to live longer, healthier lives. Optimists are not just delusional, they are also less likely to take proper health and safety precautions. So, all you fans of the dark side, you've got longer to stick round being miserable bastards.

One in ten transplants worldwide use black market organs harvested from the world's poorest and most vulnerable people. Can you rank these body parts in order of their estimated street value, with the most expensive first? (Award two points each for correctly guessing the most and the least valuable; one point for getting any of the rest in the correct position.)

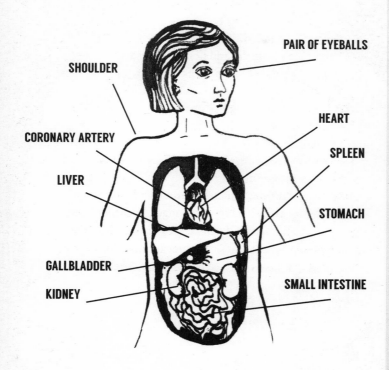

SHOULDER

PAIR OF EYEBALLS

CORONARY ARTERY

HEART

SPLEEN

LIVER

STOMACH

GALLBLADDER

SMALL INTESTINE

KIDNEY

ANSWERS
p.
250

"The guy says to the surgeon, 'Please, this transplant, make sure it's the heart of a lawyer.' The Doc says, 'Why?' Guy says, 'I want one that's never been used.'" Unknown

I. In *Huckleberry Finn*, **Mark Twain** based the character of the laughably bad poet Emmeline Grangerford on a real-life rotten rhymester named Julia A. Moore. Which of the odious odes below are Twain's inventions, and which are genuine Miss Moore at her most worst ?

> **A.** *Ode to Stephen Dowling Bots, Dec'd...*
> such was not the fate of
> Young Stephen Dowling Bots;
> Though sad hearts round him thickened,
> 'Twas not from sickness' shots.
> No whooping-cough did rack his frame,
> Nor measles drear with spots;
> Not these impaired the sacred name
> Of Stephen Dowling Bots.
> O no. Then list with tearful eye,
> Whilst I his fate do tell.
> His soul did from this cold world fly
> By falling down a well.

> **B.** *Hattie House*
> Come all kind friends, wherever you may be,
> Come listen to what I say,
> It's of a little girl that was pleasant to see,
> And she died while out doors at play.

> **C.** *Lord Byron*
> Lord Byron was an Englishman
> A poet I believe
> His first works in old England
> Was poorly received
> Perhaps it was Lord Byron's fault
> And perhaps it was not.

ANSWERS
p.
251

D.   *Little Libbie*

While eating dinner, this dear little child
Was choked on a piece of beef.
Doctors came, tried their skill awhile,
But none could give relief.

2 The verse below was composed by 'Poet to the Queen' William McGonagall in 1897. Fill in the blanks.

Oh! It was a most gorgeous sight to be seen
Numerous foreign magnates were there for to see the Queen
And to the vast multitude there of women and men
Her M------ for two hours showed h ------ to t---.

And have a go at this one, too:

Calamity in London; Family of Ten Burned To Death.
Oh, Heaven! it was a frightful and pitiful sight to see
Seven bodies charred of the Jarvis family;
And Mrs. Jarvis was found with her child,
    and both ----------,
And as the searchers gazed thereon they were surprised.
And these were lying beside the fragments of the bed,
And in a chair the tenth victim was sitting dead;

3. J. Gordon Coogler, described in his 1901 obituary as 'an excellent young man, who unfortunately thought he was a poet', inspired what?

A. Francis Xavier Enderby, the titular hero of Anthony Burgess' novel, *Inside Mr Enderby.*

B. British performance poets Pam Ayres and John Hegley.

C. An annual literary award in his name, for the 'worst book of the year'.

D. Graham Fellows' 1978 punk hit, 'Gordon Is A Moron'.

4. Which of these verses did Poet Laureate Alfred Austin write:

A. *On the illness of the Prince of Wales 1871*
Along the wires the electric message came
He is no better, he is much the same.

B. *The Jameson Raid 1896*
So we forded and galloped forward,
As hard as our beasts could pelt
First eastward, then tending northward,
Right over the rolling veldt.

5. Which word often occurred in capital letters, underlined, in the industrial verse output of Joseph Gwyer – sometimes called 'the McGonagall of Penge', since he was Queen Victoria's second poetic stalker?

A. Victoria (also Victory/Victor/Victorious, etc.)
B. Penge
C. Noble (Queen Victoria's favourite collie dog, and subject of 72 sonnets by Gwyer)
D. Potato

For a bonus point, finish this verse composed by Gwyer for his son:

I wish you Alfred now a good night;
You gives your mother great delight;
Don't you wake and ask for baa
Or you'll offend your – – – – – – –

6(i) Which of these statements about Irish poet and novelist Amanda McKittrick Ros is untrue?

A. She had a thing for alliteration, and her two poetry volumes were entitled *Poems of Puncture* and *Fumes of Formation*.
B. She wrote a series of romantic novels in which most characters had alliterative names. In her first book *Irene Iddesleigh*, the main character was Osbert Otwell; other novels were called *Delina Delaney* and *Helen Huddlestone*.

C. In *Helen Huddlestone*, McKittrick Ros combined alliteration with a fishy theme, naming characters Tim O'Tench, Sir Percival Perch, Lily Lamprey and Mattie Monkfish.

D. During meetings of The Inklings, an Oxford University literary circle, the likes of C.S. Lewis and J.R.R. Tolkien staged Ros-reading bouts, to see who could recite her works for the longest without laughing.

6(ii) Which of these quotes is NOT taken from a genuine review of McKittrick Ros' work?

    A. 'A kind of literary diabetes'

    B. 'Uniquely dreadful'

    C. 'The book of the century'

    D. 'File under farce, folly, flimflam and forget-it-why-not'

7. Responding to a bad review of her first novel by the novelist Barry Pain, she called him a 'clay crab of corruption' and alleged what?

    A. He was secretly in love with her.

    B. He had stolen the plot of two horror stories, along with a silver spoon, from her home in County Antrim.

    C. 'Barry Pain' was a pseudonym for a group of influential literary types who had made it their mission to ruin her career.

    D. She had once been his teacher, and had to reprimand him for doing something obscene during a Scripture lesson.

8. Why was eccentric country squire Henry James Pye given the job of Poet Laureate by Prime Minister William Pitt in 1790?

    A. Pitt was marrying Pye's daughter, Henrietta.

    B. Pye was a staunch Pitt supporter, but had just lost his seat in Parliament.

    C. With an increasingly volatile German King on the throne, Pitt couldn't risk giving the job to the Scottish Robbie Burns or the Irish William Blake.

    D. Clerical error: the invitation went to Pye instead of top contender, Samuel Jackson Pratt.

9. On which subject matter did the fame of poet James McIntyre (1827-1906) chiefly focus?

   A. Donkeys   **B.** Cheese
   C. Wrestling   **D.** Canadian achievements

10. What are the last three words of McIntyre's 'Ode on the Mammoth Cheese Weighing over 7,000 Pounds', composed in honour of an enormous dairy display at the 1878 Toronto Industrial Exposition?

> We have seen the Queen of cheese,
> Laying quietly at your ease,
> Gently fanned by evening breeze
> Thy fair form no flies dare seize.
> All gaily dressed soon you'll go
> To the great Provincial Show,
> To be admired by many a beau
> In the ---- -- -------

11. Which Poet Laureate wrote these lines?

> And to the left, three yards beyond,
> You see a little muddy pond
> Of water – never dry
> I measured it from side to side:
> 'Twas four feet long, and three feet wide.

   A. Wordsworth   **B.** Tennyson
   C. Masefield   **D.** Cecil Day-Lewis

12. And which Poet Laureate wrote this?

> Better stand back
> Here's an age attack,
> But the second in line
> Is dealing with it fine.

1. To what remedy did Qin Shih Huang, the first emperor of China, owe his untimely death?

   A. Blood-letting: the Emperor's medics went at it so vigorously that, eventually, one of his bodyguards interrupted them to point out that he was dead.

   B. Mercury pills – in order to ensure his eternal life.

   C. Sex with two virgins: the traditional remedy for tiredness and bloating.

   D. Cupping: instead of stimulating the flow of *qi*, a glass suction cup applied to the Imperial thigh shattered, slicing an artery and stimulating a fatal flow of blood.

2. What did Richard the Lionheart do as he lay dying from blood poisoning in 1199, following an attempt by his physician to remove a crossbow bolt in his shoulder?

   A. He forgave his doctor, endowing the man with lands that remained in his family's possession until the 1930s.

   B. He forgave the young archer who had shot the fatal arrow, but ordered his doctor's execution.

   C. He spent his last hours with his horse, Carus, and his terrier Septimus: 'beestes [being] fyner physick than an horde of chirurgeones'.

   D. Wild with pain, the King tipped the contents of a chamber pot onto his wound; its effects were irrelevant, as he died doing it.

3. Which two of these remedies were NOT applied to Charles II in the aftermath of a massive stroke?

   A. Plasters infused with crushed cantharides beetles – causing burns and blisters.

   B. Twice-hourly enemas of rock salt, buckthorn syrup and orange infusion of metals in white wine.

   C. Tinctures of bezoar stone – gallstones from the stomach of a goat.

ANSWERS p. **254**

"The art of medicine consists of amusing the patient while nature cures the disease." Voltaire

D. A head-to-toe ointment composed of nuns' urine and fresh placentas.

E. Spirits boiled inside a human skull.

F. Toads placed in the mouth and anus.

4. **What fatal advice did Robbie Burns receive from his doctor, after he contracted rheumatic fever in 1795?**

A. Stand up to his waist in the freezing waters of the Solway for as long as he could, then sink several glasses of port.

B. To take a holiday 'somewhere warm and dry'.

C. To drink a 'dram o' breist milk, warm frae the tit.'

D. Bed rest, fluids, fresh fruit and amusing company.

5. **As George Washington lay dying with a throat infection in December 1799, what proposals did the architect and inventor William Thornton turn up with?**

A. He asked the president to endorse a 'Rejuvenating Elixir' he'd developed with the aid of an Apache medicine man.

B. To halt the President's deterioration by placing him in a 'mesmeric trance'.

C. The founder of 'Thorntonism', a mix of geometry, numerology and sheer hogwash, was convinced that Washington just needed to move his bed.

D. He intended to pinch the President's skin, blow air into his nostrils and give him a transfusion of lamb's blood.

6. **In the autumn of 1881, why was the inventor of the telephone Alexander Graham Bell rushed to the bedside of the recently-shot US President James Garfield?**

A. So that the President could make an inaugural, PR-winning 'first' telephone call.

B. The medics hoped that Bell's other great invention – the metal detector – could locate the bullet, which they'd failed to find by rummaging around inside the wound.

C. Garfield insisted he had something very important to tell his boyhood friend, Bell, but refused to use the telephone.

D. It was a cock-up. Garfield's executor, Alexander Grainger Ball, was staying at the same hotel as the inventor.

7. **What was the unusual 'medical' defence offered by Charles Guiteau, when he went on trial for assassinating Garfield?**

A. A Chinese doctor in Baltimore had inserted the idea of assassinating the President into Guiteau's brain whilst lancing a boil.

B. He'd been told the President had weeks left to live, so he had not murdered him, just changed the departure date.

C. It was the 80 days of medical tampering that did for the President, not the small wound made by Guiteau's bullet.

D. The President would soon be resurrected, which would make Guiteau's execution unlawful.

8. **Name the ancient cataract-removing technique employed by John Taylor, self-styled 'Opthalmister to the Pope and every crowned head in Europe' – and which finished off Johann Sebastian Bach.**

A. Crochet   **B.** Crewel   **C.** Couching   **D.** Bordure

9. **What watery fate did Thailand's Queen Sunandha Kumariratana meet in 1880?**

A. She was advised to drink the water from a sacred well to cure a nasty chest infection, and contracted typhoid.

B. She was sent to recover from an illness at the family retreat on Koh Prong island, but instead succumbed to the December 1880 *tsunami*.

C. The elephant belonging to her court physician went berserk and knocked her carriage into a river.

D. Numerous people watched her drown when her boat capsized: touching a monarch was a capital offence.

10. What circumstances led to a member of the British Royal family dying from a 'speedball' of morphine and cocaine?

A. In December 1861, rival British and German doctors couldn't agree on the best treatment for Prince Albert, resulting in the sedative/stimulant combo that – in all probability – finished him off.

B. Just before midnight on 20 December 1936, George V's doctor Lord Dawson slipped the deadly dose, so that the Royal death would be announced in the respectable morning papers and not the trashy evening tabloids.

C. In 1892, the public were told that Prince Albert Victor, eldest son of Edward VII, had succumbed to the flu pandemic; medical papers unearthed later suggest he was just partying too hard.

D. In 1942 George, Duke of Kent, a medal-winning swimmer, drowned in a lake at a Swiss spa centre, where strong narcotics were being used to 'cure' alcoholism and depression.

"You fall out of your mother's womb, you crawl across open country under fire, and drop into your grave." Quentin Crisp

Which of the following are conditions recognised by medical experts, and which are fake?

1. **Textitis** – the pain you get throughout your wrist and hands after constant mobile phone use.

2. **Brexit-induced depression** – the cause of a 13.5% rise in UK prescriptions for anti-depressants since June 2016.

3. **Cyberchondria** – Googling obsessively for health care information in fear that you could have some rare disease you have read about on a health-oriented website, regardless of the reliability of the information.

4. **Instagram Disorder** – a 2020 study found a consistent link between posting edited selfies and eating disorder risk factors.

5. **FOMO syndrome (Fear of Missing Out)** – psychological disorder characterised by anxiety that you are missing out on some important or exciting experience e.g. not staying up to date on your Facebook or Twitter feeds.

6. **Phantom vibration syndrome** – a sign of mobile phone dependency, it manifests as the sensation that your phone is vibrating in your pocket when it isn't.

7. **3D psychosis** - eye strain, blurred vision, dizziness, headaches, nausea or hallucinations after viewing 3D content.

8. **Shit-life syndrome** – a set of symptoms such as depression, alcoholism and lower life expectancy, caused by being poor.

9. **Photoshop Blindness** – in 2021, a pan-European study found a link between screen-time and an impaired ability to spot when images of humans had been airbrushed.

10. **Selfitis** – condition that causes people to post too many selfies on the internet.

ANSWERS
p.
256

20 SPECIES THAT SHOULD NEVER HAVE BOTHERED TO EVOLVE

Wasps (I know, they eat harmful aphids, etc, etc, blah, blah)

20 USELESS THINGS YOU WASTED HOURS LEARNING ABOUT AT SCHOOL

Physics

1. In his 1877 book *Diseases of Women*, why did American surgeon Lawson Tait warn young ladies against music lessons?

    A. It would harm their delicate ears.

    B. It would upset their ovaries and cause 'a great deal of menstrual mischief'.

    C. It would give them muscular and unfeminine arms.

    D. It might give them 'lewd and lascivious thoughts'.

2. Which of these horror films, ranked by IMDB as among the greatest movies of all time, was ignored by the Academy Awards?

    A. Psycho   **B.** Dr. Jekyll and Mr Hyde
    C. The Exorcist   **D.** The Shining

3. Who or what are the most likely survivors of nuclear war?

    A. Humans   **B.** Rats
    C. Cockroaches   **D.** Conan the bacterium

4. Which of the following statements is false?

    A. In the Middle Ages, a child with ginger hair was assumed to have been conceived through 'unclean sex' or during menstruation.

    B. In ancient Egypt, gingers were buried alive as sacrifices to the god Osiris.

    C. The ancient Greeks believed redheads turned into werewolves after they died.

    D. Medieval paintings often depicted Judas with flaming hair and beard, fuelling centuries of discrimination.

5. Nicholas Wood, who lived in Kent in the 17th century, was a local folk hero on account of his ability to do what?

    A. Eat an entire sheep except the skin, wool, and horns.

    B. Eat seven dozen rabbits in a single sitting.

    C. Drink the contents of a 'shitte bukett'.

    D. Eat a wheelbarrow full of raw eggs.

ANSWERS
p.
257

6. In 2007 what did Welsh rugby fan Geoffrey Huish do to mark his team's victory over England?

    A. He bit the pub landlord's ear off.

    B. He bit a policeman's ear off.

    C. He tore his own ear off and ate it.

    D. He cut off his testicles and took them to show his mates.

7. Globally, which is the biggest killer?

    A. drugs   **B.** alcohol   **C.** war   **D.** work

8. In a November 2020 survey of British people aged 16-75, how many said they believed the true purpose of the Covid vaccine was to track and control the population?

    A. 14%   **B.** 27%   **C.** 39%   **D.** 42%

9. Which of the following statements about Queen Victoria is untrue?

    A. She survived eight attempts to kill or harm her.

    B. Her Coronation was marred by bad omens: an elderly peer was injured, the ring was forced onto the wrong finger, and a Bishop prematurely declared the ceremony over.

    C. She described her own children as 'ugly', 'nasty' and 'frog-like'.

    D. She wore crotchless panties: they were more hygienic.

    E. She refused to breastfeed, which she thought only suitable for women of low social class.

10. What event secured the reputation of Bartholomew Binns as 'Britain's Worst Hangman'?

    A. The drunken and myopic Binns almost succeeded in hanging Durham Gaol's chaplain before guards intervened.

    B. Binns said he 'couldn't go through' with his first strangling gig, and fled Liverpool's Walton Gaol in tears.

    C. He only lasted four months in the job – botched executions were his speciality – and it took his last customer 13 minutes to die.

    D. Binns hanged himself by mistake while attempting to fix a jammed trapdoor.

Can you recognise these ten despots from their anagrams?

1. RILL Of DEath
2. So SoFTer SLaNDERER
3. FaLSESt JOiN
4. EviL BAd OBduRacy
5. SLeek DRuNK ANaL HOAX
6. sUN Said He's MAD
7. BRUTE moB RaGe
8. DAbBLE as SANe JOKe
9. SO dAFt RELIC
10. I'M SuLKiNG

ANSWERS
p.
258

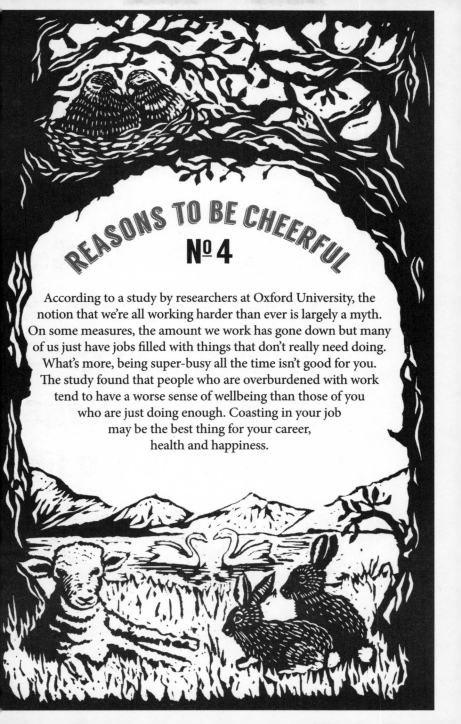

REASONS TO BE CHEERFUL
Nº 4

According to a study by researchers at Oxford University, the notion that we're all working harder than ever is largely a myth. On some measures, the amount we work has gone down but many of us just have jobs filled with things that don't really need doing. What's more, being super-busy all the time isn't good for you. The study found that people who are overburdened with work tend to have a worse sense of wellbeing than those of you who are just doing enough. Coasting in your job may be the best thing for your career, health and happiness.

How many serial killers can you pick out? There are ten to find.

KILLER WORD SEARCH #1

B	O	S	T	O	N	S	T	R	A	N	G	L	E	R
H	H	I	X	P	W	U	D	I	T	C	G	M	D	K
A	V	H	O	C	S	I	J	S	D	P	J	S	G	T
R	T	C	H	A	L	B	E	R	T	F	I	S	H	H
O	E	G	G	O	I	E	F	X	E	E	Q	W	I	E
L	D	L	J	E	L	E	F	E	F	E	U	E	U	M
D	B	R	E	K	E	M	R	R	E	T	E	R	P	A
S	U	K	M	Q	U	D	E	D	G	E	I	N	C	D
H	N	E	M	P	E	D	Y	S	I	S	J	O	P	B
I	D	V	E	E	W	E	D	E	E	G	U	S	C	U
P	Y	W	E	E	J	V	A	U	E	M	O	O	W	T
M	G	J	S	E	C	E	H	D	I	E	C	T	K	C
A	X	T	W	D	T	E	M	O	M	S	J	O	V	H
N	E	O	G	U	I	W	E	I	C	G	K	X	I	E
Y	O	R	K	S	H	I	R	E	R	I	P	P	E	R

ANSWERS
p.
258

"One day men will look back and say I gave birth to the twentieth century."
Jack the Ripper

1. What does the formula '30-thousandths of a millimetre per minute' represent?

    A. How fast human cells grow in the first 12 weeks after conception.
    B. The rate of cell death.
    C. The speed of tumour growth in the most virulent types of cancer.
    D. The rate of weight gain in the USA from 1950 to 2010.

2. For most of us, at what age do our cognitive skills start to decline?

    A. 12   B. 27   C. 33   D. 41

3. What health milestone do most people hit at the age of 55?

    A. 87% of all people living beyond this age will do so accompanied by a chronic, life-shortening condition.
    B. If you don't need glasses, a hearing aid, daily medication or pain relief at 55, you're probably already dead.
    C. 55 is the age at which your DNA begins to degenerate, increasing your risk of cancers.
    D. It's when 'morbid' processes like fat gathering around organs and plaques building in the brain start working faster than health-sustaining ones like red blood cell production and cytokine generation.

4. Every year the NHS spends around £1 million on the removal of foreign bodies from rectums. TRUE or FALSE?

5. There are more bacteria than human cells in your body. TRUE or FALSE?

6. Which of these activities is the most dangerous?

    A. Suppressing a sneeze.   B. Holding in a fart.
    C. Yawning.   D. Holding in your pee.

ANSWERS
p.
258

"The meaning of life is that it stops." Kafka

65

7. You can fail a breathalyser test even if you haven't touched a drink. TRUE or FALSE?

8. Extreme dieting can cause your brain to eat itself. TRUE or FALSE?

9. One in a thousand people is prone to sudden eyeball explosion. TRUE or FALSE?

10 Human semen is packed with nutrients. TRUE or FALSE?

BONUS QUESTION: From how many humans would a vampire need to suck all the blood, in order to maintain a minimum daily requirement of 1500 calories?

    A. one
    B. three to five
    C. five to seven
    D. ten to twelve

What links these people and who is the odd one out? (NB. One is more widely known by her married name.)

A
Lise Meitner
1878-1968

B
Rosalind Franklin
1920-1958

C
Vera Rubin
1928-2016

D
Cecilia Payne
1900-1979

E
Chen Shiung Wu
1912-1997

F
Ida Tacke
1896-1978

G
Nettie Stevens
1868-1912

H
Esther Lederberg
1922-2006

I
Maria Skłowdowska
1867-1934

ANSWERS p. 260

"As long as she thinks of a man, nobody objects to a woman thinking."
Virginia Woolf

Can you match the global warming sceptics with their quotes?

1. 'The global warming alarmists are the equivalent of the flat-Earthers.'

2. 'The whole thing is based on a fallacy: that our fossil fuels are actually going to run out...'

3. 'An increase of two or three degrees wouldn't be so bad... we could spend less on fur coats, and the grain harvest would go up.'

4. 'Global warming, at least the modern nightmare vision, is a myth. I am sure of it and so are a growing number of scientists. But what is really worrying is that the world's politicians and policy makers are not.'

5. 'The concept of global warming was created by and for the Chinese in order to make US manufacturing non-competitive.'

6. 'The climate change argument is absolute crap.'

7. '[we should not] persuade the world to impoverish itself by moving from relatively cheap carbon-based energy to much more expensive non-carbon energy.'

8. 'If you believe in God, then intellectually you cannot believe in manmade global warming.'

9. 'Climate has been changing for four billion years. [The] Sahara has become a desert, it isn't because of industry. You need to be as arrogant as men are to believe we changed the climate.'

10. 'Climate change is to this century what eugenics was to the last century. It's hysteria and a lot of it is junk science. And when it's as discredited as eugenics, you know a lot of people are going to look very foolish and heartless.'

ANSWERS
p.
262

"Man, we could use a big fat dose of global warming!" Donald Trump

A

Tony Abbott

B

Nicolas Sarkozy

C

Vladimir Putin

D

Nigel Farage

E

Nigel Lawson

F

Ted Cruz

G

David Bellamy

H

Donald J. Trump

I

Rush Limbaugh

J

Sarah Palin

SOME LIKE IT HOT

1. **What persistent rumour attached to the Shah of Iran's state visit to the UK in 1873?**

   A. Taking offence at a stray remark from the Archbishop of Canterbury, Charles Longley, the Shah demanded his beheading.

   B. Whilst staying at a royal palace, he had one of his retinue garroted with a bowstring, and the body buried somewhere in the grounds.

   C. The Shah's visit is the persistent rumour. It was his Prime Minister, Ali Asghar Khan who made the trip in 1873, and it passed without event.

   D. Bigging up the delights of Persian tobacco to the Duchess of Kent, the Shah withdrew the pipe from his mouth and forced it between Her Ladyship's lips.

2. **What request did Idi Amin make of the Queen, by letter?**

   A. Amin asked for tape recordings of all episodes of 'The Archers' broadcast since 1952.

   B. To appoint him King of Scotland.

   C. To send shortbread – a delicacy he had not tasted since serving with the British Army in Kenya.

   D. To arrange his visit to Scotland, Ireland and Wales 'to meet the heads of revolutionary movements fighting against your imperialist oppression.'

3. **What advice did Ann-Aymone, wife of the French President, Valéry Giscard D'Estaing pass to other state leaders, following a visit from Romania's Mr and Mrs Ceausescu?**

   A. Lock up your daughters.

   B. Lock up your sons.

   C. Lock up your booze.

   D. Lock up your valuables.

ANSWERS
p.
262

4. **What inappropriate gift did Britain make to President Ceausescu?**

    A. A horse named Nicalas – in Romania, calling somebody 'cal', a horse, is an insult.

    B. A rifle and telescopic sight (he would be executed by firing squad in 1989).

    C. Instead of the memoirs of 19th-century socialist Ion Petrescu, exiled in London, he was presented with the works of Romania's wartime fascist leader Ion Antonescu.

    D. A case of British wine (he didn't drink and had twice attempted to outlaw alcohol in his country).

5. **What event marred the start of an overseas visit by President Mobutu of Zaire?**

    A. He had not bothered to pack his passport.

    B. Officials declined to issue a visa for his pet Yorkshire terrier, Cara.

    C. A Paris-Charles de Gaulle airport baggage handler named Auguste Patasse – exiled after Mobuto's violent takeover in 1960 – subjected the dictator to a curse-filled harangue in full view of dignitaries and journalists.

    D. The luggage belonging to Mobuto and his entourage got mixed up with that of an Austrian convent school bound for Lourdes.

"A leopard cannot change its spots. But it can be made into a fetching hat."
Unknown

Brush up on your mass killings and brutal massacres...

1. In 1002, the Feast Day of St. Brice (a 5th-century Frankish bishop) was a far from jolly affair for England's...

   A. **SHEEP**: the population embarked on a mass slaughter in order to prevent the Vikings from pillaging this valued resource over the winter.

   B. **DANES**: King Aethelred the Unready went after various Danish communities, fearing an insurrection among these settled incomers.

   C. **WITCHES**: in a state of heightened tension over Viking raids and bad harvests, witches were slaughtered up and down the land.

   D. **BIRDS**: flocks of starlings and swallows dropped dead from the sky in Norwich and Lincoln, an event interpreted as an omen of dynastic downfall.

2. What caused the most deaths during William the Conqueror's 1068 charm-offensive, aka 'The Harrying of the North'?

   A. The massacre of Northern settlements who'd sided with the Danish-Scots rebellions.

   B. The flu – William's Norman troops were raddled with something akin to avian flu, and passed it on.

   C. The famine that resulted after the burning of crops and killing of livestock.

   D. Floods – William needn't have bothered with the Harrying, as devastating rains came shortly afterwards, drowning cattle, washing away fields and destroying whole towns.

ANSWERS p. **263**

"I hate mankind, for I think myself one of the best of them, and I know how bad I am." Dr Johnson

3. **Was the St Bartholemew's Day Massacre...**

   A. a wave of Roman Catholic mob violence in 1572, directed against Huguenot Protestants.

   B. an Irish-American gangland killing at a wedding at the Chicago church of St Bartholemew, in 1960.

   C. the crushing of an uprising by Chinese labourers in Portuguese-owned Macao on August 24th, 1709, the Feast Day of Saint Bartolomeo.

   D. a spate of persecutions on the Feast Day of Saint Bartholomew in 1938, carried out by the Soviet authorities against the Armenian Apostolic Church, including the murder of clergy and the destruction of religious buildings.

4. **Where did Prince Dodo order his troops to slaughter approximately 800,000 people over a 10-day period in 1645?**

5. **What term entered popular usage in 1768 at the Massacre of St George's Fields, after troops fired on supporters of radical MP John Wilkes?**

   A. 'A short, sharp shock'   B. 'A line in the sand'

   C. 'Reading the Riot Act'   D. 'Angry young men'

6. **What was the motive behind the September Massacre of prisoners in Paris (and other cities) in 1792?**

   A. The Revolutionary authorities feared that Royalists would spring the prisons open, freeing a mass of people who would gratefully join the anti-Revolutionary cause.

   B. In the logic of Revolutionary thought, all criminals were enemies of the People.

   C. An outbreak of 'jail-fever' (probably smallpox), which spread via prison guards to the general population, was seen as a threat to the Revolutionary cause.

   D. Getting rid of the jailed priests and nobles.

7. Where did the original Peterloo Massacre take place?

A. At Pieterloo – in Belgium, as townsfolk took revenge on French troops injured or captured at Waterloo.

B. At Peterloo – a sugar plantation in Australia in 1890, where Pacific Islander workers turned on the bosses.

C. In Nepal in 1816, where Lt. Col. Sir James Petersleigh's treatment of Gurkha rebels was so violent that it was dubbed 'Petersleigh's Waterloo', then shortened to 'Peterloo'.

D. At St Peter's Fields, Manchester – on 16th August 1819, sabre-wielding cavalry charged a crowd protesting about voting rights.

8. What revolutionary symbol debuted during the Merthyr Rising in 1831?

A. The rebels brandished the tools of their trades – hammers and sickles – as defence against the Highland Cavalry. Later the two images started appearing on flags.

B. Red flags were made from cow's blood, symbolising the sacrifices made thus far, and the unity of all men.

C. The clenched fist – rebuked by the Judge for continually clenching and unclenching his hand, rebel miner Lewis Lewis retorted, 'Have you ever swung a pickaxe for 12 hours a day, Your Honour?'

D. The red star: Merthyr rebels tore these badges from the coats of the soldiers suppressing the revolt.

9. Which Native American chief was shot dead during the 1890 Massacre of Wounded Knee (sometimes called the 'Battle of Wounded Knee' to make it sound like a fair fight)?

A. Sitting Bull   B. Buffalo Bill
C. Geronimo   D. Tecumseh

10. What caused the British public to raise £26,000 for Brigadier Reginald Dyer, following a revolt in Amritsar, India, in 1919?

A. In the midst of a protest-turned-riot against British rule, Dyer had personally shepherded some 55 orphans to safety.

B. Dyer had been sacked after ordering the massacre of hundreds of anti-British demonstrators in the walled Jallianwala Gardens. The public wished to show their support.

C. Dyer gave the trapped rioters the option of going home – and they all did so. He was court-martialled for his actions, but the British public rewarded his act of humanity.

D. The funds were not for Dyer, but donated 'in his name' to victims of his brutality by disgusted readers of the socialist *Daily Worker*.

What links these images, and which is the odd one out?

ANSWERS
p.
263

Below are lyrics from the national anthems of **MEXICO, VIETNAM, FRANCE, TUNISIA, ARMENIA, ALBANIA, ALGERIA, HUNGARY, ITALY** and **TURKEY** – but which is which?

1.   We swear by the lightning that destroys,
      By the streams of generous blood being shed
      When we spoke, nobody listened to us
      So we have taken the noise of gunpowder as our rhythm
      And the sound of machine-guns as our melody.

      CLUE: Allegedly written in blood on a cell wall by a political prisoner, it became the official anthem in 1962.

2.   The blood surges in our veins
      We die for the sake of our land
      For the flag, for our country
      To die is a fine thing! Our past cries out to us:
      Have a disciplined soul! To die is a fine thing!

      CLUE: Read from right to left.

3.   Only he who is a born traitor
      Averts from the struggle.
      He who is brave is not daunted,
      But falls – a martyr to the cause.

      CLUE: This was published as a poem in a newspaper called *Liri e Shqipërisë* in 1912.

4.   Everywhere death is the same
      Everyone dies only once
      But lucky is the one
      Who is sacrificed for his nation.

      CLUE: This one had two lives: 1918-20, again from 1991 onwards.

ANSWERS p. **264**

5.   But no freedom's flowers return
From the spilled blood of the dead
And the tears of slavery burn
Which the eyes of orphans shed.

CLUE: Zsa Zsa knew it off by heart.

6.   Let us join in the cohort
We are ready to die!
We are ready to die!
Mercenary swords, they're feeble reeds.
The Austrian eagle has already lost its plumes
The blood of Italy and the Polish blood
It drank, along with the Cossack. But it burned its heart.

CLUE: Ends in a shouted 'Si!'

7.   Who would not sacrifice their life for this paradise of a
country?
Martyrs would burst forth should one simply squeeze the
soil! Martyrs!
May God take my life, my loved ones, my possessions from
me if He will,
But let Him not deprive me of my one true homeland in
the world.

CLUE: The fez went out when this came in.

8.   Our flag, red with the blood of victory, bears the spirit of
the country
The distant rumbling of the guns mingles with our march-
ing song
The path to glory is built by the bodies of our foes
For too long have we swallowed our hatred. Be ready for all
sacrifices!

**CLUE: A rival contender for the anthem was a song called
'Killing Fascists'.**

9. The bloody flag is raised, the bloody flag is raised.

Do you hear in the countryside, the roar of these savage
   soldiers,

They come right into our arms, to cut the throats of your sons!

May a tainted blood irrigate our furrows!

**CLUE: Shares a certain quality with 'New, York, New York' and
'London Calling' .**

10. War, war without quarter to any who dare

to tarnish the coats of arms of the country!

War, war! Let the national banners

be soaked in waves of blood.'

**CLUE: Sung in the second-most widely spoken language in
the world.**

BONUS QUESTIONS

1. Were the words to 'God Save The Queen/King' first written in:

   A. 1745 – to inspire loyalty to King George II at the time of
   the Jacobite Rebellion.

   B. 1067 – adapted from the Saxon ditty *Gottas swyf fulkens
   kung* to encourage obedience to the new Norman regime.

   C. 1558 – a hymn composed by Andrew Rush to mark the
   coronation of Queen Elizabeth I.

   D. 1819 – by Poet Laureate Robert Southey to replace
   Victoria's obviously Teutonic predecessor, George ze
   Third.

**2. Which of these countries has also used the *'God Save'* tune for its
own national anthem?**

   A. Switzerland   **B.** Liechtenstein   **C.** Sweden
   D. Norway   **E.** Russia

"If you live long enough, you'll see that every victory turns into a defeat."
Simone de Beauvoir

79

34

OR NOT TO BE...

1. On 7 November 1910, the 82-year-old novelist Leo Tolstoy left his home on foot, intending to 'put aside his worldly life and spend his last days in solitude and contemplation'. What happened next?

    A. He was run over by a train.
    B. After falling ill on a train, he spent his final days at a rural railway station, besieged by Pathé film crews, fans and secret policemen.
    C. He ended up on a Moscow railway station where, confused, lost and about to be deported for vagrancy, he was eventually recognised by a bookish policeman.
    D. He caught flu waiting for a train, went home, recovered and lived another decade before choking on *pirogi*.

2. In which great English river did Virginia Woolf drown herself?

    A. The Uck   B. The Arun
    C. The Tamar   D. The Ouse

3. Philip Larkin once wrote: 'Depression hangs over me as if I were...' What?

    A. Ireland   B. Eeyore
    C. Iceland   D. Wellington

4. What is the modern name of the Baltimore tavern where macabre tale-teller Edgar Allen Poe was allegedly found in a semi-conscious state four days before his death in 1849?

    A. The Nevermore
    B. Usher's House
    C. The Arthur Gordon Pymm
    D. The Horse You Came In On

ANSWERS
p.
265

5. According to the terms of his will, how were the remains of playwright Tennessee Williams to be laid to rest?

    A. His ashes were to be shot out of a circus cannon 'somewhere south of San Diego, direction of Tijuana'.

B. By being 'put outside on a Monday, with all the other trash.'

C. They were to be sewn into a canvas bag and dropped in the sea 'as close as possible to where [the poet] Hart Crane was given by himself to the great mother of life which is the sea.'

D. Despite no prior connection to the faith, he wanted a Jewish funeral and burial at Brooklyn's Beth Olam cemetery.

6. **All the below happened to Ernest Hemingway, but which one actually killed him?**

A. anthrax	**B.** a fractured skull
C. pneumonia	**D.** a ruptured kidney
E. diabetes	**F.** two plane crashes
G. hepatitis	**H.** a gunshot to the head
I. skin cancer	**J.** a ruptured spleen
K. malaria	**L.** a crushed vertebra

7. **What was the name of the cocktail sunk in vast quantities by Dylan Thomas shortly before his death in New York in November 1953?**

A. Boilermaker

B. Black and Tan

C. Bootmaker

D. Bronx

E. Manhattan

8. **Which of these statements about poet Emily Dickinson is NOT true?**

A. Wrote over 1,800 hundred poems yet less than a dozen were published in her lifetime.

B. Became so reclusive that she would only speak to visitors through a closed door.

C. Invented the term 'Purple Haze' later immortalised by Jimi Hendrix.

D. Her father bought her books but begged her not to read them, in case they would 'joggle her mind'.

"Life is first boredom, then fear." Philip Larkin

9 On October 4th 1974, the Pulitzer-prize winning poet Anne Sexton donned her mother's fur coat, downed a glass of vodka, and asphyxiated herself in her garage. Which of these statements about her is **NOT** true?

   A. She is acknowledged as an influence by both Morrissey and Peter Gabriel.

   B. She had a bit-part in the Halloween episode of the first (1962) season of 'The Beverly Hillbillies'.

   C. She was greatly encouraged by 1960 Pulitzer winner W.D. Snodgrass (who wrote under the pseudonym S.S. Gardons).

   D. She was a member of a jazz-rock combo that played at a fundraising gig for Senator Eugene Joseph McCarthy.

10. TRUE or FALSE? Sylvia Plath's *Bell Jar* is/was/has been...

   A. initially published under the pseudonym 'Victoria Lucas', and met a lukewarm response.

   B. adapted into Bislama pidgin by Ken Campbell.

   C. Hollywood slang for a project to avoid, after being optioned 22 times for film adaptations that never appeared.

   D. the only literary work besides the Harry Potter series to have been mentioned on 'Match of the Day'.

How many potentially deadly diseases can you find in the puzzzle below? There are 11...

S	Z	S	X	A	P	P	N	E	U	M	O	N	I	A
I	A	R	A	B	I	E	S	I	T	E	U	M	D	K
T	T	L	O	C	S	I	J	S	D	N	J	M	G	T
I	T	C	M	A	L	B	E	A	T	I	I	S	P	H
R	O	Y	G	O	I	E	R	X	E	N	Q	W	I	S
E	E	L	P	E	N	E	F	E	F	G	U	E	U	M
T	N	O	C	H	L	E	R	R	E	I	E	Y	P	A
N	T	K	M	O	O	D	L	D	G	T	I	N	C	D
E	E	H	P	E	I	Y	L	I	I	J	O	P	G
O	R	C	E	E	W	E	D	E	O	S	U	S	C	U
R	I	W	E	J	V	A	U	E	S	O	O	W	O
T	T	U	B	E	R	C	U	L	O	S	I	S	K	P
S	I	S	H	I	G	E	L	L	O	S	I	S	V	S
A	S	O	G	U	I	W	E	I	C	G	K	X	I	Y
G	O	N	O	R	R	H	O	E	A	I	P	U	S	E

ANSWERS p. 266

"Start every day off with a smile. Get it over with." W.C. Fields

36

Can you name these tragic fictional heroines?

1. Hands and tongue cut off, she writes her rapists' names with a stick held in her mouth, before her enraged father breaks her neck.

2. Thrown in jail with her mad, blind father, she is hanged during a rescue attempt.

3. Her paranoid husband, convinced she's been having an affair, smothers her in their bed.

4. Grieving her father, she climbs a willow tree whose branch snaps, dropping her into a watery grave.

5. Dumped by her lover, shunned by society and prevented from seeing her son by her cuckolded husband, she jumps under a train.

6. Choosing to die with honour rather than live with shame, she sings a song about it before it impaling herself on a sword.

7. Locked in the attic by her husband, she sets fire to the house and jumps off the roof.

8. Starves herself to death then haunts her beloved to the end of his life.

9. Murdered by her violent lover, her corpse is so mutilated that the friend who identifies the body has to be led away in a straitjacket.

10. Shocked by her new husband's infatuation, fate intervenes when she is struck by a passing car.

ANSWERS p. **266**

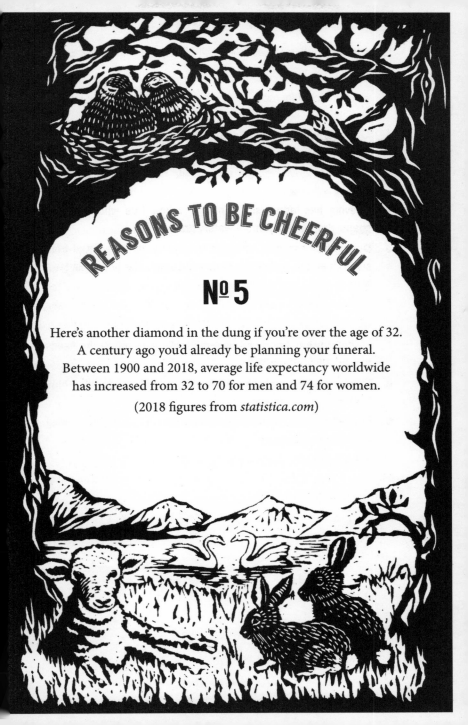

REASONS TO BE CHEERFUL

№ 5

Here's another diamond in the dung if you're over the age of 32.
A century ago you'd already be planning your funeral.
Between 1900 and 2018, average life expectancy worldwide
has increased from 32 to 70 for men and 74 for women.

(2018 figures from *statistica.com*)

37

IT'S BEHIND YOU!

Can you match these much-loved children's tales and characters to their rather less lovely original versions?

1. Violent, alcoholic racist goes on a murder spree, killing his wife and child.

2. After his friend is murdered, the hero has his feet burned off and dies gruesomely, hanged by villagers.

3. Raped by a king at her most vulnerable, the heroine bears twins. Furious about the infidelity, the queen has the babies boiled and served to her husband.

4. Goes to extreme lengths to arrange a tryst with her prince, then is abandoned by him, pregnant and a prisoner.

5. A conniving creature tricks a princess into striking a deal, then tries to jump into bed with her, before being smeared up the bedroom wall.

6. Two of the heroine's relations have their eyes pecked out by doves.

7. She escapes being raped by a predator by claiming she needs to pop outside for a sh*t.

8. Sees her prince marry someone else, considers stabbing him, but opts for a strangely apt method of suicide.

9. Her stepmother is forced dance in a pair of red-hot iron shoes until she drops dead.

10. He murders his friends, rather than watch them grow old.

ANSWERS
p.
267

"As a child I thought I hated everybody. But when I grew up I realised it was just children I didn't like." Philip Larkin

A

B

C

D

E

F

G

H

I

J

1. The Nazis promoted the Grimms' tales, not just as authentic Germanic folk culture, but as a way to get their propaganda drummed into little Aryans. That bit is TRUE. But which of the following fascist-fairy-tale-factoids is FALSE?

    A. In the jackbooted re-boot of *Snow White*, released a month before Poland was invaded, the heroine's father can't be with his daughter because he's off invading an 'eastern' enemy.

    B. To big up the honour of death in battle, young audiences had to watch Hans Christian Andersen's 'Brave Tin Soldier' being burned to death.

    C. 'Puss in Boots' ends with adoring crowds greeting the goose-stepping kitty at a Nurembergish rally, chanting 'Heil Puss in Boots!'

    D. Little Red Riding Hood's cloak is emblazoned with swastikas, and a SS man rescues her from the wolf.

    E. Cinderella has three Ugly Sisters – one greedy, one stupid, one sly – bearing a resemblance to Churchill, Stalin and Roosevelt.

2. What childhood event inspired J.M. Barrie's creation of Peter Pan?

    A. Barrie dreamt the entire thing – aged 10, whilst delirious with diphtheria.

    B. On a trip to Glasgow's Hunterian Museum, Barrie became infatuated with a sculpture of the god Pan, 'boy-like and old as time.'

    C. Barrie tried to please his grieving mother by dressing and acting like his brother, who died suddenly, aged 14.

    D. A *Glasgow Herald* headline of July 1870: They Shall Never Grow Old – referring to children who drowned on a Sunday School river trip.

PART I. Each year since 1993 the *Literary Review*'s 'Bad Sex in Fiction Award' has honoured an author who has produced 'an outstandingly bad scene of sexual description'. Which of these excerpts won the prize in various years since the award's inception, and which were merely deemed bad enough for the long list?

1. And then we would be on the bed and I touching you, hungry. Eyes closed, fingers inside you, reaching into the melting fluid rubbered silk – a relief map of mysteries – the eager clitoris, reeking of you, our tongues imitating the fingers, your hands gripping and stroking me but also careful not to excite too much. [...] and so I would fuck you gently and then more strongly and finally thrust in hard and suddenly let everything go. 'Slam into me,' you used to say. 'How you just slam into me!'

2. He closed his eyes and heard himself make a gurgling sound. And as his trousers slipped down his legs all the burdens of his life to date seemed to fall away from him; he tipped back his head and faced up into the darkness beneath the ceiling, and for one blessed moment he felt as if he could understand the things of this world in all their immeasurable beauty. How strange they are, he thought, life and all of these things. Then he felt Anezka slide down before him to the floor, felt her hands grab his naked buttocks and draw him to her. 'Come, sonny boy!' he heard her whisper, and with a smile he let go.

3. Then she was on him. She did not know if this would resuscitate him or end him, but the same spite, sharp as a needle, that had come to her after Fanni's death was in her again. Fanni had told her once what to do. So Klara turned head to foot, and put her most unmentionable part down on his

ANSWERS
p.
269

hard-breathing nose and mouth, and took his old battering ram into her lips. Uncle was now as soft as a coil of excrement. She sucked on him nonetheless with an avidity that could come only from the Evil One – that she knew. From there, the impulse had come. So now they both had their heads at the wrong end, and the Evil One was there. He had never been so close before.

4. The actual lovemaking was a series of cryptic clues and concealed pleasures. A sensual treasure hunt. She asked for something, then changed her mind. He made adjustments and calibrations, awaited further instruction.

5. 'I'm going to have you now,' Leon said. He led her back up the beach to where the sand was dry. Then he took off his coat, placed it on the ground and she lay down upon it.
   'Christ!' he muttered, placing himself on top of her. 'It's bloody cold. I might get frostbite on my cock.'
   She gave a low purring laugh. 'Silly man. Why don't you put it somewhere hot?'

6. When his hand brushed her nipple it tripped a switch and she came alight. He touched her belly and his hand seemed to burn through her. He lavished on her body indirect touches and bitter-sweet sensations flooded her brain. She became aware of places in her that could only have been concealed there by a god with a sense of humour.

7. Adrift on warm currents, no longer of this world, she became aware of him gliding into her. He loved her with gentleness and strength, stroking her neck, praising her face with his hands, till she was broken up and began a low rhythmic wail … The universe was in her and with each movement it unfolded to her. Somewhere in the night a stray rocket went off.

8. Looking down, she unbuckled his belt. 'We're grown-ups.' Perhaps he wasn't quite in the moment, because he thought of Kierkegaard and Socrates. If there wasn't great wisdom gained by lust, by love, its consummation – the aesthetics of all this – then you were doing it wrong. 'Kiss me again.'

9. At this, Eliza and Ezra rolled together into the one giggling snowball of full-figured copulation, screaming and shouting as they playfully bit and pulled at each other in a dangerous and clamorous rollercoaster coil of sexually violent rotation with Eliza's breasts barrel-rolled across Ezra's howling mouth and the pained frenzy of his bulbous salutation extenuating his excitement as it whacked and smacked its way into every muscle of Eliza's body except for the otherwise central zone.

10. Katsuro moaned as a bulge formed beneath the material of his kimono, a bulge that Miyuki seized, kneaded, massaged, squashed and crushed. With the fondling, Katsuro's penis and testicles became one single mound that rolled around beneath the grip of her hand. Miyuki felt as though she was manipulating a small monkey that was curling up its paws.

11. 'Do me a favour,' she says as she turns. She covers her breasts with her swimsuit. The rest of her remains so delectably exposed. The skin along her arms and shoulders are different shades of tan like water stains in a bathtub. Her face and vagina are competing for my attention, so I glance down at the billiard rack of my penis and testicles. 'Let's not tell Charlie and Sonny about us. Let's leave them out of it. You know how this kind of thing can become a telenovela for everyone else.'

12. I'm hard and deep inside her fucking her on the bathroom sink her tight little black dress still on her thong on the floor my pants at my knees our eyes locked, our hearts and souls and bodies locked. Cum inside me.

Cum inside me.

Cum inside me.

Blinding breathless shaking overwhelming exploding white God I cum inside her my cock throbbing we're both moaning eyes hearts souls bodies one.

One.

White.

God.

Cum.

Cum.

Cum.

I close my eyes let out my breath.

Cum.

I lean against her both breathing hard I'm still inside her smiling. She takes my hands lifts them and places them around her body, she puts her arms around me, we stay still and breathe, hard inside her, tight and warm and wet around me, we breathe. She gently pushes me away, we look into each other's eyes, she smiles.

PART II. For double points, can you fit the authors to the filthy prose?

A. Dominic Smith **B.** Ben Okri   **C.** Christopher Bollen
D. Norman Mailer **E.** Wilbur Smith   **F.** Morrissey
G. Melvyn Bragg   **H.** Neil Griffiths **I.** Jeffrey Archer
J. Didier Decoin **K.** Robert Seethaler **L.** James Frey

Fill in the missing Letters.

1. Give – – r – – – words; the grief that does not speak
   knits up the o–er wrought – – – a – – and bids it
   break.
   (Macbeth – William Shakespeare)

2. When sorrows come, they come not single – p – – s,
   but in b – – – ll – – – –.
   (Hamlet – William Shakespeare)

3. A grief without a pang, void, – a – – and drear,
   A stifled, drowsy, unimpassioned – r – – –,
   Which finds no natural outlet, no relief,
      In word, or sigh, or – – – –
      ('Dejection: An Ode' – Samuel T. Coleridge)

4. I have experienc'd
   The worst, the World can wreak on me – the worst
   That can make Life indifferent, yet disturb
   With whisper'd Discontents the dying p – a – – –
   I have beheld the whole of all, wherein
   My Heart had any interest in this – – – e
   To be disrent and torn from off my Hopes
   That n – – – – n – now is left. Why then live on ?
   ('Despair' – Samuel Taylor Coleridge)

5. Nothing begins, and nothing ends,
   That is not paid with m – – –;
   For we are born in others' – – i –,
   And perish in our own.
   ('Daisy' – Francis Thompson)

ANSWERS
p.
269

"The world is a comedy for those who think, but a tragedy for those who feel."
Horace Walpole

6. I sit in one of the dives
On Fifty–second Street
Uncertain and – f – a – –
As the clever hopes expire
Of a low dishonest d – – – – –
('September 1, 1939' – Philip Larkin)

7. Preacher was a–talkin', there's a sermon he gave
He said every man's conscience is vile and depraved
You cannot depend on it to be your – u i – –
When it's you who must keep it – – – i – – – – –
   ('The Man in the Long Black Coat' – Bob Dylan)

8. Don't turn away, in – – l – – – –
Your confusion
My illusion
Worn like a mask of s – – f   – – – e
('Atmosphere' – Joy Division)

9. If you are the dealer, I'm out of the game
If you are the – – a – – –, it means I'm broken and lame
If thine is the glory then mine must be the s – – – –
You want it darker
We kill the – – – m –
('You Want it Darker' – Leonard Cohen)

10. Oh, oh, oh
I just can't – – – – – tonight
Knowing that things ain't right
It's – n the – – – e – –, it's – n the – – , it's – – – – – – – – – e I
go.
Oh, oh – –
('Pray' – Justin Bieber)

1. Theo Walcott: 'I've been consistent in – this season.' What's the missing word?

2. Former cricketer Ronnie Irani: 'Who will win the league? It's a toss of a coin between – – – .' (three words)

3. Complete the wise quote of Tony Cottee with the missing three words: 'The thing about goalscorers is – – –'

4. Complete this dazzling insight from Ray Parlour: 'The last six games of the Invincibles season were the most pressurised, because they were – –' (two words)

5. Graham Beecroft: 'He's got a lot of self-belief in –' (one word)

6. 'They were numerically – .' Finish the sentence for poor Garry Birtles. (one word)

7. Did West Ham skipper Mark Noble say...

    A. Not to win is rutting… we're all rutted
    B. Losing is fu- I mean, it's frotten, it's frotting, isn't it?
    C. Not to win is guttering
    D. Losing…not to win, it's like guts

8. Ian Darke: 'Amongst them some very attractive-looking ladies. I mean women. Girls. Can I say that anymore?' TRUE or FALSE?

9. Ron Atkinson: 'I'm going to make a prediction – it could go either way.' TRUE or FALSE?

10. 'Certain people are for me and certain people are – me.' What's the missing word from Terry Venables?

11. 'Reading won't have the confidence to be – .' Paul Merson is missing a word, what is it?

12. 'If we played like this every week, we wouldn't be so – .' Help Bryan Robson out – what's the missing word?

13. Gary Lineker: 'At Anfield today we've seen something no one's ever seen at Anfield before. And that's football.' TRUE or FALSE?

14. David Acfield: 'Strangely, in slow motion replay, the ball seemed to hang in the air for even longer.' TRUE or FALSE?

ANSWERS
p.
270

15. Ron Greenwood. 'Glenn Hoddle hasn't been the Hoddle we know. Neither has Bryan Robson.' TRUE or FALSE?

16. 'I don't think there is anybody bigger or − − Maradonna.' What two words are missing from Kevin Keegan's quote?

17. John Motson: 'There he is, the star of Chelsea, Lamp Frankard.' TRUE or FALSE?

18. Ron Atkinson: 'In my view, at this level, there are round balls and there are square balls.' TRUE or FALSE?

19. 'I would not say he [David Ginola] is the best left winger in the Premiership, but − − −.' What three words is Ron Atkinson missing?

20. Stuart Hall: 'What will you do when you leave football, Jack – will you stay in football?' TRUE or FALSE?

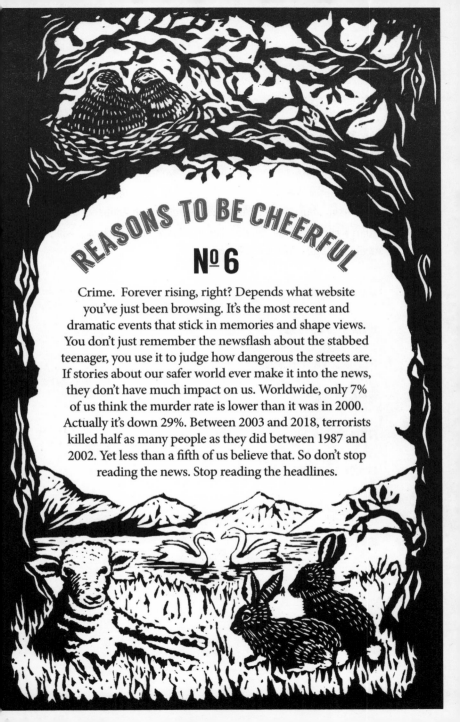

REASONS TO BE CHEERFUL

№ 6

Crime. Forever rising, right? Depends what website you've just been browsing. It's the most recent and dramatic events that stick in memories and shape views. You don't just remember the newsflash about the stabbed teenager, you use it to judge how dangerous the streets are. If stories about our safer world ever make it into the news, they don't have much impact on us. Worldwide, only 7% of us think the murder rate is lower than it was in 2000. Actually it's down 29%. Between 2003 and 2018, terrorists killed half as many people as they did between 1987 and 2002. Yet less than a fifth of us believe that. So don't stop reading the news. Stop reading the headlines.

Which of these musicians were responsible for these put-downs of their fellow artists?

HECTOR BERLIOZ

SIR THOMAS BEECHAM. (The bitchiest of all classical musicians, he once likened the sound of someone's harpsichord to 'two skeletons copulating on a tin roof in a thunderstorm' and dismissed Beethoven's 7th Symphony as 'like a lot of yaks jumping about.' When asked if he had ever conducted anything by the avant-garde Karlheinz Stockhausen, Beecham replied, 'No, but I once trod in some.')

RICHARD STRAUSS

MAURICE RAVEL

GIOACHINO ROSSINI

PYOTR ILYICH TCHAIKOVSKY

RICHARD WAGNER

FREDERIC CHOPIN

GIACOMO PUCCINI

CAMILLE SAINT-SÄENS

IGOR STRAVINKSY

ANSWERS
p.
271

1. 'A composer for one right hand.'

    _____ on Frédéric Chopin

2. 'Monsieur Wagner has good moments, but awful quarters of an hour.'

    _____ on Richard Wagner

3. 'What a giftless bastard.'

    _____ on Johannes Brahms

4. 'A tub of pork and beer.'

    _____ on George Frederic Handel

5. 'Berlioz composes by splashing his pen over the manuscript and leaving the issue to chance.'

    _____ on Hector Berlioz

6. 'The work of an idiot.'

    _____ after the world premiere of Stravinsky's 'The Rite of Spring'

7. 'If he'd been making shell-cases during the war it might have been better for music.'

    _____ on Ravel

8. 'He'd be better off shoveling snow than scribbling on manuscript paper.'

    _____ on Arnold Schoenberg

9. 'Written by a deaf man and should only be listened to by a deaf man.'

    _____ on Ludwig van Beethoven

10. 'All you need to write like him is a large bottle of ink.'

    _____ on Oliver Messiaen

INGRATITUDE JOURNAL NO. 7

20 HUMAN BEINGS WHOSE VERY PRESENCE ON THIS PLANET FILLS YOU WITH DESPAIR AND INGRATITUDE

Me

INGRATITUDE JOURNAL NO. 8

20 HOUSEHOLD CHORES TO BE PROFOUNDLY UNGRATEFUL FOR

Cleaning the fridge

1. Which founder member of Booker T. & the M.G.s known as 'The Human Timekeeper' was shot dead in his home in 1975?

2. Which British drummer managed not to kill himself whilst dynamiting hotel lavatories only to overdose on drugs prescribed to help him kick booze?

3. Which hard-drinking drummer took the stairway to heaven in 1980, choking on his own vomit?

4. Allegedly the only member of his ocean-loving band who could swim, which drummer drowned retrieving drugs from under his boat in 1983?

5. After Hanoi Rocks drummer Nicholas 'Razzle' Dingley died in a car crash in 1984, what 'tribute' was paid to him by another glam metal band?

6. Toto drummer Jeff Porcaro died in a bizarre gardening accident in 1992. TRUE or FALSE?

7. In 1998, who fatally crashed his car whilst on the phone to his girlfriend, drunk driving at 104 mph without a seatbelt, through bad weather on the M4?

8. In 1995, who told American music magazine *Seconds* he wanted to be remembered as 'the baddest of the bad'?

9. 65-year old drummer Thomas Erdelyi died in 2014. By what name was he better known?

10. Which drummer and last surviving member of Elvis Presley's band died in 2018?

ANSWERS
p.
272

"God knows. I don't know. I don't listen to music." Cream drummer Ginger Baker when asked by *Rolling Stone* magazine what record last excited him.

Can you name the artists who covered – that is to say, desecrated – these classic songs in the year mentioned?

1. 'Lucy in the Sky with Diamonds', 1968
2. '911 Is A Joke', 1995
3. 'Smells Like Teen Spirit', 1995
4. 'American Pie', 2000
5. 'My Generation', 2004
6. 'Wild Horses', 2009
7. 'In My Life', 2009
8. 'Let It Be', 2011
9. 'Fairytale of New York', 2015
10. 'Bohemian Rhapsody', 2015

ANSWERS
p.
272

"Two things are infinite: the universe and human stupidity. And I'm not sure about the universe." Albert Einstein

1. **What, according to the Greek historian Herodotus, did Egyptian men do to prove their manliness?**

   A. They had sex with bears.

   B. They had sex with crocodiles.

   C. They attached heavy weights to their testicles.

   D. They threw themselves off pyramids.

2. **Marlboro cigarettes were known by what nickname in the 1970s?**

   A. Cowboy Killers   **B.** Ole Reds

   C. Marble Rows   **D.** Last Gaspers

3. **Why did Jeffrey Hudson lose his job as court dwarf to English royalty in the 1620's?**

   A. He shot a man in the head.

   B. He refused to sit in between two halves of a loaf so the king could pretend to eat him.

   C. He became a hopeless alcoholic.

   D. He insulted King Charles I's French wife Henrietta.

4. **Adolf Hitler once ordered his medical experts to...**

   A. take measurements of his skull to prove his superiority.

   B. make him taller.

   C. investigate the possibility of making him immortal.

   D. issue a statement that he had complete set of gonads.

5. **During Napoleon's 1813 retreat from Moscow, why did only 10,000 of a half-million-strong army make it home?**

   A. They had plentiful tins of peaches, and no tin-openers.

   B. Snow-blindness made them march the wrong way.

   C. They froze because, like their Emperor, they wore no underwear.

   D. They froze when the buttons on their uniforms fell off.

ANSWERS
p.
273

6. **Which of the following was not a genuine fertility treatment?**

   A. Ancient Egyptians placed a woman in a bucket of dates and beer. If she vomited, she would conceive.

B. The ancient Greek Hipponax advised that a wife struggling to conceive should whip her husband's testicles with the branch of a fig tree.

C. Swiss doctor Paracelsus prescribed a potion made from the pus of a diseased goat to prevent difficult births.

D. To be assured of a male heir, German friar Albertus Magnus advised men to eat two goat testicles before sex.

7. **What is the most popular song played at British funerals?**

   A. 'My Way' – Frank Sinatra
   B. 'My Heart Will Go On' – Celine Dion
   C. 'Another One Bites The Dust' – Queen
   D. 'Wish You Were Here' – Pink Floyd

8. **Which 21st-century phenomenon did Nostradamus purportedly predict?**

   A. 9/11
   B. Hurricane Katrina
   C. The Indian Ocean Tsunami
   D. Greta Thunberg

9. **What were Syrian army recruits required to do to in front of President Hafez al-Assad to prove loyalty?**

   A. Males had to stab puppies, females to bite the heads off snakes.
   B. Run over 100 metres of broken glass.
   C. Remove their own teeth.
   D. Swear an oath that they would kill their own mothers.

10. **What was the childhood hobby of Tsar Ivan 'the Terrible'?**

    A. Archery practice on his household servants.
    B. Strangling kittens.
    C. Needlepoint.
    D. Throwing live dogs off the Kremlin roof.

Can you spot the fake tweet in each group from Big Don?

1. **A.** I have never seen a thin person drinking Diet Coke.
   B. Bambi's mother was careless and deserved to die.
   C. Despite the constant negative press covfefe
   D. Healthy young child goes to doctor, gets pumped with massive shot of many vaccines, doesn't feel good and changes — AUTISM. Many such cases!

2. **A.** Sorry losers and haters, but my I.Q. is one of the highest — and you all know it! Please don't feel so stupid or insecure, it's not your fault
   B. Throughout my life, my two greatest assets have been mental stability and being, like, really smart. Crooked Hillary Clinton also played these cards very hard and, as everyone knows, went down in flames. I went from VERY successful businessman, to top T.V. star
   C. How much BETTER is my hair than every other President?
   D. My twitter has become so powerful that I can actually make my enemies tell the truth.

3. **A.** Everyone knows I am right that Robert Pattinson should dump Kristen Stewart. In a couple of years, he will thank me. Be smart, Robert.
   B. I ran a great meeting w/ Angela Merkel. But she is very out of shape
   C. .@ariannahuff is unattractive both inside and out. I fully understand why her former husband left her for a man — he made a good decision.
   D. .@katyperry Katy, what the hell were you thinking when you married loser Russell Brand. There is a guy who has got nothing going, a waste!

4. **A.** An 'extremely credible source has called my office and told me that @BarackObamas's birth certificate is a fraud.

ANSWERS
p.
275

B. How amazing, the State Health Director who verified copies of Obama's "birth certificate" died in plane crash today. All others live.

C. The polls have shown that DEAD PEOPLE voted for President Obama overwhelmingly and without hesitation — he must be doing something right!

D. Very unfair New York Times listing boring Obama book No.1 bestseller. I have like 88 million followers whatever

5. A. The Oscars were a great night for Mexico & why not — they are ripping off the US more than almost any other nation

B. Do you think Putin will be going to The Miss Universe Pageant in November in Moscow — if so, will he become my new best friend?

C. Congratulations to France, who played extraordinary soccer, on winning the 2018 World Cup. Additionally, congratulations to President Putin and Russia for putting on a great World Cup Tournament — one of the best ever!

D. Take a look at what happened in England to incredible Kate and her family it is such an incredible thing

6. A. We should be focusing on beautiful, clean air & not on wasteful & very expensive GLOBAL WARMING bullshit! China & others are hurting our air

B. The concept of global warming was created by and for the Chinese to make US manufacturing non-competitive.

C. Windmills are the greatest threat in the US to both bald and golden eagles. Media claims fictional 'global warming' is worse.

D. Thank you coal industry! Thank you for all of the United States as they manufacture inefficient and costly wind turbines are destructive to tourism etc.

7. A. I conquered the China Virus and not one person noticed but okay

B. A total and complete sign off from White House Doctors yesterday. That means I can't get it (immune., and can't give it. Very nice to know!

C. Tonight, @FLOTUS and I tested positive for COVID-19. We will begin our quarantine and recovery process immediately. We will get through this TOGETHER!

D. I always treated Chinese Virus very seriously, and have done a very good job from the beginning, including my very early decision to close the borders from China— against the wishes of almost all. Many lives were saved. The Fake News news narrative is disgraceful & falsee

8 A. 26,000 unreported sexual assaults in the military-only 238 convictions. What did these geniuses expect when they put men & women together?

B. Lowest rated Oscars in HISTORY. Problem is, we don't have Stars anymore — except your President (just kidding, of course!

C. If you are lucky enough to catch a knockout assaulter before getting slugged, and you carry a gun, shoot the bastard (teach them a lesson.!

D. Melinda Gates was very concerned about her husband's dealings with Jeffrey Epstein. Fortunately, my wife Melanie had no such concerns.

These film classics were overlooked Academy voters for Best Picture. Can you name the films that beat them to the Oscar?

1. 'Citizen Kane' directed by Orson Welles, 1941

    (Clue: The 20th century's only coal-mining-themed Oscar winner.)

2. 'High Noon' – Fred Zinnemann 1952

    (Clue: A big top big flop.)

3. 'Doctor Zhivago' – David Lean 1965

    (Clue: When the bee stings, when the film sucks...)

4. 'Taxi Driver' – Martin Scorsese 1976

    (Clue: He did it all for Adriaaaan.)

5. 'Raging Bull' – Martin Scorsese 1980

    (Clue: Family bereavement, attempted suicide, all very ordinary.)

6. 'Goodfellas' – Martin Scorsese 1990

    (Clue: The best acting comes from the buffaloes.)

7. 'Pulp Fiction' – Quentin Tarantino 1994

    (Clue: You never know what you're going to get.)

8. 'L.A. Confidential' – Curtis Hanson 1997

    (Clue: You can't Winslet them all.)

9. 'Saving Private Ryan' – Steven Spielberg 1998

    (Clue: Bard or bored?)

10. 'The Social Network' – David Fincher 2010

    (Clue: Extremely privileged old white guy pays another white guy to sort out a problem.)

ANSWERS
p.
275

"Whenever a friend succeeds, a little something in me dies." Gore Vidal

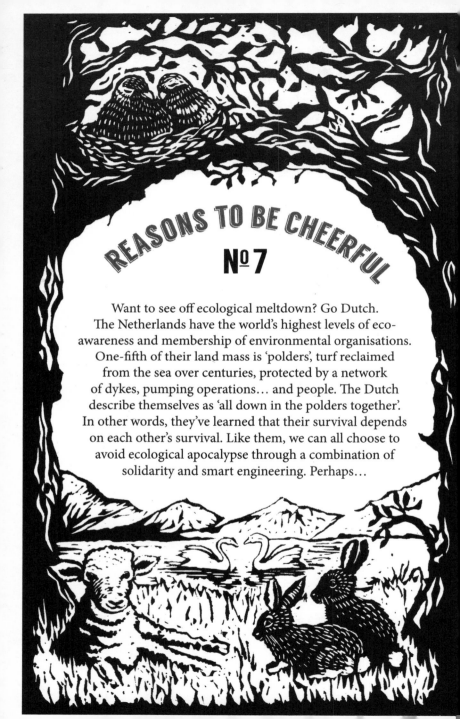

REASONS TO BE CHEERFUL

№ 7

Want to see off ecological meltdown? Go Dutch. The Netherlands have the world's highest levels of eco-awareness and membership of environmental organisations. One-fifth of their land mass is 'polders', turf reclaimed from the sea over centuries, protected by a network of dykes, pumping operations… and people. The Dutch describe themselves as 'all down in the polders together'. In other words, they've learned that their survival depends on each other's survival. Like them, we can all choose to avoid ecological apocalypse through a combination of solidarity and smart engineering. Perhaps…

THE UGLY TRUTH #3

TRUE or FALSE?

1. The Greek philosopher Pythagoras became a vegetarian, motivated by his concern for healthy eating and compassion for animals.

2. Professor Steven Hawking's final prediction was that science would ultimately save the planet.

3. Statistically, it's better to be born rich than talented.

4. An American who has a gun in his or her home is more likely to use it in a suicide or accidental shooting than in defence against intruders.

5. Westlife have had nearly twice as many Number One singles as The Rolling Stones.

6. According to Weight Watchers, almost two-thirds of dieters regain all the weight they lost within three years.

7. Men are more likely to be fatally struck by lightning than women.

8. Air pollution from vehicles is making us more stupid.

9. One of the world's roughly 7,000 languages dies out every year.

10. 25% of the world's people have no electricity.

ANSWERS
p.
276

WORDS FAILED HIM

Can you match these bitchy authors with their take-downs?

A

Samuel Johnson

B

Kingsley Amis

C

Percy Wyndham Lewis

D

Mark Twain

E

Virginia Woolf

F

William Makepiece Thackeray

G

Germaine Greer

H

Oscar Wilde

I

W. H. Auden

J

Thomas Carlyle

ANSWERS p. **277**

1. 'To me, Poe's prose is unreadable, like Jane Austen's. No, there is a difference. I could read his prose on a salary, but not Jane's.

   _____ on Jane Austen

2. 'Horrible, shameful, blasphemous, filthy in word, filthy in thought.'

   _____ on Jonathan Swift

3. 'There are two ways of disliking poetry. One way is to dislike it, the other is to read Pope.'

   _____ on Alexander Pope

4. 'I don't think Browning was very good in bed. His wife probably didn't care for him very much. He snored and had fantasies about twelve-year-old girls.'

   _____ on Robert Browning

5. 'The work of a queasy undergraduate scratching his pimples.'

   _____ on James Joyce's *Ulysses*

6. 'The Hitler of the book racket.'

   _____ on Arnold Bennett

7. 'He was dull in company, dull in his closet, dull everywhere... he was a mechanical poet.'

   _____ on Thomas Gray

8. 'A poor creature who has said or done nothing worth a serious man taking the trouble of remembering.'

   _____ on Percy Bysshe Shelley

9. 'An outstandingly unpleasant man, one who cheated and stole from his friends and peed on their carpets.'

   _____ on Dylan Thomas

10. 'When his cock wouldn't stand up he blew his head off. He sold himself a line of bullshit and he bought it.'

   _____ on Ernest Hemingway

49

THE WISDOM OF CROWDS

PART I. TRUE or FALSE?

1. Over half of Americans believe there was a conspiracy behind the assassination of President John F. Kennedy in 1963.

2. One in ten Americans believes chemicals in fruit juice cartons are turning children gay.

3. 12.5 million Americans believe Lizard People, aka 'Reptilians' are running the world.

4. Fewer than half of Britons think Princess Diana's death was a genuine accident.

5. One in ten Americans believes The Illuminati are controlling the world.

6. More than one in ten Americans believes the 9/11 attacks were an inside job.

7. In a 2011 poll, 51% of Americans said they approved of God's handling of natural disasters.

8. In an IPSOS poll of January 2021, 33% of Russians said they woud not get vaccinated against Covid.

9. Two-thirds of the world's population either don't know the Holocaust happened or deny that it did.

10. 5% of Americans (12.5 million people) believe the real Paul McCartney died in 1966.

11. In an October 2020 survey, more than one in three Americans said they believed Covid-19 had caused fewer deaths than the figure reported, or was a hoax.

12. The same survey found one in four Americans believed powerful people had intentionally planned the coronavirus outbreak.

13. Some 5% of US citizens believe that Microsoft founder Bill Gates is using 5G to brainwash Americans.

14. Nearly 10% of Americans believe tighter gun controls would actually cause more mass shootings.

15. A similar percentage believe that marijuana should never be legalised or decriminalised for any purpose.

ANSWERS p. **277**

"We only have to look at ourselves to see how intelligent life might develop into something we wouldn't want to meet." Stephen Hawking

PART II. How well do you know the great American public? Provide the correct percentages for the following poll questions

    A. A UFO crashed at Roswell.

    B. The government controls minds with TV.

    C. Fluoride is dangerous.

    D. The CIA developed crack.

    E. The moon landing was faked.

    F. Airplane contrails are sinister chemicals.

Percentages: 19%, 21%, 9%, 7%, 5%, 15%

BONUS BEATLES-BASED TWADDLE MINI-ROUND

Some claim Paul McCartney died in a road accident on a rainy night in 1966. The survivors replaced Paul with a lookalike so that their musical careers wouldn't be scuppered, yet couldn't resist dropping heavy clues about the cover-up on their next three albums, Sergeant Pepper's Lonely Hearts Club Band (1967), The White Album (1968) and Abbey Road (1969).

Which of these are further, widely circulated details of the 'Paul is Dead' theory and which did we just make up?

    A. The White Album song 'Glass Onion' includes the stanza 'Here's another clue for you all/the walrus was Paul'. And since the walrus is the Viking symbol for death...

    B. On the Sergeant Pepper's cover, the band name is laid out wreath-like in flowers, while the Beatles gaze downwards, next to a priest. Dressed in white crossing Abbey Road meanwhile, Lennon resembles a priest, Ringo, in black, is a gravedigger and the barefoot Paul is a corpse.

    C. On the Abbey Road cover, the car number plate LMW 281F stands for 'Linda McCartney Weeps'.

    D. Reverse the order in which the lads cross Abbey Road, turn the initial letters of their surnames into Hebrew, which is read right to left, and you get the phrase 'Thus Saul [Hebrew version of Paul] departed'.

E. Take a Sergeant Pepper's album cover, put the edge of a mirror on the centre of the band's drum, and an arrow points directly to McCartney.

F. You can hear Lennon say 'Paul's in Anfield' if you play 'Ob-la-di Ob-la-da' backwards. (Anfield being the name of Liverpool's largest cemetery.)

Who said...

1. 'Your whole life is on the other side of the glass. And there is nobody watching.'

   A. Alan Ayckbourn   **B.** Alan Bennett
   C. Harold Pinter   **D.** Tom Stoppard

2. 'If you live long enough, you'll see that every victory turns into a defeat.'

   A. Simone de Beauvoir   **B.** Albert Camus
   C. Charles Baudelaire   **D.** Alexandre Dumas

3. 'The thought of suicide is a great consolation: by means of it one gets through many a dark night.'

   A. Friedrich Nietzsche   **B.** David Hume
   C. John Locke   **D.** Thomas Hobbes

4. 'If you want to know what God thinks of money, just look at the people he gave it to.'

   A. Dorothy Parker   **B.** Edith Wharton
   C. Harper Lee   **D.** Louisa May Alcott

5. 'Life is not having been told that the man has just waxed the floor.'

   A. Allen Ginsberg   **B.** Ogden Nash
   C. Sylvia Plath   **D.** Gertrude Stein

6. 'The basis of optimism is sheer terror.'

   A. Thomas Hardy   **B.** Charles Dickens
   C. Aubrey Beardsley   **D.** Oscar Wilde

ANSWERS p. **281**

7. 'If it's true that our species is alone in the universe, then I'd have to say that the universe aimed rather low and settled for very little.'

   A. William Faulkner   **B.** George Carlin
   C. John Steinbeck   **D.** David Attenborough

8. 'Man is the only animal that laughs and weeps; for he is the only animal... struck with the difference between what things are, and what they ought to be.'

    A. Walter Scott   **B.** Elizabeth Gaskell
    C. William Hazlitt   **D.** Charles Dickens

9. 'You fall out of your mother's womb, you crawl across open country under fire, and drop into your grave.'

    A. Quentin Crisp   **B.** Anthony Burgess
    C. Doris Lessing   **D.** Samuel Beckett

10. 'Blessed is he who expects nothing, for he shall never be disappointed.'

    A. Henry Fielding   **B.** Samuel Johnson
    C. Frances Burney   **D.** Alexander Pope

What links these people and who is the odd one out?

A

Vladimir Nabokov

B

Thora Hird

C

Ronald Colman

D

Albert Trott

E

Philippa Fawcett

F

David Bowie

G

Eva Gore-Booth

H

Isadora Duncan

I

Neville Cardus

ANSWERS
p.
282

"To want fame is to prefer dying scorned than forgotten." Emil Cioran

BEYOND BELIEF

1. It was the 18th-century French Royal Court philosopher Voltaire who said, 'Man will never be free until the last king is strangled with the entrails of the last priest.' TRUE or FALSE?

2. As 17th-century mathematician and theologian Blaise Pascal put it, 'Men never commit evil so fully and joyfully as when they do it for — —.' What are the missing two words?

3. 'Is God willing to prevent evil, but not able? Then he is not omnipotent. Is he able, but not willing? Then he is malevolent. Is he both able and willing? Then whence cometh evil? Is he neither able nor willing? Then why call him God?' Which philosopher put it so neatly?

   A. Zenobius
   B. Socrates
   C. Plato
   D. Epicurus
   E. Aristocreon
   F. John Locke
   G. Eric Cantona

4. Supply the missing words to this quote by the late American particle physicist, Victor Stenger: 'Science flies you to the —. Religion flies you into —.'

5. 'With or without religion, you would have good people doing good things and evil people doing evil things. But for good people to do evil things, that takes religion.' Which scientist said this?

   A. Steven Weinberg
   B. Richard Feynmann
   C. Richard Dawkins
   D. Roger Penrose

ANSWERS
p.
283

6. 'Jealous and proud of it; a petty, unjust, unforgiving control-freak; a vindictive, bloodthirsty ethnic cleanser; a misogynistic, homophobic, racist, infanticidal, genocidal, filicidal, pestilential,

megalomaniacal, sadomasochistic, capriciously malevolent bully.'
Was Richard Dawkins talking about...

    A. The Reverend Ian Paisley

    B. God

    C. Pope Alexander VI (born Rodrigo Borgia in 1431)

    D. St. Paul

7. 'Simply evolved out of fraud, fear, greed, imagination and ------.'
Can you supply the missing 6-letter word from Edgar Allen Poe's
quote about religion?

8. Who or what did sci-fi writer and scientist Isaac Asimov describe as
'The most potent force for atheism ever conceived'?

    A. The Russian Orthodox Church

    B. Polio

    C. U.S. Televangelist Oral Roberts

    D. The Bible

9. Napoleon on religion: 'Religion is what keeps the poor — — — —'
What are the four missing words?

10. Which wag said, 'If it turns out that there is a God... the worst that
you can say about him is that basically he's an underachiever.'

    A. Mel Brookes

    B. James Thurber

    C. Woody Allen

    D. Jackie Mason

"Life has to be given a meaning because of the obvious fact that it
has no meaning." Henry Miller

Can you identify these morbid pop hits from their descriptions?

1. The narrator's 16-year-old girlfriend is pulled from their car when it stalls on a railway in front of an oncoming train, but returns to look for a missing ring (1960).

2. Tommy's plan to win cash for a wedding ring in a car race ends when his vehicle overturns and bursts into flames (1960).

3. A soldier on leave waits for his fiancée to join him so they can be married, but she is lost in a tragic aviation disaster (1961).

4. After a lovers' tiff, the boy speeds off on a motorcycle to his death (1964).

5. Young lovers perish when their car hits a tractor trailer on a road. The gas station attendant helping to recover the bodies fails to recognise his own dead daughter (1964 & 1999).

6. Betty's parents force her to ditch unsuitable biker-boy Jimmy, who roars away on his bike, leading to inevitable death on a rain-slicked surface (1965).

7. The narrator meets a quiet girl with cold hands at a dance, only to find out later she was dead all along (1965).

8. The stricken teenage narrator can't finish her dinner when she learns of the apparent suicide of the boy next door, while her father only observes, 'Well, Billie Joe never had a lick o' sense; pass the biscuits, please' (1967).

9. Husband mourns his wife, who died shortly after planting a tree, and is consequently reminded of her every time he sees it (1968).

10. Chap with an unspecified terminal illness says goodbye to family and friends (1974 & 1999).

ANSWERS p. **283**

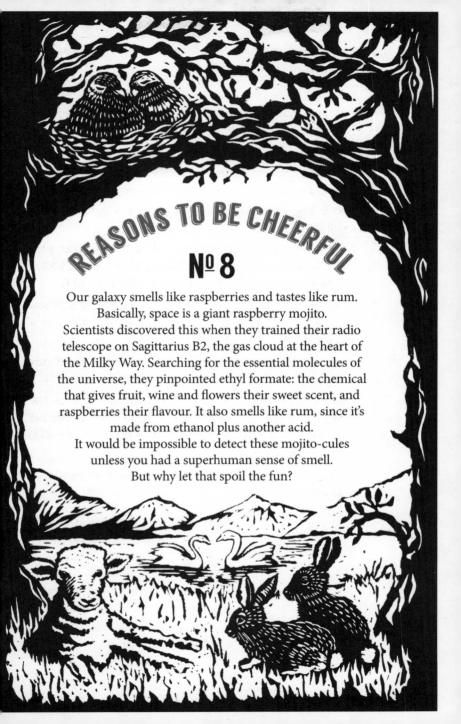

REASONS TO BE CHEERFUL

№ 8

Our galaxy smells like raspberries and tastes like rum.
Basically, space is a giant raspberry mojito.
Scientists discovered this when they trained their radio
telescope on Sagittarius B2, the gas cloud at the heart of
the Milky Way. Searching for the essential molecules of
the universe, they pinpointed ethyl formate: the chemical
that gives fruit, wine and flowers their sweet scent, and
raspberries their flavour. It also smells like rum, since it's
made from ethanol plus another acid.
It would be impossible to detect these mojito-cules
unless you had a superhuman sense of smell.
But why let that spoil the fun?

1. What was the verdict of the psychologists hired by the US government in World War II to write a report on Adolf Hitler?

   A. Excessive toilet training
   B. Repressed homosexuality
   C. Sadistic paraphilia
   D. Delusional psychosis

2. In Paraguay, dictator Alfredo Stroessner's imaginative torturer-in-chief, Pastor Coronel conducted interrogations while his interviewees were...

   A. on the edge of a cliff.
   B. immersed in a bathtub full of human excrement.
   C. suspended above a tank of snakes.
   D. being slowly pulled apart by motorbikes.

3. Stalin's career lowlight was being left to die in a puddle of urine on the floor by attendants who were too afraid to enter his bedroom uninvited. TRUE or FALSE?

4. Stroessner is the only dictator to have had a dance named after him. TRUE or FALSE?

5. Alexander Lukashenko, President of Belarus, swept to power with the slogan, 'You will live badly, but not for long.' TRUE or FALSE?

6. What made Robert Mugabe call the Blair government in November 1999 'the gay gangster government of the gay United gay Kingdom'?

   A. They refused to extradite Peter de Hoff, a British-born Zimbabwean who fled after allegedly funding a coup.
   B. Peter Mandelson had called for Mugabe's knighthood to be withdrawn.
   C. The British Foreign Policy think-tank had categorised Zimbabwe as deficient in its human rights record.
   D. Peter Tatchell had attempted a citizens' arrest on Mugabe's wife while she was shopping in London.

ANSWERS
p.
284

7. Jean-Bedel Bokassa, President for Life of the Central African Republic from 1966 to 1979, once claimed that he was the 13th apostle of the Catholic Church secretly appointed by the Pope. TRUE or FALSE?

8. Which of these measures was NOT among the 638 CIA plots to bump off or depose Fidel Castro?

A. Dusting his wetsuit with a fungus that caused a disabling skin disease.

B. Luring the avid shell collector to pick up a beautiful and explosive-packed conch from the ocean floor.

C. Fitting an electromagnetic device into Castro's Czech-made shoes to make the leader feel disoriented and unwell.

D. Making him speak gibberish by spraying an LSD aerosol around him as he made a broadcast to the Cuban people.

9. Asked once if he wore a bullet-proof vest, Castro replied:

A. 'Why bother? If anyone could get a bullet into me it wouldn't kill me.'

B. 'I have a moral vest.'

C. 'I have two – Felipe and Hector.' (His bodyguards)

D. 'Our soldiers and sailors don't wear them, so why would I?'

10. Which of these claims has NOT been made about former North Korean leader Kim Jong II?

A. In the womb, the unborn Kim communicated with his mother using a series of taps and kicks.

B. While at university he wrote 1,500 books over a period of three years, along with six full operas.

C. A double rainbow and a new star appeared on the day he was born.

D. The first time he picked up a golf club, he shot a 38-under-par round on North Korea's only course, including 11 holes-in-one. Each of his 17 bodyguards verified the feat. He then decided to retire from the sport forever.

1. In a survey, Thomas Cook and ABTA agents reported the following genuine communications from disgruntled, baffled or simply brain-dead holidaymakers. Well, some of them are genuine. We made a few up. Can you spot them?

    A. 'The brochure says "no hairdressers at the accommodation." We are both trainee hairdressers. So will we be okay staying there?'

    B. 'It is your duty to warn us of noisy or unruly guests before we travel.'

    C. 'Your brochure stated that Kos was in Greece but it isn't. It is an island, which made travel very difficult.'

    D. 'Your brochure shows the sand as yellow but it was white.'

    E. 'The local store does not sell proper biscuits like custard creams.'

    F. 'We were told the town had numerous options for eating out but there was no KFC, no Burger King, no Mcdonald's, just a lot of foreign restaurants.'

    G. 'We had to queue outside without air conditioning.'

    H. 'The aeroplane landed early and my daughter was not allowed to finish the film she was watching.'

    I. 'We hold you responsible for the fact that I find myself pregnant. This would not have happened if we had been given the room we had booked.'

    J. 'After my two-week holiday turned into a fourteen-month prison nightmare, I can honestly say your travel reps are useless.'

2. Operating Manuals set out guidelines for the permissible number of screws that can be missing from an aeroplane in use. TRUE or FALSE?

3. On some airlines, the crew only get paid if the plane takes off. TRUE or FALSE?

4. If you hear the announcement 'Operation Rising Star' on a cruise ship, it means that a passenger has died. TRUE or FALSE?

Which of the following are real jobs currently held in the British royal household?

1. Warden of the Swans
2. Chocolate Maker to the Queen/King
3. Keeper of the Lions in the Tower
4. Master of the Queen's/King's Music
5. Astronomer Royal
6. The Piper to the Sovereign
7. The Queen's/King's Bargemaster
8. Surveyor of the Queen's/King's Pictures
9. Necessary Woman to the Corridor and Entrance Hall
10. Groom of the Stool

ANSWERS
p.
285

1. Which actor left the following message? 'Dear World, I am leaving because I am bored. I feel I have lived long enough. I am leaving you with your worries in this sweet cesspool. Good luck.'

   A. George Sanders   **B**. George Raft
   C. George Peppard   **D.** George Hamilton

2. 'Anne, I love you. Blair, I love you. I will not be allowed to love and trust everybody. This is better. P.S. Stan Polley is a soulless bastard. I will take him with me.' Which singer-songwriter and guitarist wrote this?

   A. Pete Burns   **B.** Pete Ham
   C. Pete Seeger   **D.** Pete Shelley

3. Which American writer wrote this? 'No More Games. No More Bombs. No More Walking. No More Fun. No More Swimming. 67. That is 17 years past 50. 17 more than I needed or wanted. Boring. I am always bitchy. No Fun for anybody. 67. You are getting Greedy. Act your old age. Relax. This won't hurt.'

   A. John Steinbeck   **B.** Henry Miller
   C. Ernest Hemingway   **D.** Hunter S. Thompson

4. Comedian whose final verdict on his life was: 'Things just seemed to go too wrong too many times.'

   A. Lenny Bruce   **B.** Freddy Prinze
   C. Tony Hancock   **D.** Robin Williams

5. 'We had a death pact, and I have to keep my half of the bargain. Please bury me next to my baby. Bury me in my leather jacket, jeans and motorcycle boots. Goodbye.' Who was the departing rocker?

ANSWERS p. **287**

   A. Keith Emerson   **B.** Michael Hutchence
   C. Sid Vicious   **D.** Kurt Cobain

6. One psychiatric study examined suicide notes left between 1972-3 in an unnamed Australian city. There were 135 suicides that year. How many left notes behind?

   A. 93   **B.** 71   **C.** 53   **D.** 27

7. Which painter uttered the words 'La tristesse durera toujours' ('the sadness will last forever') before dying of a wound self-inflicted two days previously?

    A. Diane Arbus   **B.** Richard Gerstl

    C. Arshile Gorky   **D.** Vincent van Gogh

8. What did poet Hart Crane do just after declaring 'Goodbye everybody!' on 27 April 1932?

    A. Swallowed snake venom.

    B. Got in his aeroplane, took off and flew it into a hillside.

    C. Jumped off a cruise ship in the Gulf of Mexico.

    D. Blew himself up.

9. What was unusual about the suicide of Christine Chubbuck?

    A. The TV news reporter overdosed during a White House press conference with President Gerald Ford.

    B. The TV anchorwoman told viewers they were about to witness a live suicide, before shooting herself in the head.

    C. On a Houston-Hong Kong flight, the Pan-Am stewardess washed barbiturates down with a bottle of vintage 1959 Salon Le Mesnil in the First Class toilet.

    D. The magician staged her own death during a Las Vegas show so that it seemed at first to have been a tragic accident.

10. Why did ancient Greek lawgiver Charondas commit suicide at a meeting of the Assembly?

    A. He had made a minor error on a document.

    B. Accused of lying to his fellow Assembly members, he said he would prefer to die than answer such a charge.

    C. He mistakenly believed that he had killed his own brother, Iamblichus, en route to the Assembly.

    D. Having passed a law that punished by death anyone who brought a weapon into the Assembly, he forgot, and showed up with a knife after a morning of hunting.

1. In 1664 Samuel Pepys noted in his diary that his wife was using the fashionable cosmetic of the day, made from...

   A. puppy water, i.e. the urine of a young dog
   B. a stillborn child
   C. blood from the nose of a live mole
   D. leeches drowned in red wine

2. The ocean liner RMS Queen Mary is said to be haunted by

   A. the ship's cook
   B. Queen Mary
   C. Queen Alexandra
   D. her first captain, Sir Edgar T. Britten

3. When Winston Churchill was Home Secretary in 1910, he proposed...

   A. that striking miners should be shot.
   B. transportation with hard labour for Suffragettes.
   C. identity cards for ethnic minorities.
   D. neutering of the 'mentally incompetent' and penal camps for 'tramps and wastrels'.

4. How was the Greek philosopher Anaxarchus executed?

   A. He was tied to a horse and dragged to death.
   B. He was covered in honey and eaten by insects.
   C. He was pounded to death in a mortar with iron pestles.
   D. He was drowned in a barrel of white wine.

5. What, in 1998, was newsworthy about the death of Reverend Melvyn Nurse, in Jacksonville, Florida?

ANSWERS
p.
287

   A. He took his own life in the pulpit after one of his flock 'outed' him as gay.
   B. He shot himself in the head while delivering a sermon to young people about the dangers of carrying guns.
   C. He fell from his steeple fixing a lightning conductor.
   D. He tumbled from his church roof whilst filming the 'Satanic' activities at the strip-club across the road.

6. In history and in folklore, what are *comprachicos*?

   A. People who manipulated the physical attributes of growing children to satisfy the craze for human 'freaks'.
   B. Extreme circus performers.
   C. A group of overseas assassins working for Franco's regime.
   D. Exceptionally oversexed males.

7. How did Bridget 'the Midget' Powers earn her fame?

   A. As George Washington's mistress.
   B. As America's smallest hardcore porn star.
   C. As America's smallest bodybuilder.
   D. As America's shortest professional basketball player.

8. In 1867, how did the Methodist missionary Reverend Thomas Baker fatally offend his hosts in Fijian village?

   A. He removed a comb from a chief's hair, unaware that touching the head of a chief was a grievous insult.
   B. He bared his buttocks, believing this to be a sign of respect.
   C. He refused their offer of the local delicacy, shark gonads.
   D. He brushed his teeth in public.

9. Can you match each of the following artists with the comments taken from their original BBC audition notes?

   A. Elton John   B. David Bowie
   C. Marc Bolan   D. Led Zeppelin

   1. 'Old-fashioned' and 'unsuitable for daytime radio.'
   2. 'Crap, and pretentious crap at that.'
   3. 'Sung in an extremely dull fashion without any feeling and precious little musical ability.'
   4. 'Amateurish and out of tune.'

10. What proportion of Americans believes the government is keeping natural cures for cancer off the market due to pressure from drug companies?

    A. one in ten   B. a quarter
    C. more than a third   D. more than half

1. Which novelist said: 'The meaning of life is that it stops'?

   A. Franz Kafka   **B.** Joseph Heller
   C. Saul Bellow   **D.** Philip Roth

2. Fill in the blanks in this Chekhov quote: 'You ask me what life is. That's like asking what a — is. A — is a — and there's nothing more to know'?

   A. Carrot   **B.** Tit
   C. Potato   **D.** Goose

3. Philosopher Nicholas Chamfort advised: 'A man should be sure to swallow a — every morning...'

   A. glass of strong brandy   **B.** handful of dust
   C. toad   **D.** sword

4. Complete the Schopenhauer quote: 'Men are by nature merely indifferent to one another... women are by nature – -'

   A. allies   **B.** enemies
   C. sisters   **D.** curious

5. Which writer said, 'I think that God, in creating Man, somewhat overestimated his ability'?

   A. Oscar Wilde   **B.** George Bernard Shaw
   C. Ralph Waldo Emerson   **D.** Edgar Allan Poe

6. It was Ezra Pound who wrote, 'Since I no longer expect anything from mankind except madness, meanness, and mendacity; egotism, cowardice, and self-delusion, I have stopped being a misanthrope.' TRUE or FALSE?

ANSWERS
p.
288

7. Which writer's headstone reads: 'Here lies one who meant well, tried a little, failed much'?

   A. Robert Louis Stevenson   **B.** John Keats
   C. Jonathan Swift   **D.** Douglas Adams

8. Who thought that 'the sooner the party breaks up, the better'?

   A. Charlotte Bronte   **B.** Jane Austen
   C. Mary Shelley   **D.** Elizabeth Gaskell

9. Complete the F. Scott Fitzgerald quote. 'Show me a hero and I will write you a...'

   A. bore   **B.** farce
   C. tragedy   **D.** zero

10. Who wrote: 'Man is the only animal that laughs and weeps: for he is the only animal... struck with the difference between what things are, and what they ought to be'?

   A. Walter Scott   **B.** Charles Dickens
   C. Rudyard Kipling   **D.** William Hazlitt

"There are no beautiful surfaces without a terrible depth." Friedrich Nietzsche

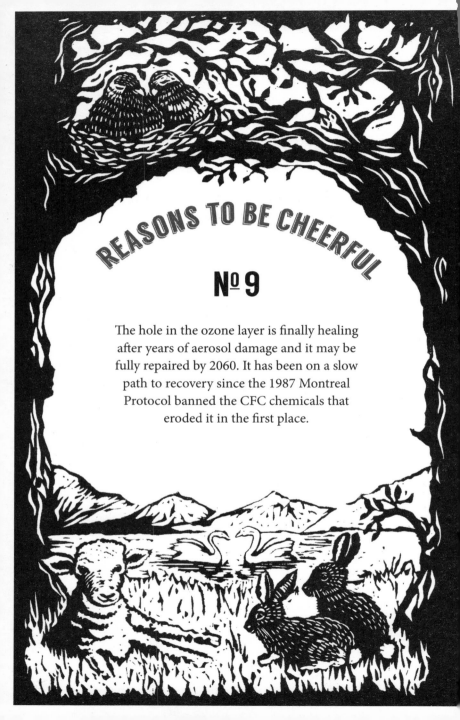

REASONS TO BE CHEERFUL

№ 9

The hole in the ozone layer is finally healing after years of aerosol damage and it may be fully repaired by 2060. It has been on a slow path to recovery since the 1987 Montreal Protocol banned the CFC chemicals that eroded it in the first place.

1. **How did Emperor Nero secure his reputation as a champion chariot racer?**

   A. He had the reins of his opponents laced with poison.

   B. He bribed judges to let him run a ten-horse team in a four-horse race.

   C. By murdering anyone stupid enough to beat him.

   D. He won once, by a fluke, then banned all future chariot racing.

2. **Why was Fred Lorz stripped of the gold medal in the Marathon event at the 1904 St Louis Olympic Games?**

   A. Lorz didn't so much compete in the 26-mile race as spend it actively fleeing police officers.

   B. On the winners' podium, he confessed to being fuelled by a cocktail of heroin, cocaine and brandy.

   C. He'd ridden 11 miles of the course in a car.

   D. He'd put the wrong date on his entry form.

3. **What sport-related ruckus gave rise to the line, 'Say it ain't so, Joe'?**

   A. A baseball fan shouted it to disgraced Chicago White Sox outfielder 'Shoeless' Joe Jackson in 1919, after he was accused of match-throwing and bribery.

   B. It was a 1962 *LA Times* headline after baseball legend Joe di Maggio banned dozens of VIPs from the funeral of his ex-wife, Marilyn Monroe.

   C. It was a *Wall Street Journal* headline following boxer Joe Frazier's shock defeat to Muhammad Ali at the 'Thrilla in Manila' match in 1975.

   D. It was the title of a 1971 song penned by Kris Kristofferson in tribute to Joe Namath, the dandy New York Jets quarterback, who abruptly quit the sport after being banned from wearing his trademark fur coats on the sidelines.

ANSWERS
p.
289

4. Polish sprinter Ewa Klobukowska became the first person ever to fail a sport sex test in 1967. TRUE or FALSE?

5. For what reason was Russian fencing ace and KGB Colonel Boris Onischenko disqualified from the 1976 Olympic Games?

    A. He stabbed his opponent and ran at the judges with his foil.

    B. There were of two of him. An identical twin brother named Sasha exhausted the opponents, before Boris sailed in fresh as a daisy for the *coup de grace*.

    C. Boris was a woman, something the KGB had been as unaware of as the Olympic committee. She defected shortly after competing in the Games.

    D. Boris had an electrical device hidden inside his *epée* which could hack into the judges' scoring boxes.

6. Which event at the Seoul Olympics in 1988 became known as 'the dirtiest race in history', and why?

7. Which of these did NOT happen to track and field athlete Marion Jones in the aftermath of the Sydney Olympics in 2000?

    A. Her marriage ended.

    B. She was stripped of five gold medals.

    C. She served a six-month prison sentence for lying to Federal Agents.

    D. She broke her ankle.

8. What explanation did former South Africa cricket captain Hanse Cronje give when found guilty of bribe-taking and match-fixing?

    A. That the money he'd received had funded an orphanage in Cape Town's poorest area.

    B. That he was in 'shitloads of debt to the Portuguese mafia'.

    C. That he had briefly taken his eyes off Jesus, and listened to Satan.

    D. That he needed money for a sex change and – given his public profile and the rigid attitudes in South Africa – a new identity abroad.

9. Why was the Women's Olympic Technical Figure Skating on 23 February 1994 one of the most watched sporting events in US TV history?

10. For which specific type of unsporting match behaviour has footballer Luis Suarez received 39 bans?

   A. Spitting
   B. Hair-pulling
   C. Whispering threats whilst tackling
   D. Biting

1. **In what respect was the Holy Roman Emperor Charles V a perfectionist?**

   A. He took part in rehearsals for his own funeral.
   B. He had members of his orchestra shot if they played out of tune.
   C. He owned 2,200 pairs of shoes which required daily cleaning and polishing.
   D. A stickler for punctuality, he imprisoned a senior minister for three years for being three minutes late.

2. **How many people live without an adequate supply of water?**

   A. 200 million   **B.** 600 million
   C. 750 million   **D.** 1.2 billion

3. **In 1847 Thomas Holmes was the first American to develop and use embalming fluid, having honed his technique on soldiers during the Civil War so their remains could be shipped home for burial. After the war he opened a shop selling his home-made embalming fluid. What did he display in his window as an example of his work?**

   A. His wife's leg
   B. The pickled head of a young girl
   C. His own leg
   D. A fetus

4. **According to philosopher Friedrich Nietzsche, why did women become scholars?**

   A. There was something wrong with their sexual organs.
   B. They were ugly and couldn't find husbands.
   C. They were naturally curious.
   D. To avoid motherhood.

ANSWERS
p.
291

5. **How did Vedius Pollio, a Roman official under Emperor Augustus, punish his slaves?**

   A. He threw them into a pool of lampreys trained to eat human flesh.

   B. He made them sing until they died of exhaustion.

   C. He had them mauled to death by lions.

   D. He crucified them upside down.

6. **How did the Nazi race theorist Professor Hermann Gauch embarrass the Nazi leadership?**

   A. He married a black woman.

   B. He said that Hitler was 'very likely Jewish'.

   C. He was so racist he offended some of the Nazis' allies.

   D. After studying the earliest texts, he concluded that the 'Aryans' were brown-skinned ancestors of today's Iranians.

7. **In 1900, German naturalist Carl von Hagen went to Papua New Guinea and found the bright green Paradise Birdwing, said to be the most beautiful butterfly in the world. But what became of von Hagen?**

   A. He died after ingesting a very poisonous moth.

   B. Shortly after von Hagen's netting of *Onithoptera Paradisea*, men of the Wari tribe netted him, pinned him to a tree with spears and finally ate him.

   C. He set off home anticipating a hero's welcome, but drowned at sea in a severe storm.

   D. He fell off a cliff while pursuing a butterfly specimen.

8. **Which is the most popular flavour of edible underwear?**

   A. cherry   B. banana   C. chocolate   D. strawberry

9. **Which of the following statements is false?**

   A. A piece of bubblegum spat out by Britney Spears at a Wembley concert in 2000 sold for $14,000 on eBay.

B. On Mount Everest there are around 200 corpses of failed climbers. They are useful markers for those on their way up.

C. Approximately 5% of office mugs contain fecal matter.

D. Nazi experiments on concentration camp inmates are the reason we know so much about the stages of hypothermia.

10. Which of the following is FALSE?

A. In 1932 Hungarian Szilveszter Matuska came to the attention of the court due to his symphorophilia – arousal from watching a tragedy, such as a fire or a traffic accident.

B. In 1986, the *Journal of Sex and Marital Therapy* reported on a young Buddhist male with formicophilia – sexual stimulation from being nibbled by small insects

C. The case of Arwin Meiwes – whose victim consented to being cooked and eaten in March 2001 – caused prosecutors a headache, as cannibalism is not a crime in Germany.

D. In 1991, the end of the Prime Minister's 11-year reign prompted a flurry of articles in the British Journal of Human Sexuality concerning 'penelopophiliacs', or people aroused by Margaret Thatcher.

1. What do these animals have in common and which is the odd one out?

A
B
C
D
E
F
G
H
I

ANSWERS
p.
291

2. Having cracked question 1, can you match the critter to the country?

1. Hawaii	2. Switzerland	3. Cameroon
4. France	5. Australia	6. Bengal/Bangladesh
7. Peru	8. China	9. Tunisia/Morocco

20 THINGS YOU WISH YOU'D KNOWN ABOUT YOUR PARTNER BEFORE TAKING OUT A JOINT MORTGAGE

Bites toenails

20 THINGS YOU LOATHE ABOUT CHRISTMAS

Literally everything

1. In 1938, a month after the German campaign to round up all of the Jews began, who invited Nazi film-maker Leni Riefenstahl to his Californian HQ for a personal guided tour?

2. Which US industrialist came over from the mid-West to be the first recipient of a medal created by Hitler for foreign friends of the Third Reich, the Cross of the German Eagle Order?

3. Which high-flying hero was an outspoken Hitler fan in the late 1930s?

4. Who did Himmler commission to make his soldiers a uniform that would inspire fear in men and 'success with girls'?

5. During German occupation, which couturier kept more than little black dresses in her closet?

6. A Hitler Youth member, but 'not an enthusiastic one', he later became head of another movement fond of dressing-up and ceremonies. Who was he?

7. Which two Mitford sisters had fascist leanings, and what happened to them after WWII broke out?

8. The only MP interned during WWII, Scottish Unionist Archibald Maule Ramsay, marked the outbreak of hostilities by singing 'Land of Dope and Jewry' in the House of Commons. TRUE or FALSE?

9. Jeeves and Wooster creator P.G. Wodehouse passed the war in comfort in Paris, making pro-Nazi radio broadcasts to be beamed to Britain. TRUE or FALSE?

10. Which pop legend collected Nazi memorabilia, thought 'Hitler was a genius orator' and 'great showman' and that he could have helped heal *der Führer* if only they had met.

ANSWERS
p.
293

Which of these 'facts' about RMS Titanic are TRUE and which are FALSE?

1. Titanic's first victim was never on board.

2. Titanic's 706 third-class passengers had four bathtubs between them – one for males and three for females.

3. Before the maiden voyage, Titanic's owners extensively promoted their ship as 'unsinkable'.

4. The inventor of the radio, Guglielmo Marconi, should have been on the Titanic but arrived too late.

5. Titanic's captain, Edward John Smith was widely considered to be the finest sea captain of his generation.

6. The final song played by the band was 'Nearer, My God, to Thee'.

7. Although there were insufficient lifeboats for human passengers, three dogs found room on them and were rescued.

8. The surviving crew members were awarded a pay rise.

9. Even in death, class barriers were observed: proper coffins were reserved solely for Titanic's first-class passengers.

10. Almost all the bodies were recovered and given a proper burial on land.

Bonus Question

Public subscription raised funds for a statue to be erected in honour of Captain Smith in his hometown, Stoke-on-Trent. What happened next?

ANSWERS
p.
294

65

HOMO DISAPPOINTUS

Can you match these quotes with the downhearted people opposite?

1. 'The world is a comedy for those who think, but a tragedy for those who feel.'

2. 'You fall out of your mother's womb, you crawl across open country under fire, and drop into your grave'.

3. 'In three words I can sum up everything I've learned about life. It goes on.'

4. 'To travel hopefully is a better thing than to arrive.'

5. 'Life has to be given a meaning because of the obvious fact that it has no meaning'.

6. 'Always borrow money from a pessimist, he won't expect it back.'

7. 'Happiness in intelligent people is the rarest thing I know'.

8. 'Always examine the dice.'

9. 'I have never made but one prayer to God, a very short one. "O Lord, make my enemies ridiculous." And God granted it.'

10. 'You tried your best and you failed miserably. The lesson is, never try.'

ANSWERS
p.
295

A

Oscar Wilde

B

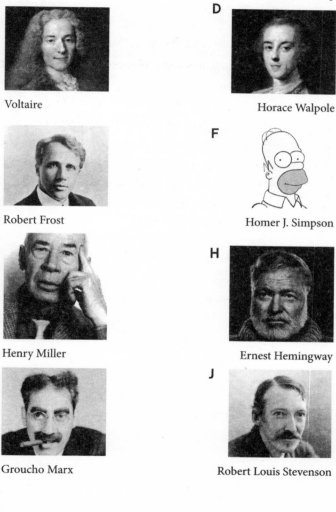

Quentin Crisp

C

Voltaire

D

Horace Walpole

E

Robert Frost

F

Homer J. Simpson

G

Henry Miller

H

Ernest Hemingway

I

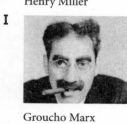

Groucho Marx

J

Robert Louis Stevenson

1. How many hours a week – including lunch – did 45th US President Donald Trump work, on average, over his first two years in office?

   A. 17   **B.** 20   **C.** 29   **D.** 33

2. What percentage of his time did the orange-quiffed psycho-POTUS spend playing golf?

   A. 11%   **B.** 16%   **C.** 23%   **D.** 34%

3. Philosopher René Descartes came up with the wisecrack 'Cogito ergo sum' ('I think therefore I am') and famously did most that of thinking in bed. Why?

   A. He believed exertion shortened human life, so decades of lie-ins would ensure a long existence. He was 89 when he died, in 1650.

   B. As above, but it misfired – Descartes' lazy life ended when he hit 54.

   C. Whilst tutoring the Queen of Sweden, Descartes found his castle lodgings savagely cold, so he stayed in bed to keep warm.

   D. Descartes absorbed this basic soldiers' wisdom while serving as a mercenary in the Dutch army: if you're off duty, stay in bed.

4. As Cambridge University's Lucasian Professor of Mathematics, Charles Babbage had just one duty, which he nevertheless neglected to perform. What was it?

   A. To deliver one 8-week course of lectures a year. (He didn't deliver any – for 11 years.)

   B. To widen public understanding of mathematics by delivering lectures across the country. (He never left Cambridge.)

   C. To visit Buckingham Palace twice yearly, at the vernal and autumnal equinox. (The Lucasian Professor was automatically also Royal Astronomer.)

ANSWERS
p.
296

D. To chair a monthly advisory panel to the Bank of England. Babbage would eat and drink heavily at the luncheon before each meeting, then sleep through the proceedings.

5. On 15 April 1865 John Frederick Parker got plastered in a pub. How did that affect history?

    A. The inebriated Salford signalman caused what was then the world's largest railway disaster – leading to the red-amber-green traffic light system used everywhere today.

    B. A tipsy P.C. Parker arrested the wrong dissident in a Stepney pub, while his true target – one Joseph Dzhugashvili, aka Stalin – slipped out the back and home to Russia.

    C. Newspaper articles about feckless Parker, killed by a horse as he staggered home, leaving behind a wife and seven kids, inspired eugenics founder Francis Galton.

    D. President Abraham Lincoln was shot dead at the theatre because his police guard, Parker, was in the pub.

6. After being sworn in on 2 August 1923, what was the first thing the 30th U.S. President, Calvin Coolidge did?

    A. Went back to bed.

    B. Took a week's holiday in Florida.

    C. Declared 12 new Public Holidays, one a month, all Mondays.

    D. Raided the White House dispensary for opiates.

7. How many sentences a day did James Joyce consider a good output?

8. Which TWO were favoured work habits of the poet W.H. Auden?

    A. He wrote between midnight and 2 am, fuelled by biscuits.

    B. He would never work beyond 5 pm.

    C. He rose just before lunch, had a swim and a snooze, and hit the rhymes at about 5 pm.

    D. He used amphetamines, which he termed his 'labour-saving device in the mental kitchen'.

9. Which 20th-century leader was allegedly unreachable before 2pm, had ministers chasing him for meetings for months, and rarely put any effort into anything, except his carefully-crafted speeches?

    A. Mussolini   **B.** Hitler   **C.** Franco   **D.** Churchill

10. Why, in 2010, did a Judge sentence a Coventry teenager to spend Christmas – and another three months after it – in prison?

    A. He said he 'couldn't be arsed' to stand up in court.

    B. He fell asleep in the dock and when rebuked for it said, 'Whatevs bruv innit.'

    C. He said he'd rather go to prison than do 100 hours unpaid community service.

    D. He changed plea four times, offering in explanation the fact that he'd 'toked this like massive fat blunt' on the way to court and was consequently 'proper mashed'.

IDLE WORSHIP

'Kids, you tried your best and you failed miserably. The lesson is, never try.'
Homer Simpson

These classic singles got to No. 2 in the UK charts. Can you name the songs that kept them off the top spot?

1. 'Heartbreak Hotel' – Elvis Presley, 1956

    A. 'I'll Be Home' – Pat Boone

    B. 'Giddy Up A Ding Dong' – Freddie Bell and the Bellboys

    C. 'The Ying Tong Song' – The Goons

    D. 'Never Do A Tango With An Eskimo' – Alma Cogan

2. 'My Generation' – The Who, 1965

    A. 'Pop Go The Workers' – The Barron Knights

    B. 'The River' – Ken Dodd

    C. 'The Minute You're Gone' – Cliff Richard

    D. 'The Carnival is Over' – The Seekers

3. 'Brown Sugar' – The Rolling Stones, 1971

    A. 'Knock Three Times' – Dawn

    B. 'Ernie, The Fastest Milkman In The West' – Benny Hill

    C. 'Grandad' – Clive Dunn

    D. 'Chirpy, Chirpy, Cheep, Cheep' – Middle of the Road

4. 'The Jean Genie' – David Bowie, 1972

    A. 'Long-haired Lover from Liverpool' – Little Jimmy Osmond

    B. 'I'd Like To Teach The World To Sing' – The New Seekers

    C. 'Leeds United' – Leeds United Football Team

    D. 'Ooo-Wakka-Doo-Wakka-Day' – Gilbert O'Sullivan

ANSWERS
p.
296

5. 'Killer Queen', Queen, 1974

    A. 'Jet' – Paul McCartney and Wings

    B. 'The Wombling Song' – The Wombles

    C. 'Gonna Make You A Star' – David Essex

    D. 'Ma, He's Making Eyes At Me!' – Lena Zavaroni

6. **'God Save The Queen' – The Sex Pistols, 1977**

   A. 'Mull of Kintyre' – Wings
   B. 'I Don't Want to Talk About It' / 'The First Cut is the Deepest' – Rod Stewart
   C. 'Halfway Down The Stairs' – The Muppets
   D. 'Don't Cry For Me, Argentina' (from the musical 'Evita') – Julie Covington

7. **'Vienna' – Ultravox, 1981**

   A. 'Shaddapaya Face' – Joe Dolce Music Theatre
   B. 'There's No-one Quite Like Grandma' – St. Winifred's School Choir
   C. 'Making Your Mind Up' – Bucks Fizz
   D. 'The Birdie Song' – The Tweets

8. **'Fairytale of New York' – The Pogues 1987**

   A. 'Hold Me Now' – Johnny Logan
   B. 'Star Trekkin'' – The Firm
   C. 'The Look Of Love' – Madonna
   D. 'Crockett's Theme' (from the TV series 'Miami Vice') – Jan Hammer

9. **'Wonderwall' – Oasis, 1995**

   A. 'I Believe'/'Up On The Roof' – Robson and Jerome
   B. 'Anywhere Is' – Enya
   C. 'The Gift of Christmas' – Childliners
   D. 'Whoomph! There It Is' – Tag Team

10. **'Common People' – Pulp, 1995**

   A. 'Cotton Eye Joe' – Rednex
   B. 'Unchained Melody'/'White Cliffs Of Dover' – Robson and Jerome
   C. 'Living Next Door To Alice (Who The F*ck Is Alice?)' – Smokie, feat. Roy 'Chubby' Brown
   D. 'Don't Stop (Wiggle,Wiggle)' – The Outhere Brothers

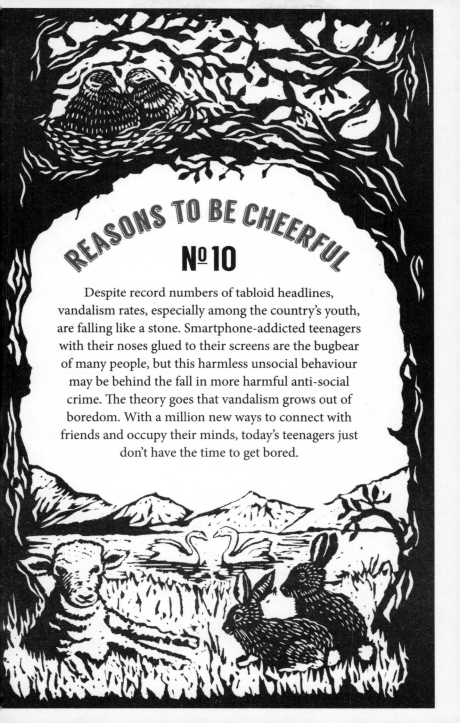

REASONS TO BE CHEERFUL
№ 10

Despite record numbers of tabloid headlines, vandalism rates, especially among the country's youth, are falling like a stone. Smartphone-addicted teenagers with their noses glued to their screens are the bugbear of many people, but this harmless unsocial behaviour may be behind the fall in more harmful anti-social crime. The theory goes that vandalism grows out of boredom. With a million new ways to connect with friends and occupy their minds, today's teenagers just don't have the time to get bored.

1. In 400 BCE, why did Greek artist Zeuxis 'laugh himself to death' after painting a portrait of an elderly woman?

    A. After realising he'd painted all women with the same face for his entire career, he laughed himself into hysterical delirium and jumped out of his studio window to his death.

    B. She had insisted on being made to look like Aphrodite.

    C. Unable to explain or curb his giggles, Zeuxis abandoned the portrait and consulted his doctor, who prescribed a tincture of henbane. He soon stopped laughing, and indeed breathing.

    D. She kept telling him jokes.

2. In 206 BCE the Greek stoic philosopher Chrysippus of Stoli keeled over and died laughing after giving his donkey some wine, then....

    A. Watching it trying to eat figs.

    B. Trying to ride it.

    C. Tying a bell to its tail.

    D. Playing a melody to it on the zither.

3. In 1410 King Martin I of Aragon retired to bed, unwell after eating a whole goose, and called for his jester to cheer him up. The joke the jester told on arrival caused King Martin to die, after three hours of giggles. Did it involve...

    A. Mothers-in-law

    B. Farts

    C. Randy nuns, monks, cardinals, etc.

    D. Figs

ANSWERS
p.
297

4. What prediction, by a fellow soothsayer, apparently caused ancient Greek soothsayer Calchas to laugh himself to death?

5. What news from Venice caused Nanda Bayin, King of Burma, to chortle himself into an early grave in 1599?

A. A Venetian merchant told him the streets were canals.

B. A Venetian merchant tried to explain ice cream.

C. A Venetian merchant told him that men stood up to urinate, and women sat down.

D. A Venetian merchant told him that Venice was a republic and therefore had no king.

6. In 1660, the Scottish Royalist Thomas Urquhart laughed himself to death upon hearing what news?

7. In November 2020, US comedian Robyn Schall broke the internet with a video of herself revisiting the 2020 Goals List she'd written at the start of the year. Which particular missed goal sent Robyn into ironic hysteria and straight to the top table in the TikTok Hall of Fame?

A. Spend less time at home.

B. Spend less time worrying about health.

C. Spend more time with Grandma.

D. Spend more time in China.

8. Following the death of Alex Mitchell, a 50-year-old Norfolk bricklayer whose last 25 minutes were spent laughing non-stop during an episode of 1970s TV comedy show 'The Goodies', what did his widow do?

A. She wrote to 'The Goodies' to thank them for making her late husband's last moments so happy.

B. She wrote to the BBC to demand a refund of her £8 television licence fee.

C. She wrote to MPs and the House of Lords, to the BBC 'Points of View' complaints programme, the Broadcasting Complaints Commission, and to every national newspaper, demanding that comedy shows carry warnings.

D. She wrote a comic poem about the event, which she then performed on the BBC One Sunday night entertainment show 'That's Life'.

9. Following the death in 1984 of British comedian Tommy Cooper during a live, televised performance at Her Majesty's theatre...

   A. A time delay became standard practice for all 'live' broadcast events.

   B. YouTube came under pressure to remove footage of the moment – mistaken by many for a part of Cooper's act – from the website.

   C. Trained medical staff and resus kits became mandatory for all venues over a certain size.

   D. Arrests were made after a 'mini-riot' at a comedy club in Lewisham, South London, when a visiting stand-up made an ill-advised quip about Cooper's act 'dying on stage'.

10. In 1989 which box office hit comedy caused the easily amused Danish audiologist, Ole Bentzen, to die laughing?

   A. 'The Naked Gun'

   B. 'Coming to America'

   C. 'A Fish Called Wanda'

   D. 'Critters 2: The Main Course'

1. In 1935, Percy Grainger, composer of the ditties 'An English Country Garden' and 'Danny Boy', founded the Grainger Museum at the University of Melbourne. What was it intended to display?

    A. 30,000-plus notebooks, music sheets, scribbled-on fag packets, receipts and other scraps of paper.

    B. Items he'd 'collected' from hotels all over the world.

    C. Fan mail and 'items of intimate apparel sent by lady admirers'.

    D. His collection of porn, along with sex aids, photographs of his own buttocks, and naked *papier-maché* models of his closest friends.

2. Who recorded in his journal: 'Bath. Continued experiment with dog after and discovered that a dog will join with a man'?

    A. Eric Gill   **B.** Hans Holbein the Younger
    C. Wassily Kandinsky   **D.** Aubrey Beardsley

3. Which early 20th-century novelist had a stash of upmarket hardcore porn which he kept under lock and key in a safe on their bookshelf?

    A. L. Frank Baum   **B.** John Buchan
    C. Franz Kafka   **D.** E. M. Forster

4. Which of these renowned leaders and independence icons retained a number of young virgins to sleep with him in the nude?

    A. Ernesto 'Che' Guevara   **B.** Haile Selassie
    C. Mohandas K. Gandhi   **D.** Michael Collins

5. Who fantasised about constructing 'a lethal chamber as big as the Crystal Palace' for disposing of the sick and the maimed'?

    A. D. H. Lawrence   **B.** Winston Churchill
    C. George Bernard Shaw   **D.** Francis Crick

ANSWERS
p.
297

6. Which beloved children's writer was described by her daughter as 'arrogant, insecure, pretentious... and without a trace of maternal instinct'?

A. Richmal Crompton   **B.** E. Nesbitt
C. Enid Blyton   **D.** Beatrix Potter

7 'He [Adolf Hitler] didn't just pick on [the Jews] for no reason... there is a trait in the Jewish character that does provoke animosity.' Who pronounced these charming words?

A. Roald Dahl   **B.** A.A. Milne
C. Noel Streatfeild   **D.** Johanna Spyri

8. Who wrote in his diaries about 'bandit-like, filthy Levantines' and described the Chinese as 'a peculiar herd-like nation, more like automatons than people...'?

A. Alexander Fleming   **B.** Max Planck
C. Erwin Schrödinger   **D.** Albert Einstein

9. Which of these charges/criticisms has NOT been levelled at Mother Teresa?

A. Secretly baptising the terminally ill without their consent.
B. Failure to provide painkillers and other malpractices aimed at glorifying suffering and death rather than relieving discomfort.
C. Backing the Indian government's 1970s crackdown on civil rights.
D. Providing a character witness statement for Imelda Marcos.

10. Which of these much-loved British actors has NOT been accused of making racist, homophobic, anti-semitic, sexist or otherwise 'problematic' comments?

A. Martin Freeman   **B.** Idris Elba
C. Jeremy Irons   **D.** Charlotte Rampling

1. **How did the famous French chef Bernard Loiseau die in 2003?**

    A. He blew his brains out after learning that his third Michelin star was in jeopardy.

    B. A venomous snake, destined for the evening's exotic *hors d'oeuvres*, bit Louiseau's left hand.

    C. He choked to death during a marshmallow-eating contest in Paris.

    D. He was murdered by a patron of his restaurant, '*Loiseau et Moi*', after serving an over-cooked steak.

2. **What proportion of the Earth's vertebrates – mammals, fish, birds, amphibians and reptiles – was wiped out between 1970 and 2014?**

    A. 10%   B. 25%   C. 35%   D. 60%

3. **'Women belong to us, just as a tree that bears fruit belongs to a gardener. What a mad idea to demand equality for women! Women are nothing but machines for producing children.' Which charmer wrote these words in 1817?**

    A. Tsar Alexander I   B. George, Prince Regent
    C. Duke of Wellington   D. Napoleon Bonaparte

4. **'Zabernism' means abuse of military power or authority or unjustified aggression. From what incident in 1912 in Zabern (the German name for Saverne, in Alsace) does it derive?**

    A. An overzealous German officer killed a cobbler for smiling at him.

    B. German infantrymen beat up some nuns because they refused to show their papers.

    C. German officers took offence when they lost a football match to local Frenchmen and had them all shot.

    D. A grammar-obsessed officer punished the townsfolk for an error on a local road sign.

ANSWERS
p.
298

5. In 1906 the dying Spanish general Ramón Blanco y Erenas was asked by a priest, 'Do you forgive your enemies?' What was the general's reply?

  A. Go home, priest, before I bite your head off.

  B. I don't have any enemies, I've had them all shot.

  C. My enemies can go fuck themselves. My only regret is that there aren't more of them.

  D. Can't you see I'm busy dying, you fool?

6. In the 1870s, what product was adorned with the name, face and official endorsement of Pope Leo XIII?

  A. Vin Mariani – a wine laced with cocaine.

  B. The 'Il Papa' brand of Pecorino Romano cheese, produced in Leo XIII's hometown of Carpineto.

  C. A brand of tooth-cleaning powder called 'Piu Bianco Del Bianco' ('whiter than white').

  D. 'Vaticano' cigars – the tobacco was imported from Cuba and 'baptised' in Holy Water in St Peter's, Rome, before being rolled into cigars for the faithful.

7. In 1973 how did Ugandan dictator Idi Amin enliven a TV interview with the journalist John Simpson?

  A. He confessed to having eaten a former cabinet minister.

  B. He confessed to having erotic thoughts about the Queen.

  C. He left one of his testicles hanging out of his shorts.

  D. He gave an impromptu demonstration of his strangling technique.

8. What were the last words written by the Antarctic explorer Robert Falcon Scott?

  A. Blizzard bad as ever.

  B. It has turned out nice again.

  C. For God's sake look after our people.

  D. I have decided to have a lie-in.

9. On which of these dates are you most likely to commit suicide?

    A. 1 January   **B.** 8 April
    C. 16 July   **D.** 26 December

10. Which miserly misdeed of oil magnate J. Paul Getty is a myth?

    A. He kept a payphone in his house for the use of guests.

    B. He refused to pay his grandson's ransom, even after they sent the boy's ear to him.

    C. He paid it, but only once his accountants had confirmed it was tax-deductible, and his son had promised to return the sum, with interest.

    D. At his Surrey mansion, he deducted 10% from his servants' wages for their use of heat, light and toilet facilities.

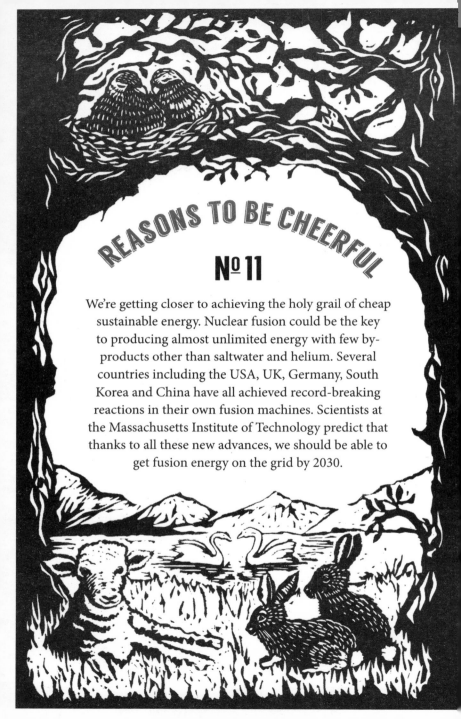

REASONS TO BE CHEERFUL

№ 11

We're getting closer to achieving the holy grail of cheap sustainable energy. Nuclear fusion could be the key to producing almost unlimited energy with few by-products other than saltwater and helium. Several countries including the USA, UK, Germany, South Korea and China have all achieved record-breaking reactions in their own fusion machines. Scientists at the Massachusetts Institute of Technology predict that thanks to all these new advances, we should be able to get fusion energy on the grid by 2030.

1. **Which of these are genuine jibes, which falsified fulminations?**

   A. Suck butter out of my arse – Spain
   B. Ugly as a salad – Bulgaria
   C. Ladybird face – China
   D. Go threaten the geese – Yiddish
   E. May they build a market on the graves of your ancestors – Afghanistan
   F. You are the fatty layer on my warm milk – Ethiopia
   G. May the cat eat you, and the Devil eat the cat – Ireland
   H. Feet of nori (edible seaweed) – Japan
   I. May rats ejaculate upon you – Armenia
   J. Bitter-tasting tits – Finland

And what do these splendid German insults actually mean?

2. **A 'Taker of Warm Showers' is...**

   A. a free-loader
   B. a wimp
   C. a person who likes to be dominated
   D. a spendthrift

3. **A 'Grater of Liquorice' is...**

   A. someone who takes unnecessary measures/goes too far/into too much detail
   B. someone with a pointless occupation
   C. someone who lays on the charm
   D. an ungenerous host

4. **A 'Piss Carnation' is...**

   A. someone/something superficially pleasant, nasty underneath
   B. a nerd
   C. a gift that conveys an insult
   D. a flamboyant but shallow person

ANSWERS p. **299**

5. A 'Driller of Thin Planks' is...

    A. a fool

    B. a person trying to look busy

    C. a control freak

    D. a seducer who is sexually inept

6. A 'Tarzan of Asparagus' is...

    A. someone who is skinny and weak

    B. someone who talks tough but lacks courage

    C. a teller of tall tales

    D. a big fish in a small pond

7. Match the curse to the country (or language...)

    A. '250!'

    B. 'A shoe is upon your head!'

    C. 'May your mother recognise you in a meat pie!'

    D. 'I fart on your balls!'

    E. 'Go comb your monkeys!'

    1. Greece

    2. Arabic

    3. Portugal

    4. Mandarin

    5. Serbia

"I'm tired of this back-slappin' 'isn't humanity neat?' bullshit. We're a virus with shoes." Bill Hicks

Below are ten members of the '27 Forever Club'. Can you identify them and the reason why they didn't live to see their 28th birthdays?

A

B

C

D

E

F

G

H

I

J

ANSWERS
p.
300

1. For which insult against Anne Boleyn was the shoe-maker William Bolton arrested in 1536?

   A. Saying that she was a man.
   B. Saying that she had used witchcraft to seduce the King and would use it to drive him mad.
   C. Saying that her bottom was 'worm-eaten'.
   D. Calling her a 'minger' (yes, it's a very old word).

2. In 1585 Jeremy Vanhill, a labourer from Kent, was hanged for saying, 'I would to God she were dead so that I might shit on her face.' Who was he talking about?

3. What choice expression does Falstaff reserve for the Prince of Wales in 'Henry IV, Part 1'?

   A. A cock-swipe (or cocks-wipe)
   B. A cocks-drip
   C. A groin-flea
   D. A bull's pizzle

4. Which of these insults did Martin Luther NOT hurl at King Henry VIII?

   A. pig
   B. ass
   C. dunghill
   D. spawn of an adder
   E. suet dumpling
   F. basilisk
   G. lying buffoon
   H. mad fool with a frothy mouth

ANSWERS p. **301**

5. Sir Thomas More, meanwhile, described Martin Luther as having a 'beshitted tongue... his shitty mouth (is) truly the shit-pool of all shit'. TRUE or FALSE?

6. In 1676 Ottoman Sultan Mehmed IV wrote to the Zaporozhian Cossacks, in Ukraine, demanding they submit to his authority. They wrote an extremely rude reply, immortalized in a 19th-century painting by Ilya Repin, and using all the insults listed below. Can you fill in the missing words?

  A. Secretary to --c--e- himself
  B. Canst thou not slay a hedgehog with your naked ----?
  C. B---l----- scullion
  D. --c----ian wheelwright
  E. Goat- ------ of Alexandria
  F. -w---he-- of Greater and Lesser Egypt
  G. P-- of Armenia
  H. Podolian -hi--
  I. C-t---t- of Tartary
  J. Hangman of Kamyanets and --o- of all the world and u---------
  K. --io- before God, grandson of the --rp---, and the crick in our ----
  L. Pig's -----
  M. Mare's ----
  N. -u-
  O. ---- thine own ------!

7. The 18th-century French pamphleteer Jacques Hébert had a prose style that would make today's tabloid columnists wet their breeches. Which of the below did the rabid revolutionary NOT say?

  A. 'Fuck The Pope' (the title of one of his publications, in 1790)
  B. 'The greatest of all joys: the head of the female veto removed from her fucking tart's neck.' (On the execution of Marie-Antoinette)
  C. 'Knicker-wearers, midgets of the boutiques, little clerics, you're underestimating your host. Cowardly bandits, expect to receive a beating; you won't escape us, dammit.' (1793)

D. 'And one up the bum, also, to that choucroute guzzling, sweating, farting, jib-jabbering fat bucket on the throne.' (1794, on George III of England).

8. In 1809 Napoleon told de Talleyrand-Périgord, his chief diplomat:

   A. You are a shit in a silk stocking.
   B. When they circumcised you, they threw the wrong bit away.
   C. If I had been given the choice between hiring you, and hiring leprosy, guess which I'd have gone for?
   D. I know one person more vain, more greedy and false than you – she's an old brothel-madam in Ajaccio.

9. In 1861 who received hate mail from Mr A. G. Frick inviting them to 'suck my prick', 'buss my ass' and 'call my Bolics your uncle Dick'?

   A. Queen Victoria   **C.** Charles Darwin
   B. Abraham Lincoln   **D.** Mark Twain

10. Authentic political mud-slinging or made up?

   A. 'The son of 60,000 whores.' Syrian Defence Minister Mustafa Tlass on Yasser Arafat.
   B. 'You are a donkey, Mr Danger.' Venezuelan leader Hugo Chavez to George W. Bush.
   C. 'A turd in fart's clothing.' Alastair Campbell on Gordon Brown.
   D. 'An angry, evil and embittered little bishop.' Robert Mugabe on Desmond Tutu.
   E. 'He would make a drum from the skin of his own mother in order to sound his own praises.' Lloyd George on Winston Churchill.
   F. 'Like his nation: wet, windy and given to long, singsong strings of melodious gibberish.' Winston Churchill on Lloyd George.

G. 'A shiver looking for a spine to run up.' Australian PM Paul Keating on his rival John Howard.

H. 'Joan Rivers with a dick. And missiles.' U.S. Secretary of State Colin Powell, on Colonel Gadaffi.

I. 'Living proof that a pig's bladder on a stick can be elected to Parliament.' Labour MP Tony Banks on Tory counterpart Terry Dicks.

J. 'If that reaper-faced thug hadn't got into politics, he'd be kicking the sh*t out of people for a Chingford bookmaker.' Labour MP Dennis Skinner on Lord Tebbit of Chingford.

K. 'The charisma of a damp rag and the appearance of a low-grade bank clerk.' Nigel Farage to European Council President Herman van Rompuy.

1. Onan, struck down by God in the Book of Genesis, is the first recorded wanker. TRUE or FALSE?

2. Spot the fib. Renowned diarist and dick-diddler Samuel Pepys...

   A. recorded each successful pocket-party in his diaries.

   B. once did the five-finger fandango in Church on Christmas Eve, sitting next to his wife.

   C. was prescribed a tincture of opium, brandy and arsenic to curb his todger-tampering tendencies.

   D. once shot his bolt whilst being rowed up the Thames, without laying a finger on himself, merely thinking about a girl he'd seen in the street.

3. Physicians have linked masturbation (in males) to all of the below, except one. Which is it?

   A. An increased risk of prostate cancer.

   B. A decreased risk of prostate cancer.

   C. Peyronie's Disease: a build-up of scar tissue deforming the penis, making urination and ejaculation painful.

   D. Blindness – not in the Victorian sense, but from bacteria-laden ejaculate getting into the eyes.

4. Fill in the blanks in the lyrics below, taken from anti-wanking song 'The Big M' by the Texan punk Christian band Lust Control.

   'It's --t--a-. It's a release. Release from ----? Forget it. Get ---. It's -r--f----- sex.'

5. When a young André Gide, later winner of the 1947 Nobel Prize for literature, was taken to the family doctor due to his excessive love of pocket hockey, what remedy was prescribed?

   A. The doctor advised Gide's father to take him to the brothel for 'a taste of the real thing'.

   B. The doctor threatened the boy with castration.

ANSWERS p. 301

C. The doctor took him to see 'the consequences of lust': patients dying of syphilis and other ghastly STDs at the Hôtel Dieu de Paris hospital.

D. The doctor gave him 'a small book, full of daguerreotypes of females, all without a stitch on, and told [him] to study it until [he] felt no more lust towards them than towards [his] Geometry book.'

6. Which band not only sang in harmony but also occasionally cracked one off in chorus too?

    A. The Beatles   **B.** The Beach Boys
    C. The Kinks   **D.** The Bay City Rollers

7. Which one of these patented masturbation preventers is fake?

    A. Sohn's Mechanical Sheath (1906): a bear trap for a boy's best friend, activated by 'engorgement'.

    B. Stephenson's Spermatic Truss (1876): a means of strapping penis and testicles towards the back of the thigh.

    C. Kellogg's Corn Flakes (1894): Seventh Day Adventist Dr K. believed plain foods dampened unhealthy passions.

    D. Orth's Cooling Apparatus (1893): erections triggered a jet of cold water to the offending parts.

    E. Dudley's Erectile Alarm Bell (1899) – a.k.a. 'How To Look Really Embarrassed at the Breakfast Table'.

    F. Klinefelter's Gauntlets (1901): fingers were locked into mittens with a surface that was 'corrugated and mildly abrasive'.

    G. Ellen E. Perkins' Sexual Armor (1908): a big zip-up onesie, into which no hand could trespass.

8. What experience, in the summer of 1948, did a quick bout of bishop-beating induce in the beat poet Allen Ginsberg?

    A. A minor stroke, causing him to walk with a slight limp for the rest of his life.

B. A vision of God, alternating with the voice of William Blake reciting 'Ah, Sunflower'.

C. 'A primal, empty howl, from within but beyond me…' – in other words, a noisy bout of bratwurst-bothering which became the inspiration for Ginsberg's most famous poem, 'Howl'.

D. 'The knowledge, as if I had read it in the newspaper, that [baseball legend] Babe Ruth was dead, and that as my own essence snaked out in silken chains from my body, Babe's had evaporated, too. He died that evening.'

9. According to the USA's National Survey of Sexual Health and Behaviour, 80% of males have, by the age of 17, engaged in the harmless, healthy and tax-free activity of masturbation. What's the percentage of females?

A. 88   **B.** 78   **C.** 68   **D.** 58

10. In 1994, what comments about masturbation forced the resignation of Jocelyn Elders, Surgeon-General of the United States?

A. It was ungodly, sullying young men and women's minds and bodies.

B. It was harmless, healthy and should be taught in schools.

C. It caused infertility: this was why groups who rejected the practice, like the Amish and the Hasidic Jews, had large families.

D. Everybody did it – 'teachers, preachers, pastors, Senators, hell, even Barbara Bush, probably'.

"Man first walked upright in order to free his hands for masturbation."
Lily Tomlin

1. **Plato described love as...**

   A. a grave mental disease.
   B. a fever during which the animal soul regained control over the human one.
   C. something which afflicted children, but soon passed.
   D. suffering, cleverly disguised as joy.

2. **According to Shakespeare's *Twelfth Night*, 'Many a good hanging prevents a — —'** (2 words)

3. **According to Plato, 'The hottest love has the — —'** (2 words)

4. **The American writer and Civil War veteran Ambrose Bierce wrote that love was 'a temporary insanity curable by... '**

   A. Death   B. Sex   C. Marriage   D. Children

5. **Who wrote, 'When one is in love one begins by deceiving one's self, and one ends by deceiving others. That is what the world calls a romance.'**

   A. Oscar Wilde   B. George Bernard Shaw
   C. Tennessee Williams   D. Arthur Miller

6. **Somerset Maugham: 'Love is only the — — played on us to achieve — of the species.'** (3 words)

7. **'God gave men both a penis and a brain, but unfortunately not enough blood supply to run both at the same time.' Said...**

   A. Norah Ephron   B. Richard Pryor
   C. Joan Rivers   D. Robin Williams

8. **Prince Philip: 'When a man opens a car door for his wife, it's either — — — or — — —'** (6 words)

9. **Chris Rock: 'A man is only as faithful as his —'** (1 word)

10. **Novelist Chuck Palahniuk: 'If you love something, set it free. But don't be surprised if it comes back with —'** (1 word)

ANSWERS
p.
302

169

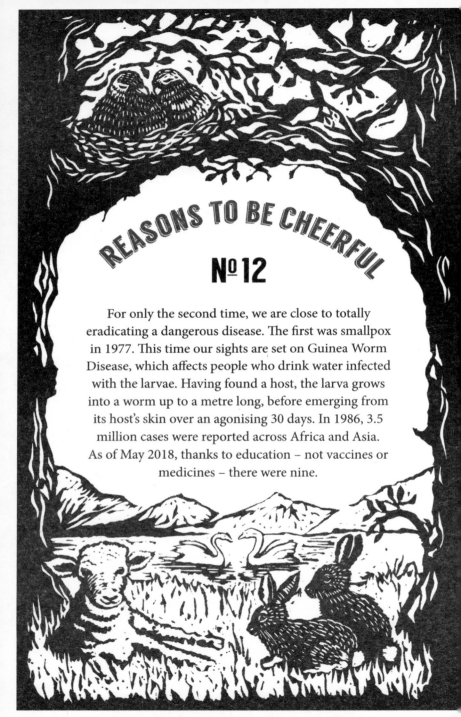

REASONS TO BE CHEERFUL

Nº 12

For only the second time, we are close to totally eradicating a dangerous disease. The first was smallpox in 1977. This time our sights are set on Guinea Worm Disease, which affects people who drink water infected with the larvae. Having found a host, the larva grows into a worm up to a metre long, before emerging from its host's skin over an agonising 30 days. In 1986, 3.5 million cases were reported across Africa and Asia. As of May 2018, thanks to education – not vaccines or medicines – there were nine.

1. How many Americans believe global warming is a hoax?

   A. 7%   **B.** 27%   **C.** 37%   **D.** 47%

2. TRUE or FALSE? One in ten Americans believes that aliens have visited their country – and that their government knows it.

3. Out of a survey of 1,003 British people, what percentage said they believed the Apollo 11 Moon Landings to be faked?

   A. More than 10%   **B.** More than 25%
   C. More than 35%   **D.** More than 50%

4. To which age-group did those space-dream believers predominantly belong?

   A. 16-24   **B.** 25-34   **C.** 35-49   **D.** 50-64   **E.** 65+

5. In a 2018 BBC survey, 64% of respondents claimed...

   A. to have a Guardian Angel.
   B. to believe in an afterlife.
   C. that dinosaurs never existed.
   D. that spells and curses 'worked'.

6. In the same survey, 3 in 5 British adults said they believed in...

   A. fairies, pixies or other 'little folk'   **B.** miracles
   C. virgin births   **D.** auras

7. According to a 2009 Harris Poll, 26% of Americans believe that the movement of the planets determines people's personalities and their destinies (that is, in astrology). Is this MORE or LESS than...

   A. the number of Americans who believe in witches
   B. the number of Americans who believe in UFOs
   C. the number of Americans who believe in Creationism
   D. the number of Americans who believe in ghosts

(ANSWER ALL FOUR QUESTIONS.)

ANSWERS
p.
303

8. TRUE or FALSE? Homeopathy...

    A. is based on the same 'logic' as magic.

    B. is free on the NHS.

    C. was, in 2018, being used by around 120 UK practitioners to 'cure' children of autism.

    D. was found by a House of Commons Committee in 2010 to perform 'no better than placebos'.

    E. claims all disorders and diseases stem from a few underlying chronic 'miasms' (e.g. a single, itching-type miasm causes cancer, deafness, jaundice and epilepsy).

9. What skill was (allegedly) practised by Florida-based Willard Fuller of the Lively Stones World Healing Fellowship?

    A. Psychic dentistry.

    B. Whistling at warts and skin tags until they dropped off.

    C. Spiritual organ transplants.

    D. Faith-based cosmetic surgery.

10. Studies have found that, as a treatment for back pain, paracetamol works...

    A. about as well as placebos.

    B. only slightly better than placebos.

    C. significantly better than placebos.

    D. less well than placebos.

11. In 2017, how much money did NHS England spend on paracetamol?

    A. £0   **B.** £70 million

    C. £50 million   **D.** £1 billion

"Two possibilities exist. Either we are alone in the Universe or we are not. Both are equally terrifying." Arthur C. Clarke

1. Sir Walter Raleigh spent 15 years on death row writing a History of the World, but...

   A. never got further than 1300 BCE.

   B. entrusted the manuscript to his jailer, who burnt it.

   C. abandoned it to write a sonnet about blackbirds, also unfinished.

   D. made most of it up.

2. TRUE or FALSE? Mozart's unfinished final work, 'Requiem', was...

   A. commissioned by Count Franz von Wallsegg, an amateur musician who planned to claim it as his own work, written in tribute to his deceased wife.

   B. farmed out by Mozart's widow to another composer, Franz Süssmayr, for completion, then submitted with Mozart's forged signature so she could claim payment.

   C. sampled by Austrian drag artiste Conchita Wurst in the 2015 Eurovision entry, 'Rise Like A Phoenix'.

   D. torn by an unknown person when on display at the World's Fair in Brussels 1958. The lost fragment has never been found.

3. Haydn's 68th string quartet was left incomplete when he fell fatally ill. What else was less-than-complete after the composer's death in 1809?

4. Which Beethoven Symphony was left incomplete when he slipped into unconsciousness and died in 1827?

5. What prevented Franz Schubert completing his Symphony No. 8 in B minor, his 'Unfinished Symphony', in 1828?

   A. Measles

   B. Tuberculosis

   C. A Russian shell (Schubert had unwisely chosen to holiday in the Black Sea resort of Varna during the Russo-Turkish War.)

   D. Syphilis and/or the mercury given to 'cure' it.

ANSWERS p. **303**

6. **What stopped Arnold Bennet from finishing his final novel?**

  A. Salvador Dali's 'The Persistence of Memory' – disturbed after seeing the painting unveiled in Paris in 1931, Bennett was flattened by a tram on leaving the gallery.

  B. The taxman – Bennett became obsessed with a £21 rebate he felt was owing to him and spent his final weeks feverishly writing letters about it.

  C. Politics – Bennett became so depressed by the 1931 election defeat of the Labour Party that he stopped writing.

  D. A glass of water – Bennett ignored a Parisian waiter's advice and drank a glass of unboiled *eau*, dying of typhoid soon afterwards.

7. **After he'd sketched out the first draft of his 'Symphony No. 10' what sudden event ended the life of Gustav Mahler in 1911?**

  A. A bacterial infection
  B. A virus
  C. A bullet (from a crazed fan)
  D. A wasp sting

8. **Whose unfinished portrait has remained on display since his death in 1945?**

  A. Adolf Hitler
  B. Franklin D. Roosevelt
  C. Lord Alfred Douglas
  D. Jerome Kern

9. **What fate met Richard Pryor's subversive film, 'Uncle Tom's Fairy Tales'?**

  A. Pryor died in 2005 before it could be edited, and his widow has blocked all attempts to finish and screen the film.

  B. Pryor's lawyers have the only copy, but due to an ongoing family feud, nobody can access the deceased's archives.

  C. Whilst watching a rough cut, Pryor started rowing with his wife about the time and money he was spending on the film, and in a fit of rage, he destroyed it.

D. As a finale to the marital tiff mentioned above, Pryor did not destroy the film, but posted the only copy to a 'Mrs Bitch, Bitch Drive, Bitchville, Bitchigan'. Despite a lengthy search, it has never been found.

10. On 7 June 1926, during construction of Barcelona's La Sagrada Familia, Gaudi was returning from confession when he was struck by a tram. He might have recovered, and completed one of the world's greatest, strangest buildings, except that...

    A. his dishevelled appearance and lack of ID led people to assume he was a beggar, therefore not worth saving.

    B. first on the scene were a pair of priests, who administered the Last Rites instead of trying to save Gaudi's life.

    C. opponents of the fantastical cathedral bribed medical staff at the Hospital del Mar to administer a fatal overdose of morphine.

    D. Gaudi's unconscious body rolled into a gully dug to drain water from the cathedral site, and he was already dead by the time he was found.

Can you match these dying words with the people opposite?

1. 'On the contrary.'

2. 'Go on, get out! Last words are for fools who haven't said enough!'

3. 'Hold me up, I want to shit.'

4. 'Channel 5 is all shit, isn't it? Christ, the crap they put on there. It's a waste of space.'

5. 'Go away. I'm all right.'

6. 'I knew it. I knew it. Born in a hotel room and God damn it died in a hotel room.'

7. 'Tomorrow, I shall no longer be here.'

8 'I think I could eat one of Bellamy's veal pies.'

9. 'I'd hate to die twice, it's so boring.'

10. 'Don't let it end like this. Tell them I said something interesting.'

ANSWERS
p.
304

"The universe that we observe has precisely the properties we should expect if there is, at bottom, no design, no purpose, no evil, no good, nothing but pitiless indifference." Richard Dawkins

A

Karl Marx, philosopher

B

Walt Whitman, American poet

C

Adam Faith, actor and singer

D

William Pitt the Younger

E

Eugene O'Neill, playwright

F

Nostradamus

G

Francisco 'Pancho' Villa,
Mexican revolutionary

H

Henrik Ibsen, poet
and playwright

I

H. G. Wells, author

J

Richard Feynman, theoretical physicist

AND ANOTHER THING...

177

1. **In 1194 what extreme measure did Leopold V, Duke of Austria take to try and save his own life?**

    A. He drank snake venom to protect him from bites.

    B. During a Holy Crusade, he converted to Islam.

    C. After receiving an arrow in his skull during a battle, he simply plugged the hole and fought on.

    D. He held an axe head against his gangrenous foot while a servant struck it with a mallet.

2. **What did Samuel Pepys do on 19 December 1664?**

    A. He urinated inside St Olave's church after spending the day celebrating his promotion.

    B. He kissed a dead queen.

    C. He 'bantered rashly' with the sergeants of the Royal Dockyard, and got himself locked in the cells.

    D. He apologised to his wife for giving her a black eye, then went off to meet his mistress.

3. **After the Battle of Edessa in 260, what did Persian King Shakur do to his vanquished foe, Roman Emperor Valerian?**

    A. He freed him in exchange for 100 Roman virgins.

    B. He used him as a living human footstool.

    C. He cut off his ears and ate them fried in garlic.

    D. He forced him to perform as court jester.

4. **During King Leopold's reign of terror in the Belgian Congo, how did Leon Rom, District Commissioner of Matadi, upset his neighbours?**

    A. He played his new saxophone through the night.

    B. He deflowered every virgin in the region.

    C. He decorated his flowerbeds with human heads.

    D. He played polo with a severed head.

ANSWERS p.
305

5. What was special about Martin Bormann's copy of *Mein Kampf*?

    A. It had a bookmark made from human hair.

    B. It was bound in human skin.

    C. It was printed in Yiddish.

    D. It was the only copy ever made in Braille.

6. In what circumstances did two of Oscar Wilde's half-sisters die?

    A. They were run over by taxis.

    B. Their petticoats caught fire.

    C. They caught Spanish flu.

    D. They died of tuberculosis within 24 hours of each other.

7. Which one of these great writers did NOT die in poverty?

    A. Thomas Paine   **B.** Herman Melville

    C. Elizabeth Gaskell   **D.** Edgar Allen Poe

8. Who wrote of the British: '[They are] Cold-blooded queers with nasty complexions and terrible teeth... They warm their beers and chill their baths and boil all their food, including bread'?

    A. Mark Twain   **B.** P. J. O'Rourke

    C. Edgar Allen Poe   **D.** Ernest Hemingway

9. Which of these was NOT a genuine Stuart-era patent medicine?

    A. Toenails and pubic hair

    B. Goose turds

    C. Oil of badger

    D. The hand of a corpse

10. Which of the following sub-optimal outcomes for the human race did Professor Stephen Hawking NOT foresee?

    A. The temperature on Earth will rise to 250°C, with regular sulphuric acid showers.

    B. Robots will take over.

    C. Plants will evolve to uproot themselves, and wreak a terrible revenge on humanity.

    D. Nuclear war.

INGRATITUDE JOURNAL NO. 11

20 SONGS THAT SHOULD NOT NEVER HAVE BEEN ALLOWED TO SULLY THE WORLD'S EARDRUMS

SONG	TWO-WORD DISMISSAL
You're Beautiful	No words

20 ACCLAIMED FILMS THAT ARE IN FACT SHITE

FILM	TWO-WORD DISMISSAL
Citizen Kane	Unending tedium

1. TRUE or FALSE? Jehovah's Witnesses originally predicted that the world would end in 1873, then 1914, 1925, and 1975.

2. Who were the original 'Seekers' (i.e. before the Australian folk-influenced quartet adopted the name)?

    A. A cult featured in a 1962 episode of 'The Twilight Zone', attracting criticism from the Mormon church whose members, officially at least, didn't watch television.

    B. An offshoot of Spiritualism, whose adherents believed it possible to visit and have 'relations' with the dead, as well as communicate with them.

    C. Followers of 'false Messiah' Jacob Frank in 17th-century Turkey, mistakenly called 'Seekers' by English travellers due to their Arabic nickname '*siqa*', meaning 'idiots'.

    D. Followers of Dorothy Martin, a Chicago housewife, who claimed in 1954 that aliens had warned her about a world-ending flood, from which a lucky few would be saved in spaceships.

3. Who, aged 15 was annointed by Jesus Christ to be 'the father of all humanity', subsequently serving 13 months in a US prison for tax evasion, and on a single day in 1997 presiding over the simultaneous marriage of 30,000 couples in Washington, DC.?

4. Kentucky farmer's son Edgar Cayce (1877-1945) could allegedly learn a book's contents by resting his head on it and was dubbed 'Sleeping Prophet' due to his habit of receiving portentous visions whilst having a nice long kip. Which of the below did Cayce NOT foresee?

    A. The merger of various US telecommunications firms.

    B. The shifting of the polar axes in the early years of the 2nd millennium.

    C. World War II.

    D. A wall to prevent migration from Mexico.

ANSWERS p. **306**

5. According to the grand-daddy of daft predictions, Nostradamus, what virtually incomprehensible event would happen in July 1999?

    A. 'A Great King of Terror will come from the sky to bring back the Great King of the Mongols, before and after Mars, forever.'

    B. 'The Great Tomb of the people of Aquitaine will approach Tuscany.'

    C. 'The nuptials will take some arranging... the upside-down place where they transport the shit, both young and old consort in an uncontaminated way.'

    D. 'Saturn will change from gold to iron, the reverse Raypoz will exterminate everyone, before the attack there will be signs in the sky.'

6. Ronald Weinland, founder of the Church of God – Preparing for the Kingdom of God (COG-PKG), predicted the world would end on 30 September 2008, and when it didn't, he amended the date to 27 May 2012. What happened to Weinland a few days after this second prophecy?

    A. He left a message saying he'd 'gone to the wilderness to ask God what had gone wrong' and vanished, never to be seen again.

    B. He was tried for tax evasion and concealing a Swiss bank account containing church funds.

    C. He renounced his ministry, handed back the money his followers had given him, and opened a tackle shop in the Colorado town of Fruita.

    D. He was killed by a man who had (twice) given away all his possessions and quit his job after believing Weinland's predictions.

7. Who has **NOT** been revered as a living god, saint or messiah?

   A. The Imperial Japanese Army during World War II.

   B. Victor Hugo.

   C. Kaiser Wilhelm II.

   D. HRH the Prince Philip, Duke of Edinburgh.

8. What is the significance of the Mayan date 13.0.0.0.0 4 Ahau 3 K'ank'in (21-23 December 2013 in the Western calendar)?

   A. It concludes a 5,126 year-old cycle in the Mayans' Long Count calendar.

   B. The Mayans predicted this date would begin a cycle of renewal for the planet.

   C. The Mayans predicted that the world would end for ever on this date.

   D. The Mayans predicted that this was when the god Bolon Yokte' K'uh would descend to earth.

9. What did Rasputin claim would happen on 23 December 2013?

   A. The end of monarchy in Russia.

   B. A 'Russian whose name was known around the world' would die.

   C. Most of the planet would be consumed by fire, and Christ would return to comfort the few who remained.

   D. Nothing. According to Rasputin, the world would have ceased to exist in 1922.

10. What's the missing word (it's all the same word) from the following prediction by Thomas Edison?

    'The house of the next century will be furnished from basement to attic with -----. The baby of the 21st century will be rocked in a ----- cradle... and his mother's boudoir will be sumptuously equipped with ----- furnishings.'

APOCALYPSE NOW AND THEN

11. In 1951, US Magazine *Popular Mechanic* claimed that many hard-working middle-class American families could own a helicopter if it weren't for what?

   A. President Truman's personal aversion to choppers.
   B. The Cold War.
   C. The objections of the communist-infiltrated Air Traffic Controllers Union.
   D. Concern that women would demand to be allowed to fly them.

12. Fill in the missing word in the following quote from pioneer of radio, Guglielmo Marconi:

   'The wireless era will make war impossible because it will make war –i--c----–.'

13. Robert Metcalfe, co-inventor of Ethernet, in 1995: 'I predict that X will soon go supernova and in 1996 will catastrophically collapse.'. What was X?

14. Which company are the two pundits below talking about?

   '... two options. The first is to break itself up, selling off the hardware side. The second is to sell the company outright.' *The Economist*, 1995.

   'I'd shut it down and give the money back to the shareholders.'
   Michael Dell, CEO, Dell Computers, 1997

"It's the end of the world, every day. For someone." Margaret Atwood

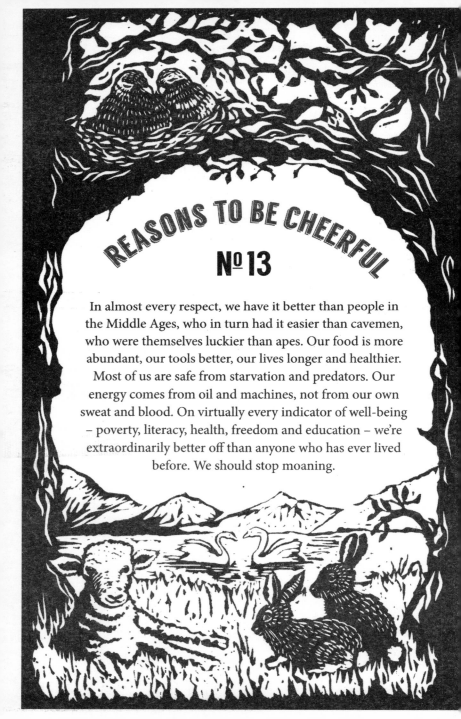

REASONS TO BE CHEERFUL

№ 13

In almost every respect, we have it better than people in the Middle Ages, who in turn had it easier than cavemen, who were themselves luckier than apes. Our food is more abundant, our tools better, our lives longer and healthier. Most of us are safe from starvation and predators. Our energy comes from oil and machines, not from our own sweat and blood. On virtually every indicator of well-being – poverty, literacy, health, freedom and education – we're extraordinarily better off than anyone who has ever lived before. We should stop moaning.

1. Complete Lord Byron's stirring epitaph on Lord Castlereagh...

> 'Posterity will ne'er survey
> a Nobler grave than this:
> Here lie the bones of Castlereagh:
> Stop, traveller, and —'

2. 'Oh?' About whose death did Queen Mary make this heartfelt utterance?

3. 'An old Wykehamist who ended up as a moderately successful Chelsea —' Which word is missing from critic Kenneth Tynan's post-mortem verdict on the author William Donaldson.

   A. Comedian   **B.** Pervert   **C.** Joke   **D.** Pimp

4. 'Good career move.' Gore Vidal in 1984, on whose death?

5. 'Fourteen heart attacks and he had to die in my week.' Why was Janis Joplin so disgruntled about the death of President Dwight D. Eisenhower?

   A. She was close to death herself and didn't want anyone else stealing the limelight.
   B. His death bumped her off the cover of *Newsweek*.
   C. The news overshadowed her only Number One hit, 'Me and Bobby McGee'.
   D. 'Death Of A President', the film in which she had a small – and, she hoped, career-reviving – cameo, was abruptly shelved.

6. 'X died when he joined the army.' About which newly-departed, fellow musical legend did John Lennon make this comment?

7. 'To be giving this much coverage to him day in and day out, what does it say about us as a country?' Peter King, Republican State Congressman for New York, on the death of whom?

ANSWERS
p.
308

8 'Everything about X's life has been a pernicious confection.' Playwright John Osborne on the death of...

    A. author Roald Dahl
    B. actress Jill Bennett
    C. actress Jill Esmond
    D. actor Leonard Sachs

9. 'It is no longer an event; it is only a piece of —' Complete Marshall Talleyrand's comment on the death of Napoleon.

    A. gossip
    B. tittle-tattle
    C. news
    D. entertainment

10. What comment by a director did actress Bette Davis have engraved on her tombstone?

    A. There goes a lady.
    B. There goes a bitch who was proud of the title.
    C. She won't live for ever. It'll be far longer than that.
    D. She did it the hard way.

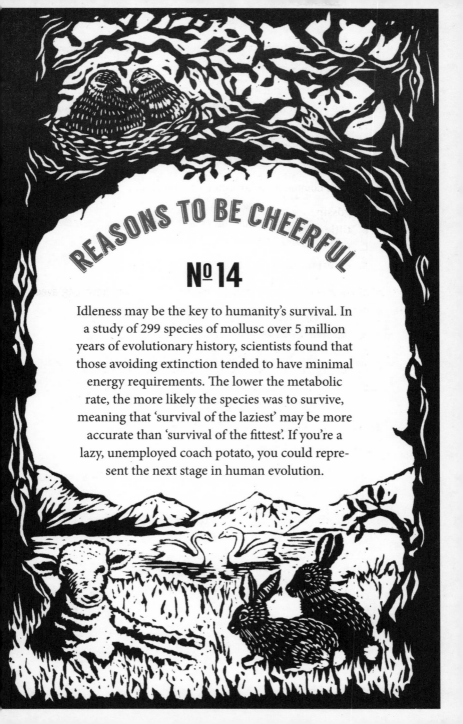

REASONS TO BE CHEERFUL

№14

Idleness may be the key to humanity's survival. In a study of 299 species of mollusc over 5 million years of evolutionary history, scientists found that those avoiding extinction tended to have minimal energy requirements. The lower the metabolic rate, the more likely the species was to survive, meaning that 'survival of the laziest' may be more accurate than 'survival of the fittest'. If you're a lazy, unemployed coach potato, you could represent the next stage in human evolution.

1. **Why did Anna Jarvis campaign against Mother's Day?**

   A. She'd invented it, but then became horrified at its commercialism.

   B. She felt it discriminated against women who couldn't, or didn't want to be mothers. And men.

   C. She was against all 'secular' events, and wanted the calendar to be strictly Christian.

   D. She said it encouraged people to think they deserved to be rewarded just for doing their duty.

2. **Roughly how much of all the plastic that has ever been created (about 8.3 billion metric tons) has never been recycled?**

   A. 61%   **B.** 71%   **C.** 81%   **D.** 91%

3. **Someone takes their own life every**

   A. forty seconds   **B.** three minutes
   C. five minutes   **D.** six minutes

4. **Which is the most popular London Underground line for suicide jumpers?**

   A. Northern   **B.** Central   **C.** Piccadilly   **D.** Jubilee

5. **PART I. Continuing the theme, which is the most popular season for a London Underground suicide?**

   PART II. And which, among these tube stations, are the three most popular for suicides?

   A. Amersham   **B.** Mile End
   C. Golders Green   **D.** Balham
   E. Tooting Bec   **F.** Kentish Town
   G. Turnham Green   **H.** Cockfosters
   I. King's Cross   **J.** Vauxhall

ANSWERS p. **308**

6. **What is deipnophobia?**

    A. A morbid fear of social media
    B. A morbid fear of dinner parties
    C. Fear of being without mobile phone coverage
    D. Fear of snooker

7. **Which of these species was declared extinct in 2020?**

    A. The Smooth Handfish (Tasmania)
    B. The Splendid Poison Frog (Panama
    C. The Bonin Pipistrelle (Japan)
    D. The European Bison (Poland/Belarus)

8. **What is anhedonia?**

    A. A morbid fear of rude words and obscene gestures.
    B. A preoccupation with luxury.
    C. The inability to experience pleasure.
    D. Belief that you are dead or rotting, have lost all your blood or internal organs.

9. **The US earns 19 billion dollars a year from the export of**

    A. bovine semen
    B. blood
    C. camel steak
    D. snail slime

10. **What is agalmatophilia?**

    A. Sexual attraction to dolls or mannequins.
    B. Arousal by touching strangers surreptitiously in a public place.
    C. Arousal by the sight of oneself.
    D. Sexual attraction to caverns, crevices and valleys.

What links these people and who is the odd one out?

And here's a tiny wee clue...

ANSWERS
p.
310

Complete the following gems of footballing wisdom:

1. ALAN GREEN: 'You don't score 64 goals in 86 games at the highest level without being able to – –' (2 words)

2. PHIL BROWN: 'If you closed your eyes, you couldn't tell the – between the – –' (3 words)

3. RON ATKINSON: 'He dribbles a lot and the opposition don't like it. You can – it – – their –' (4 words)

4. KEVIN KEEGAN: 'They're the second best team in the world, and there's – – – than –' (4 words)

5. DAVID PLEAT: 'A game is not won until – – –' (3 words)

6. In 1999 David Beckham said that he definitely wanted his son Brooklyn to be christened, but he did not yet know... what?

7. PAUL 'GAZZA' GASCOIGNE. 'I do not make predictions and I – –' (2 words)

8. What reason did former Liverpool striker Ian Rush allegedly give for being unable to settle in Italy?

9. TERRY VENABLES: 'There are two ways of getting the ball. One is from your own team-mates, and that's the – –' (2 words)

10. JOHN HOLLINS: 'A contract on a piece of paper, saying you want to leave, is like a – of – – – – to –' (6 words)

11. BARRY VENISON: 'I always used to put my right boot on first, and then obviously my – –' (2 words)

12. DAVID BECKHAM: 'My parents have been there for me, ever since I was – –' (2 words)

13. MARK VIDUKA: 'I would not be bothered if we lost every game as long as we – – –' (3 words)

14. NEVILLE SOUTHALL: 'If you don't believe you can win, there is no point in – – – – – – – – – –' (10 words)

ANSWERS
p.
311

15. What did Nottingham Forest player-manager Stuart 'Psycho' Pearce once claim he could see at the end of the tunnel?

16. After allegedly calling Manchester United player Paul Ince 'an arrogant black cunt', in 1994, Pearce concluded, '[it] wasn't appropriate — — —' (3 words)

17. MARK DRAPER 'I'd like to play for an Italian club, like — ' (1 word)

18. IAN WRIGHT: 'Without being too harsh on David Beckham — — — — — ' (5 words)

19. RONNIE WHELAN: 'He's put on weight and I've lost it, and — —' (2 words)

20. According to Bobby Robson, which are the most important minutes of a football match?

Google 'stupid laws' and you will quickly be informed that it is illegal to perform oral sex in Wales on a Sunday, among much besides. Most are urban legends, but which of these UK laws are real? (Five are real and five are made up.)

1. It is illegal to enter the Houses of Parliament wearing a suit of armour.

2. It is illegal to place a stamp of the Queen upside down on a letter.

3. It is illegal to stand within 100 yards of the reigning monarch without socks on.

4. It is illegal to handle salmon in suspicious circumstances.

5. It is against the law to jump a queue while buying a ticket on the London Underground.

6. A man may legally urinate in public, as long it is against the rear offside wheel of his motor vehicle and his right hand is on the vehicle.

7. It is against the law to beat or shake any carpet or rug in any street but beating or shaking a doormat is allowed before 8 am.

8. It is illegal to impersonate a Chelsea Pensioner.

9. It is illegal to keep a lunatic without a licence.

10. It is against the law to be drunk in a pub.

ANSWERS
p.
311

And which of these laws from around the world are real?

1. In Rome it is illegal to keep a goldfish in a bowl.
2. In the Australian state of Victoria it is illegal to use a vacuum cleaner on Good Friday.
3. In Indonesia masturbation is forbidden.
4. In the Polish town of Tuszyn, Winnie the Pooh is banned from playgrounds as he doesn't wear pants and has non-gender-specific genitalia.
5. In parts of France there's a ban on the use of ketchup.
6. In Pakistan it is illegal to celebrate St. Valentine's Day.
7. In the state of Arkansas there is still a law allowing a man to beat a woman up to once a week.
8. In Germany it is an offence to deny a chimney sweep access to your home.
9. In Iran mullets and ponytails are banned.
10. In Tibet you aren't allowed to be reincarnated without permission.

ANSWERS
p.
313

Which of these were genuine calls to the UK emergency services, and which never happened?

1. A man wanted paramedics to perform a DNA test in order to prove his partner's infidelity.

2. A woman wondered if storing cracked eggs in her fridge was a health risk.

3. A caller complained that they had been waiting for a pizza delivery for 45 minutes.

4. A woman complained because Jacob Rees-Mogg was on TV again and he was frightening the children.

5. Responding to a traumatic injury callout, an ambulance crew discovered the caller just wanted her son collected from the pub.

6. A man called because his wife was snoring.

7. A man complained that his new shoes were too tight.

8. A woman complained that she had bought a cold kebab and the shop wouldn't replace it.

9. A woman had seen a clown selling balloons for £5 each, which was much more than other clowns were charging.

10. A 4am caller asked: 'Where's the best place to get a bacon sandwich?'

11. A Consett man dialled 999 because his internet signal was crap.

12. A Manchester woman complained her cat had been playing with some string for over two hours and the noise was 'doing her head in'.

13. A Gloucester woman said her cat was staring at her.

14. Merseyside Police were summoned to a home on Christmas Day by a woman disgusted at the quality of the toys in the crackers.

15. A Yorkshire man dialled to complain that a cat had eaten his bacon.

ANSWERS
p.
313

FIGHTING MAD

Which of these were genuine reasons for starting a military conflict?

1. A soldier was shot after crossing a border while chasing his dog.

2. A Spanish coastguard sliced off a British subject's ear for smuggling.

3. France went to war with a country 5,700 miles away after an expatriate pastry chef's café was ransacked by looters.

4. Country A refused to buy any more of Country B's highly-addictive drugs.

5. Some Italian soldiers stole a bucket from a well.

6. A 3-2 win in a FIFA World Cup Qualifier led to a four-day conflict and the loss of around 3,100 lives.

7. A war fought over whether napkins should be red or blue.

8. A chariot race.

9. Irreconcilable differences over grammar.

10. A dispute over which end of the egg to crack first.

ANSWERS
p.
314

"Since I no longer expect anything from mankind except madness, meanness, and mendacity; egotism, cowardice, and self-delusion, I have stopped being a misanthrope." Irving Layton

1. **Which actor and playwright collapsed and died on stage while playing the title role of a hypochondriac?**

   A. Christopher Marlowe   **B.** Ben Jonson
   C. John Dryden   **D.** Molière

2. **Which of the below is the only recorded *coulrogenic* death?**

   A. More accurately a coulrophobogenic death, Francine Glatt of Basel died in 1988 because her fear of vegetables limited her to a sausage-only diet. (The word is from *kolos,* the ancient Greek for vegetable.)

   B. William Snyder, aged 13, died in San Francisco in 1854, when a circus clown swung him by his heels. (The word is derived from *kolon*, meaning stilts.)

   C. Henry Taylor, a pall bearer at Kensal Green cemetery, was crushed to death by a coffin in 1850. (From *kouleion*, meaning grave.)

   D. In 2005, a Canadian teenager died of butane poisoning brought on by his excessive use of spray-on deodorant. (From *coullros*, meaning clean.)

3. **Who died on the day he despised the most, Christmas Day?**

   A. Bob Hope   **B.** Bing Crosby
   C. W.C. Fields   **D.** Spencer Tracy

4. **What was ironic about the death of the famous 19th-century surgeon Sir Frederick Treves?**

   A. He performed the first appendectomy in England and died from peritonitis, a disease commonly resulting from a ruptured appendix.

   B. He was physician to Joseph Merrick, the so-called 'Elephant Man', and he died from lymphatic filariasis, a human disease caused by parasitic worms, also known as elephantiasis.

ANSWERS
p.
316

C. He died from a stomach abscess, having successfully treated the Prince of Wales for a similar condition.

D. He died from septicaemia, having campaigned for cleaner hospitals to reduce deaths in childbirth.

5. How was the death of the lawmaker Draco of Athens in c. 620 BCE caused by his own popularity?

    A. Being carried aloft by a grateful crowd, he struck his head on a beam and died.

    B. Showered with cloaks and hats by the crowd at a theatre performance, he suffocated.

    C. He left his house to plead with a vast crowd of fans to go home, and was crushed in the ensuing stampede.

    D. Fellow lawmaker, Thales, grew increasingly jealous and eventually poisoned Draco.

6. What was unusual about the death of Jerome Moody in 1985?

    A. The Northamptonshire Health and Safety Officer was electrocuted 'due to many basic, fatal errors' in the wiring of his self-built home, according to the inquest.

    B. He drowned at a New Orleans pool party attended by 100 lifeguards.

    C. Having just inherited his dairy-owning family's fortunes, he died when a canister of whipped cream exploded.

    D. A member of the 1984 US Olympic swimming team, he drowned after driving his car into a pool.

7. The death of Hans Staininger, Burgomaster of Branau, in 1567 could have been avoided if only he'd...

    A. shaved: he tripped on his own, four-foot-long beard.

    B. got a cab: too drunk to make it home, he bedded down in a barn, lit his pipe and fell asleep in the inferno.

    C. listened to his wife: she'd told him not to go out, and he was swept away in a flash flood.

D. waited: he was so impatient to try the hooch he'd been brewing that he cracked open a cask too early and poisoned himself.

8. How did the health food advocate Basil Brown die?

   A. After eating raw spinach – the 'superfood' was contaminated by E.coli.

   B. The inventor of the 'cantaloupe diet' died of salmonella poisoning after eating tainted melons.

   C. Liver damage after drinking gallons of carrot juice.

   D. The man who coined the phrase 'five a day' was hit by a lorry full of lettuce.

9. Her last role was in a film where her character said: 'What can happen on a plane?' but before the film was to be released, she died in a plane crash and the studio executives cut the line from the movie. Was she...?

   A. Hedy Lamarr   **B.** Carole Lombarde.

   C. Lana Turner   **D.** Ava Gardner

10. How did convicted murderer Michael Anderson Godwin die?

   A. While his guards were watching US television series 'Prison Break', he suffocated in an escape tunnel.

   B. About to be hung for murder, he choked to death on his final meal, a *Chateaubriand* steak.

   C. Reprieved from the noose, he accidentally hanged himself while fixing a clothes line in his cell.

   D. Reprieved from the electric chair, he created his own by trying to mend a pair of headphones whilst sitting on a steel toilet.

DEATH BY IRONY

"I wish I was a cannibal, less for the pleasure of eating someone than for the pleasure of vomiting him." Emil Cioran

Genuine Shakespeare at his sweary best... or just made-up Tudorish-sounding bollocks? Bonus points if you can name the play...

1. Thou churlish full-gorged maggot-pie.

2. Thou clay brained guts, thou knotty pated fool, thou whoreson obscene greasy tallow catch!

3. Fly-bitten measle! You puling pox-marked mountebank!

4. Who is this? A mammering crook-pated bladder!

5. Thou bootless shard-borne scut, a toad-spotted harpy!

6. Thou art an embossed carbuncle in the corrupted blood of thine line.

7. Thou puking fustiliarian, a fitful half-witted gull-catcher.

8. Thou pox-marked rampallion! White-livered malkin!

9. Sodden-witted lord! Thou hast no more brain than I have in mine elbow!

10. You common cry of curs, whose breath I hate, as reek of all that rots!

11. Swag-bellied coxcomb!

12. You poor, base, fen-sucked gudgeon!

13. Away you starveling, you eel-skin, you dried neat's tongue, you bull's pizzle, you stock-fish.

14. The tartness of thy breath could curdle sour milk anew.

15. Th'art ugly and venomous as a mammering lewdster.

ANSWERS
p.
317

16. A whoreson, beetle-headed, flap-eared knave.

17. Away, clay brained maw.

18. Away, you three-inch fool.

19. Thou qualling, pilfering mange-dog.

20. Thou cream faced loon.

21. You scullion! You rampallian! You fustilarian! I'll tickle your catastrophe!

22. You hell-hated mammet! You boil-brained vassal-ketch!

23. His wit is as slow as the summer Nile.

24. Your mother wert an ill-nurtured scarts-tail and a ship's bitch that scarce stepped ashore but for business below deck.

25. Thou leathern-jerkin, crystal-button, knot-pated, gatering, puke-stocking, caddis-garter, smooth-tongue, Spanish pouch.

1. When pharma-giant Bayer discovered that a blood-clotting product they were selling, Factor VIII, was infecting people with HIV, they developed a safer medicine. What else did they do?

2. Which world famous manufacturer of everything from car parts to vacuum cleaners also made Nazi gas chambers?

3. What argument did Philip Morris use to convince the government of one small country that they should continue to sell their cigarettes there? (Bonus point if you can name the country)

    A. Smoking rarely killed anyone in countries with a lower life expectancy, because something else would get them first.

    B. Tobacco smoke deterred flies and mites and was therefore a promoter of hygiene.

    C. Shortening lives was beneficial to a cash-strapped country, because dead citizens don't cost anything.

    D. If the economy ever tanked, cigarettes would step into the breach as currency.

4. When 'Pharma Bro' Martin Shkreli purchased the rights to Daraprim – used to combat the parasitic infection toxoplasmosis in people already sick with HIV, cancer and malaria – he raised the cost of one pill from $13.50 to...

    A. $135 **B.** $270 **C.** $450 **D.** $750

5. What defence did Shkreli give for the price hike?

    A. He was a capitalist, not a saviour.

    B. It was altruistic – the profits from this price hike would fund the search for a newer, better remedies.

    C. It was 'fake news' (but he then hastily lowered the price).

    D. Making Daraprim so costly would incentivise governments to attack the root causes of HIV, malaria and cancer – prevention being better than cure.

ANSWERS
p.
317

"If you want to know what God thinks of money, just look at the people he gave it to." Dorothy Parker

6. Which prescription pill marketed as a 'low addiction painkiller' caused an overdose and dependency epidemic and made the Sackler family $4 billion richer in just over 10 years?

    A. Codeine   **B.** Fentanyl   **C.** OxyContin   **D.** Vicodin

7. In this transcript of a 2007 chat – later filed as court documents – a Singapore-based yen trader at the Royal Bank of Scotland had the following exchange with traders in other banks, about what?

> Yen Trader: 'What's the call on the X?'
> Trader 2: 'Where would you like it, X that is?'
> Trader 3: 'Mixed feelings, but mostly I'd like it all lower….'
> Trader 4: 'The whole HF [hedge fund] world will be kissing you instead of calling me if X moves lower.'
> Trader 2: 'OK, I will move the curve down 1 basis point, maybe more if I can.'

8. Which company was behind the single worst oil spill in history?

    A. ExxonMobil   **B.** BP   **C.** Royal Dutch Shell   **D.** Texaco

9. PART I. Where did the world's worst industrial disaster take place?

    A. India   **B.** China
    C. Japan   **D.** Ukraine (formerly part of the USSR)

9. PART II. According to *The Independent* in February 2019, how many years after the responsible parties had agreed to pay compensation, were victims still waiting?

10. What is the motto of Monsanto, the US Agrichem business responsible for creating DDT and Agent Orange, which has been blamed for killing millions of crop acres, while its chemicals were added to blacklists of products causing cancer and other health problems?

    A. A healthy world, a happy world
    B. A Planet Growing In Harmony
    C. GLOBAL. WELL BEING.
    D. Together We Feed the World and Protect the Planet

TRUE OR FALSE?

1. Bad eating habits account for 20% of all deaths worldwide.

2. The first effective fertility treatment was made with the urine of menopausal Italian nuns.

3. Every year, cruise ships dump around 14 billion lbs of garbage into the oceans.

4. Half the US annual military spend would solve world hunger.

5. Half the world's population lives on less than $10 per day.

6. Americans constitute less than 5% of the population on earth, but consume a third of its resources.

7. Every day, fifty species are lost due to tropical deforestation.

8. The smell of fresh-cut grass is a distress signal, your lawn's first response to the trauma you just inflicted on it.

9. In 2020, Britain recorded twice as many deaths from drug overdose than Turkey.

10. Around 350 million people in the world are suffering from depression right now.

ANSWERS p. 319

Ten of these eleven beautiful creatures are no longer with us because of human activity. Which one is still with us? And which is our most recent victim?

A. Dodo

B. Great Auk

C. Quagga

E. Carolina parakeet

D. Japanese Sea Lion

F. Tasmanian tiger

H. Falklands Islands wolf

G. Passenger pigeon

I. Atlas bear

J. Bubal hartebeest

K. West African Pygmy Herring

ANSWERS p. **320**

Bonus questions

1. How did the behaviour of the Carolina Parakeets help to seal their own fate?

   A. Mistaking gunfire for the sound of worm-producing rainfall, they flew towards the bullets.

   B. They built nests on warm roofs, bringing them into dangerous proximity of humans and their guns.

   C. Their flocking behaviour meant that they flew, en masse, to places where others of their kind had been killed.

   D. They barely needed shooting as they were prone to dropping dead out of the sky when spooked.

2. What law concerning Great Auks did the British Parliament pass in the 1770s?

   A. A charter granting a monopoly on the trade in Auk feathers to the brother-in-law of the Prime Minister, Lord North.

   B. A prohibition on the preparation of Auk feathers, down and meat in urban areas, after concerns it was causing a diphtheria epidemic.

   C. One of the earliest environmental protection laws, forbidding the killing of auks in Great Britain.

   D. Stiff penalties for traders 'vending Grate Auk meat of poor qualittye in the guise of other tastye viandes'.

3. Who first spotted the proverbially doomed dodo?

   A. Dutch sailors on Mauritius.

   B. French sailors in the Seychelles.

   C. The Arab voyager and diplomat Ahmad ibn Fadlan on the island of Anjouan.

   D. An Anglo-Dutch expedition to the island of Socotra, led by the naturalist Thomas Chaloner.

4. The dodo was considered inedible by humans, so why was it wiped out within a century?

   A. The fat reserves of these ungainly birds were an easily obtained source of lamp oil and candles.
   B. Dodo beaks were a highly prized material for brooches, miniatures and buttons.
   C. The dogs, cats and other carnivorous animals brought by European settlers weren't so choosy.
   D. Tribes on nearby islands – having never seen dodos themselves – attributed magical powers to the birds, and happily traded vanilla, cloves and precious stones for a sack of dead dodo feathers.

94

A PEST CALLED PEOPLE

PART ONE

These animals and plants were doing fine until some bright spark moved them. In which countries did these normally harmless species cause havoc?

1. THE CAT

2. THE CANE TOAD

3. THE STARLING

4. THE GREY SQUIRREL

5. JAPANESE KNOTWEED

ANSWERS p. 322

PART TWO

6. What problem is Brazil's expanding – and imported – feral pig population causing to humans?

    A. Traffic jams and road accidents
    B. An increase in hunting accidents
    C. Rabies
    D. Chewed-up electricity and telephone cables

7. Why are pigs at the root of one of China's major ecological snafus?

    A. After mass cultivation of the water hyacinth as pig feed, the plants now block drains and sewers.
    B. A scheme to harness methane gas from pig dung was abandoned after several explosions in Hunan province.
    C. European swine, brought by Western missionaries, have a greater tendency to pass nasty viruses to humans than native Chinese breeds.
    D. A quantity of banned pig vaccine ENTOC38 was sold on the black market: released into the ecosystem via pig urine, toxic compounds in the vaccine kill crops and fish.

8. What scientific discovery might mean the cane toads get a stay of execution?

    A. The toads' chlorophyll-rich excreta are making a small, but significant contribution towards reducing CO_2 emissions.
    B. The toads' toxic secretions might kill off cancer cells whilst leaving the healthy ones intact.
    C. Easily flushed of its poisonous juices, Cane Toad might one day be canned, to address our protein needs.
    D. Their ability not to be poisoned by their own poison is providing vital new insights for immunologists.

A PEST CALLED PEOPLE

209

PART THREE

10. What did wildlife researchers accidentally destroy in 2006?

    A. A clam called Ming

    B. An entire ecosystem on a tiny Pacific island

    C. Precious specimens collected by naturalist Alfred Russell Wallace – during a drunken Christmas knees-up.

    D. Their own £2.8 million research ship – by getting too close to the humpback whales they were studying.

11. Which supposedly human trait is causing major blues for the wild starling population?

    A. Depression

    B. Addiction to anti-depressants

    C. Anorexia

    D. Boredom

12. What nasty habit have bumble bees picked up from us?

    A. A love of junk food

    B. An addiction to nicotine

    C. Road-rage –airborne– in traffic-heavy polluted areas

    D. Alcoholism

95

1. Why did nobody come to the aid of the Biblical King Eglon when he was being dispatched by an assassin – Ehud – in the loo?

   A. He was so loathed by all and sundry, including his household staff, that everyone wanted him gone.

   B. His daughters were playing music, so no one could hear the Royal death screams.

   C. God wanted him dead too, and had struck him dumb shortly before Ehud arrived with his dagger.

   D. Groans and grunts as Ehud tried to remove the dagger from Eglon's fat belly were mistaken by his servants as sounds of constipation.

2. In 2002, what caused embarrassment to the city of Lauderhill, Florida, during ceremonies to mark Martin Luther King's assassination by a white supremacist drifter called James Earl Ray?

   A. A 120-strong choir of nuns and pupils from Notre Dame Convent School sang 'Ave, Maria', wearing misprinted T-shirts that simply said 'Martin Luther'.

   B. For leading the remembrance ceremonies, actor James Earl Jones was given a plaque reading 'Thank you, James Earl Ray, for keeping the dream alive.'

   C. The platform party stood for photos in front of a banner reading 'MARTIN LUTHER KING – HERO', blocking all but the letters M, I, N, G and E.

   D. The speaker's pulpit on the main stage was adorned by a flag saying 'Martin Louth. A King.'

3. What was unusual about the sentence carried out on Leon Czolgosz, who had assassinated U.S. President William McKinley, on 29 October 1901?

   A. The sentence was commuted to life in prison, but Czolgosz was still executed for killing a guard.

ANSWERS p. 324

B. It was filmed. Sort of. After he was denied permission to film the frying of Czolgosz in the electric chair, Thomas Edison combined shots of the prison exterior with a recreated studio execution.

C. Czolgosz entered the execution chamber unconscious, and a doctor pronounced him dead – probably from a heart attack – three minutes before the appointed hour.

D. A power cut in central Manhattan delayed the execution by almost an hour.

4. What had Italian King Umberto III said, shortly before his assassination by the Italian-American Gaetano Bresci on 29 July 1900?

   A. 'I'd rather be shot dead than hand out any more trophies.'

   B. The King pointed towards Bresci in the crowd, saying, 'I've seen that man before and I don't like the look of him.'

   C. That assassination was merely 'one of the little risks of our profession'.

   D. 'When will this all be over?'

1. What, according to contemporary observers, was thought to have caused the Antonine Plague?

    A. A minor earthquake in 160 CE – believed to have released 'foul vapours'.

    B. Roman troops returning home from present-day Iraq and Armenia.

    C. Marcus Aurelius had moved the Temple of Apollo in order to widen one of the city's roads, and the gods weren't happy.

    D. 'Black rain' fell on Rome over several days in the August of 160 CE. It was probably due to an ash cloud, but was interpreted otherwise when people started to fall ill.

2. What did the 6th-century Byzantine historian Procopius observe as the Justinian Plague spread around the Mediterranean?

    A. A sharp drop in temperatures, causing crops to fail.

    B. A cycle of hot, wet summers and humid conditions.

    C. A decade of good weather, bumper harvests and peak levels of cross-Mediterranean trade.

    D. A massive increase in the pigeon population – then as now regarded as flying vermin.

3. What role did the Crimean city of Kaffa – today's Feodosia – play in the spread of the Black Death in the mid-14th century?

    A. A ship from Kaffa was wrecked near Otranto in southern Italy and the washed-up cargo, infected with plague, was gleefully carted away by the locals.

    B. Contagious Genoese merchants slipped out of besieged Kaffa shortly after the Mongols began catapulting the bodies of their own infected soldiers over the walls.

    C. Kaffa was unfairly blamed as the plague source, because *kaf* was a Turkic word for 'death'.

    D. Pilgrims had flocked from all over Europe to the important shrines of Kaffa, taking the plague home with them.

ANSWERS
p.
324

4. What, according to the diarist Samuel Pepys, had a number of his fellow Londoners taken to be a warning sign of the Great Plague in 1665?

    A. A comet in the winter of 1664

    B. A pair of peregrines – a bird traditionally thought to be an omen of coming misfortune – had set up nest on the roof of St Paul's.

    C. Many believed the claims of a widely-circulated pamphlet which said King Charles II was the 'faithless ruler' predicted in the Book of Jeremiah, whose reign would lead to 'a sickness ending of all life, throughout the land'.

    D. A gypsy had cursed the King's Coronation Procession in 1661.

5. Which of the below was NOT a genuine response to the Great Plague of 1665?

    A. Multiple bonfires were built, and kept continually alight, due to the belief that the fire would purify the 'bad air' causing the disease.

    B. Cats and dogs were rounded up and slaughtered, which ironically allowed the rats who were carrying the plague to flourish.

    C. Hair, teeth and nail clippings from the plague victims were sold to make 'cures'.

    D. Tobacco was thought to be a prophylactic, and those tobacconists who stayed alive did a roaring trade.

6. Three of these places did NOT experience the Third Plague Pandemic, which began in 1855. Can you name them?

HONG KONG	CHINA	INDIA
SAN FRANCISCO	PARAGUAY	GLASGOW
ETHIOPIA	TUNISIA	LAOS
MADAGASCAR	AUSTRALIA	NEW CALEDONIA

7. **Where did the last recorded outbreak associated with the Third Plague Pandemic occur?**

    A. In Shanghai in 1908-9

    B. In Moscow in 1917

    C. In Cuba in 1912

    D. In Argentina and Peru in 1945

8. **Pressed by the British government to find a vaccine against the Third Plague Pandemic, what aided bacteriologist Waldemar Haffkine in his research?**

    A. Cows – working from a laboratory in Devon, Haffkine was instructed to 'kill as many damned cows as it takes'.

    B. Prisoners – inmates at Bombay's Byculla jail acted as guinea pigs for his vaccine.

    C. Crows – Haffkine noticed that the scavenging birds avoided the remains of human and animal plague victims.

    D. Mrs Haffkine – she did the number-crunching that backed up the experiments, but got no credit.

9. **Between 1918 and 1920, the Spanish Influenza took more lives than the just-ended Great War. But why was it called 'Spanish'?**

    A. Troops awaiting demob in Northern Europe were fed salted pork from Spain, and a few became fatally sick with food poisoning just as the first flu cases emerged.

    B. Some Catalan volunteers had fought with the allies right to the end, and they were the first to fall sick.

    C. To preserve morale, press reports only mentioned the spread of the flu in neutral Spain, where even the King was fatally ill with it.

    D. A typo. '*Parnisches Gryppe*' or 'Parnisch Flu' was first spotted in the Austrian garrison town of that name in 1917. One clumsy telegram back to *The Times*' Foreign Desk, and 'Parnisch' became 'Spanish'.

97

Can you match these anti-mask, anti-lockdown celebs with their quotes?

1. 'If every other cunt's wearing a mask, I'm not gonna catch it off them. And if I've got it, they're not going to catch it off me. I think it's a piss take.'

2. 'Lockdowns don't work and cause more harm than good.'

3. 'NOBODY IS NO F*CKER TO TELL YOU TO WEAR A MASK.'

4. 'A pack of lies to brainwash you and keep you in order.'

5. 'Take off your masks. Gather in groups, love, hug and toast each other this Christmas.'

6. 'When it's the turn of those women, many of an age to have young families, to go to the cemetery, I trust Myrie and the team will be there to record the epitaphs on their gravestones: "Loving wife and mother, died too young from lockdown."'

7. 'No more lockdown / No more government overreach / No more fascist bullies / Disturbing our peace/ No more taking of our freedom / And our God-given rights / Pretending it's for our safety / When it's really to enslave'

8. 'Who's dead? I'm not. I'm still alive. So is everybody else I know. No-one else has caught anything.'

9. 'Anyone with a half a brain cell on active duty can see coronavirus is nonsense.'

10. 'This is the reality: the virus is there. We have to face it, but face it like a man, damn it, not like a kid. We'll confront the virus with reality. That's life. We're all going to die one day.'

ANSWERS
p.
325

A. Jair Bolsonaro

B. Laurence Fox

C. Noel Gallagher

D. Piers Corbyn

E. David Icke

F. Nigel Farage

G. Lord Alan Sugar

H. Allison Pearson

I. Van Morrison

I. Ian Brown

98

Let's talk about pop music. Actually let's not. Let's talk about the spiteful slurs our pop legends so love to swap when they're not singing.

1. 'All that money, and he's still got hair like a dinner lady.' Who on whom?

   A. Elton John on Boy George
   B. Elton John on Lionel Richie
   C. Morrissey on Mick Jagger
   D. Boy George on Elton John

2. 'I'd rather eat my own shit.' Modfather Paul Weller, when asked about performing a duet with...

3. '... looks like a fairground stripper... tour has been a disaster and it couldn't happen to a bigger c**t.' Who uttered this blasphemous indictment against Madonna?

   A. Christina Aguilera
   B. Morrissey
   C. Elton John
   D. Courtney Love

4. 'Hello, I'm Pete Grant, I manage Led Zeppelin.' How did Bob Dylan respond to this friendly overture?

   A. And? What? I should invite you to my wedding now?
   B. Never heard of the guy.
   C. I don't come to you with my problems, do I?
   D. That's the last time you touch me on my arm, okay, man? The last time.

ANSWERS p. 325

5. 'Creates all that misery for himself to write songs, then he doesn't even turn up to play them.' Which female vocalist gave this rather sharp summary of Pete Docherty?

   A. Charlotte Church
   B. Lulu
   C. Cilla Black
   D. Cerys Matthews

6. Complete Pete Burns' description of Lionel Ritchie: 'He's got a chin like...'

    A. a second Lionel Ritchie
    B. an ironing board
    C. Bruce Forsyth
    D. a church hall

7. 'Running round LA with his little legs and a bottle of Volvic. He looks like a fanny.' Who said this about U2 frontman Bono?

    A. 'The Edge'
    B. Shane MacGowan
    C. Bez from the Happy Mondays
    D. Liam Gallagher

8. Complete Marc Almond's comment on Jimmy Sommerville. 'He thinks I should do more for the gay community. And he's right. I should ------- ---.' (2 words)

9. 'Is he doing a bad Elvis pout or was he just born that way?' Freddy Mercury on...

    A. Dave Vanian of The Damned
    B. Pete Shelley of Buzzcocks
    C. Paul Weller of The Jam
    D. Billy Idol

10. Which of the below was Noel Gallagher's verdict on squeaky clean pop-rock combo Keane?

    A. They sit on top of an apex of meaninglessness... don't mean anything to anyone apart from their ugly fucking girlfriends.
    B. If one of them starting injecting heroin into his cock, people would still go, 'Yeah but your Dad was a vicar.'
    C. Bedwetters.
    D. Godawful clothes – particularly the shoes. Got dreadful hair and that kind of 'mug me' look about them.

99

MIND THE GAP

1. Say half the world's poorest citizens – about 3.7 billion people – put all their money together. How many of the world's richest citizens would have to put their money together to match it?

   A. 11   **B.** 42   **C.** 27   **D.** 510

2. Which has the richest people in the world and which the poorest?

CHAD	QATAR	SAUDI ARABIA	BANGLADESH
LAOS	BELIZE	SOUTH SUDAN	CAMBODIA
CHINA	MONACO	NORTH KOREA	SWITZERLAND
HAITI	TOGO	MONGOLIA	NORWAY

3. Identify the country with the most equal distribution of wealth and the country with the least.

PANAMA	SOUTH AFRICA	CZECH REPUBLIC
ECUADOR	SLOVENIA	UNITED KINGDOM
THAILAND	UKRAINE	NAMIBIA
CHILE	KYRGYZSTAN	IRAQ

4. Who has the highest percentage of adults with literacy difficulties, and who the lowest?

SWEDEN	ITALY	AUSTRIA	BELGIUM
ESTONIA	POLAND	NORWAY	DENMARK
GERMANY	IRELAND	ENGLAND & NORTHERN IRELAND	

5. A 2018 *Lancet* study rated access to healthcare and quality of care in 195 countries. Which came top and which came bottom?

BURUNDI	CANADA	SOMALIA	SWITZERLAND
ICELAND	GERMANY	FRANCE	AFGHANISTAN
TURKEY	SWEDEN	SOUTH SUDAN	JAPAN
DEMOCRATIC REPUBLIC OF CONGO			

6. According to the World Bank, in 2016, there were 5.2 doctors for every 1,000 Austrian citizens. How many quacks per thousand were there in Uganda at the same time?

   A 1.1   **B.** 0.1   **C.** 1.8   **D.** 1.56

ANSWERS
p.
326

7. Which two of these European countries have a lower GDP than the net worth of Amazon founder Jeff 'Rocket Boy' Bezos?

HUNGARY	SLOVAKIA	BULGARIA	LUXEMBOURG
SLOVENIA	LITHUANIA	SERBIA	ICELAND
CYPRUS	ALBANIA	MALTA	MONTENEGRO
ESTONIA	BOSNIA AND HERZEGOVINA		

8. San Francisco – population 884,363 – has one billionaire for every X people. What is X, to the nearest 1,000?

9. The US government's poverty threshold is $12,140 for an individual and $25,100 for a family of four. But how much, according to the US Department for Housing and Urban Development, would you need to make a year to stay above the poverty line in San Francisco? Answer in dollars to the nearest $1,000.

10. In this list of countries by GDP, where would the net worth of Google go?

   A. Between Brazil and Canada?
   B. Between Norway and Ireland?
   C. Between the Philippines and Bangladesh?
   D. Between Mexico and Indonesia

1	UNITED STATES	14	AUSTRALIA	27	AUSTRIA
2	CHINA	15	MEXICO	28	NIGERIA
3	JAPAN	16	INDONESIA	29	UAE
4	GERMANY	17	NETHERLANDS	30	NORWAY
5	INDIA	18	SAUDI ARABIA	31	IRELAND
6	UNITED KINGDOM	19	SWITZERLAND	32	ISRAEL
7	FRANCE	20	TURKEY	33	MALAYSIA
8	ITALY	21	POLAND	34	SINGAPORE
9	BRAZIL	22	SWEDEN	35	SOUTH AFRICA
10	CANADA	23	BELGIUM	36	PHILIPPINES
11	SOUTH KOREA	24	THAILAND	37	DENMARK
12	RUSSIA	25	IRAN	39	BANGLADESH
13	SPAIN	26	ARGENTINA	40	EGYPT

ANSWERS | ROUND 1

1. ODD ONE OUTER (P. 1)

They were all sent into outer space and none survived except G – the odd one out.

BONUS DEPRESSING INFO

A. There was a giant leap for the animal kingdom in 1970 when Nasa launched the Orbiting Frog Otolith spacecraft from the Wallops Flight Facility in Virginia, containing two bullfrogs, to investigate the effects of spaceflight and weightlessness on motion sickness. It turns out that a frog's inner ear is quite a useful model for the human equivalent and the factors that induce motion sickness in frogs are the same as those for humans and other mammals. The frogs were 'demotorised' (i.e. they had their nerves in their limbs severed to stop them hopping around and dislodging any equipment) but were otherwise said to be in good health. Right up to when the onboard battery failed one week into the flight.

B. In 2014 Russia sent five geckos into space as part of zero-gravity research into reproduction. When the satellite returned to Earth, they found the geckos' bodies mummified: they had frozen to death.

C. In 2003 the space shuttle Columbia broke up on re-entry, killing all seven members of the human crew. Also on board were some bees as part of studies looking into how gene expression changes in space. The bees didn't survive either.

D. Laika, a stray dog from the streets of Moscow, was the occupant of the Soviet spacecraft Sputnik 2, launched into outer space on 3 November 1957. She was one of several, carefully chosen for her photogenic good looks (the Soviets knew that her image would soon be printed in newspapers around the world). There was rather less effort put into plans for her survival. It was reported that Laika died when her oxygen ran out on day six, or rather, as the Soviet government initially claimed, she was humanely put down prior to oxygen depletion. In fact she was dead within hours after launch, roasted alive when ground engineers failed to notice a problem with the cooling system. Her coffin lapped the earth another 2,570 times until it burned up in the atmosphere in April 1958. It was only in 2002 that the true circumstances of her death were admitted publicly. Between 1957 and 1961, at least 13 Russian canine cosmonauts followed Laika into orbit, of whom a further five died in flight.

E. On 15 August 1950 a mouse was launched into space, attaining an altitude of 85 miles, then died when the rocket disintegrated due to parachute failure. Several other mice were launched during the 1950s but had no more luck.

F. Biosatellite III was launched from Cape Kennedy on 28 June 1969 carrying a pig-tailed monkey macaque called Bonnie. After just under nine days in orbit the mission was terminated when Bonnie died due to a heart attack brought about by dehydration.

G. In 1959 a 7lb female rhesus monkey called Able and a one-pound female squirrel monkey called Baker (pictured) were fired 300 miles into space in the nose-cone of a Jupiter missile AM-18 from a launch-site in Florida. Able was recovered successfully but died during an operation to remove sensors used to transmit vital-signs data.

H. In 1968 the Soviet Zond 6 probe flew a payload of turtles plus sundry flies and bacteria around the moon. The vessel lost a gasket on the return trip resulting in a loss of cabin pressure and the death of all biological specimens.

I. In 1987 the Soviet Bion 8 carried two monkeys into space who survived the flight and several zebra fish who did not. The vehicle missed its touchdown point by 1,850 miles, and freezing weather proved deadly for the fish.

BONUS QUESTIONS (P. 2)

1. The answer is **C**. He was a keen masturbator. However, the story that this space-travelling simian celebrated his return to earth with a handjob in front of a press conference, thereby earning himself the nickname of Enos the Penis, is regrettably untrue.

2. The answer is **C** – Bobik vanished.

3. It's an Acronym from the Russian for 'Substitute for Missing Bobik'.

2. THE UGLY TRUTH #1 (P. 3)

1. TRUE. The odds against you matching all six numbers the UK lottery are 45 million to one. Being crushed by a meteor is considerably more likely (1 in 700,000). Getting hit by lightning is also almost four times more likely than winning the lottery, and you're 45 times more likely to die from flesh-eating bacteria than securing the jackpot. It could be worse, though: you're more likely to win the lottery than you are to be crushed by a vending machine, the chances of which are 1 in 112 million.

2. TRUE. The odds against you being killed at work are 3,500/1. More accidents happen at work than anywhere else – more than 25,000 serious workplace accidents a year, killing around 300 people in the UK. The odds against you being killed in a road accident are 8,000/1. Every year 1,500 car drivers and adult passengers die in road smashes, while around 1,000 pedestrians and cyclists die in road accidents. Worldwide, over 3,000 people are killed in road crashes daily.

3. TRUE. The odds against you dying from cancer are 5/1. Around 130,000 people die from cancer every year, of whom 65,000 are aged under 75. The most common killers are lung, breast, colon and prostate cancer. The odds against you dying from a heart attack or stroke are 2.5/1. Coronary heart disease and strokes are leading cause of death in Britain, accounting for over 200,000 deaths every year. Someone has a heart attack every two minutes.

4. FALSE. The odds against you drowning in your bath are 685,000/1, though more people drown in their bath water than in public swimming pools, with young children and the elderly most at risk. Around 25 babies drown in baths every year. The odds against you being killed in a train crash are calculated at 500,000/1. Despite the occasional fatal crash, public transport is still the safest way to travel. Buses are even safer than trains, with the odds of being killed 13 million to 1.

5. TRUE. The odds against dying from falling off a ladder are 2.3 million to 1. On average 15 people die falling off ladders each year in Britain. The odds against dying after falling out of bed are 2 million to 1. In Britain around 20 people die falling out of bed every year.

6. TRUE. More people in the US were killed by lawnmowers than terrorism in the decade from 2007 to 2017. However, at the time of writing at least, the US government has yet to declare a War on Lawnmowers.

7. TRUE. The odds against you being killed by a bee sting are 54,000/1. The odds against you being killed in a dog attack, which is the most likely way you might be endangered by a dangerous animal, are over 130,000/1.

8. FALSE. You are 100 times more likely to choke to death on food, with the odds against it 3,000/1. In the US choking is the fourth leading cause of unintentional injury death. The odds against you dying from food poisoning are 3 million to 1. More than 79,000 cases of food poisoning are reported annually in the UK, while every year around 200 people die as a result of eating contaminated food.

9. TRUE. According to research by academics at Chicago University excessive partying plus accidents and suicides triggered by 'birthday blues' are to blame for higher than average deaths on birthdays.

10. TRUE. Falling coconuts kill 150 people worldwide each year, 15 times the number of fatalities attributable to sharks, according to a man who knows: the Director of the University of Florida's International Shark Attack File.

3. NAMED & SHAMED (P. 4)

1. TRUE. Admittedly, though, it was only this 8th-century Byzantine Emperor's enemies who used the nickname. *Kopros* is Greek for dung.

2. FALSE. But history is dotted with monarchs who barely saw a day on the throne. The (current) record is held by Prince Louis-Antoine, who took over as Louis XIX of France when his father abdicated, pondered it for 20 minutes and then abdicated himself.

3. TRUE. The King of Galicia from 1188-1230 apparently earned his nickname because he foamed at the mouth whenever he grew angry.

4. FALSE.

5. TRUE. The Count of Rietberg in Germany from 1552-62, John earned his nickname for his violent and unpredictable nature, joining a – surprisingly short – list of monarchs so named, including Charles the Mad (King of France 1380–1422) Maria the Mad (Queen of Portugal 1777–1816) Ludwig the Mad (King of Bavaria 1864–86) and Ibrahim the Mad (Ottoman Sultan 1640–48).

6. TRUE. In seeking an annulment from the Pope, Henry proffered the testimonies of several Segovian prostitutes, who all swore he was a tiger between the sheets. The point was that the curse only affected relations between the King and his wife.

7. TRUE. Other resplendently named Ottoman Sultans include Mehmet the Affable, Selim the Sot and Abdulaziz the Unfortunate

8. FALSE.

9. TRUE.

10. TRUE.

4. ODD JOB OUT (P. 5)

All of these jobs face extinction except G.

Scientists and economists predict that billions of us face irrelevance as Artificial Intelligence and new technology push us out of the job market. According to a study from the University of Oxford, there is a 95%–99% probability that these jobs will be automated within the next two decades, apart from short-term-contract or freelance workers, such as Uber drivers. Such work requires employees to be both flexible and independent — two things robots aren't great at.

5. CENSOR SENSIBILITY (P. 6)

1. **The answer is B.** George III had his first prolonged bout of madness in 1788. People suspected something was wrong when he took to wearing a pillowcase on his head and began foaming at the mouth. His courtiers tried to keep it a secret from the outside world by pretending that the king had flu, but eventually George couldn't be trusted to perform even basic royal tasks, such as waving from the balcony at Buckingham Palace or meeting visitors and saying 'Hello, have you come far?', and he was placed in a straitjacket. The parallels with a play about an old king who gives up his throne and goes mad were just too close for anyone's comfort and 'King Lear' wasn't performed again in an English theatre until late in 1820, many months after George's death.

2. **The answer is D.** P.G. Wodehouse was accused of being a Nazi sympathizer whilst he spent the war in occupied France; ninety of his works were removed from Southport Public Libraries and destroyed.

3. **A, B, C, D,** and **E** are all **TRUE. F,** Sir Cliff's hit, 'Theme for a Dream', was banned too, not because of angel-sex-references but because it referred, openly, to kissing (which was another big no-no).

4. **The answer is C.** Charles Darwin for *On the Origin of Species*. In 1925 Tennessee banned the teaching of the theory of evolution in schools and the law remained in force until 1967.

5. **The answer is D.** In spite of the protagonist's unrelentingly bad behaviour, not to mention dislike of girls, cruelty to dogs and anti-semitism, the *Just William* stories of Richmal Crompton have never been banned – except by one headmistress, in one school, who suspected that the author had based an unflattering character upon her.

6(i) **The answer is D.** It was banned for 14 years, from 1922 to 1936.

6(ii) **Also D.** Australia – not so much because of the shitting and fucking, but because, according to a former Customs Minister, the book 'ridicule[d] the Creator and the Church... Such books might vitally affect the standard of Australian home life. It cannot be tolerated in Australia any longer.'

6(iii) The answer is **IRELAND**. The book was never officially banned, but a loophole in the customs regulations was used to ensure that no copies of the book could be brought in for sale.

7. The answer is **D**.

8. The answer is **B**. Cunt, Your Honour. Prosecution council Mervyn Griffith-Jones kept a detailed tally of the novel's profanities and asked the jury: 'Is it a book that you would even wish your wife or your servants to read?'

9. The answer is **I**. Lebanon is the only territory to have banned *The Da Vinci Code*. Regrettably, nowhere else has prohibited its sale, least of all on grounds of quality. As critics have pointed out, even the title doesn't make sense. Leonardo's surname was not Da Vinci. He was from Vinci, or of Vinci. Calling it *The Da Vinci Code* is the equivalent of calling T. E. Lawrence 'Mr. Of Arabia' or Jesus 'Mr. Of Nazareth'.

10. The answer is **A**. Despite their popularity with a worldwide audience, the first four books in J.K.Rowling's collection have the dubious honour of being the most burned books in America.

6. A BRIEF HISTORY OF TIME WASTERS (P.9)

1. **TRUE**. In September 1991 a 29-year-old poultry-dresser cut his finger with a chicken bone and the prick caused the digit to become red and smelly. Doctors treated him a variety of drugs, but the finger continued to stink. Five years later, the poor man could still stink out a waiting room with his malodorous finger. The doctors published a description of the case in the hope that someone somewhere had encountered a similar problem and could suggest a way to relieve the patient's distress. Meanwhile the finger just got better.

2. **TRUE**. When herring pass gas, the bubbles make a high-frequency sound only audible to another herring. The fish use the noise to form 'protective shoals' at night to help them stay safe, a phenomenon called Fast Repetitive Tick (FRT). The noise sounds 'like someone blowing a high-pitched raspberry'.

3. FALSE.

4. TRUE. They researched basic information on how long a blink lasts, how many times people blink per minute and how fast camera shutters go. They worked out that blinks are random and that one person's blinks don't influence another person's blinks and unless you have something stuck in your eye, your own blinks don't influence each other either. The researchers discovered that when you're taking photos of a group with fewer than 20 people you divide the number of people by three to get the required number of shots. In bad light, however, the camera shutter is open for longer, giving people more of a chance to blink. So then you need to divide the number of people by two to get the number of shots.

5. TRUE. Armadillos, hitherto receiving little attention in academic literature, make for big trouble in the wrong circumstances. The conclusion: 'Armadillos are responsible for vertical movement of archaeological materials, but the displacement of artefacts does not appear to be systematic.'

6. TRUE. Dogs tend to align themselves along the north-south axis when defecating. This discovery has a practical application. Imagine you and Fido are lost in the desert in the dark, so you can't determine your direction by the sun. It's cloudy, so you can't see the stars. Simply feed Fido and wait for nature to take its course. That way you'll narrow your direction down to a single axis.

7. FALSE.

8. TRUE. Spit is an effective cleaning solution because human saliva contains the enzyme amylase, which evolved to break down food but also works well for removing dirt and grime.

9. FALSE. Well, half false. The study focussed on the, erm, delivery sacks of naked and clothed postmen.

10. TRUE. Kissing, they found, is more highly valued in low-income regions, perhaps because it promotes lasting bonds as an insurance against adversity.

ANSWERS | ROUND 7

7. THE STATE WE'RE IN (P. 10)

1. The answer is **C**, El Salvador, according to the latest figures provided by the United Nations Office on Drugs and Crime. Home to around 6.5 million people, the small Central American country has the highest homicide rate of all countries in the world, with an average of 82.84 murders per 100,000 people.

2. The answer, according to 2020 figures from the EU's EDGAR (the Emissions Database for Global Atmospheric Research) is **A**, China, accounting for 30.34% of the world's CO_2 emissions, with the USA a not-particularly close second, on 13.43%.

3. The answer is **C**, Chicago, host to 524 homicides up to September 2020. Philadelphia, Pennsylvania came second with 306, and New York, New York was third, with 305.

4. The answer is **D**, 11.7, equating to 695 deaths currently recorded as homicide. The 2020 figure includes 39 victims of human trafficking, found dead in a single lorry, just as 2003's high of 17.9 factors in the shocking, but rare body count of one serial killer, Dr Harold Shipman.

5. The answer is **E**.

6. The answer is **A, B** and **G**. Half of all the world's prison population of about nine million is held in either the US, China or Russia. Generally, the lowest rates are in developing countries, but overcrowding is a serious problem. In May 2021, Human Rights Watch estimated Cambodia's prisons to have an occupancy level above 300% of capacity, specially bad news for those locked up during the Covid-19 pandemic.

7. The answer is **C**, Iran, according to the *CIA World Fact Book*, with heroin use at 14.32% per capita.

8. The answer is **D**, Nigeria, accordng to UNICEF's 2020 report.

9. The answer is **A**, 117, a grim statistic shared with Somalia,

10. Ethiopia (**7** cheeseburgers), Suriname (**9**), Argentina (**11**), Libya (**12**), North Korea (**8**), Bahamas (**10**), Cuba (**13**), Eritrea (**6**)

8 THE KIDS' MENU (P. 12)

1. GRIZZLY BEARS. Pandas take the opposite approach. If a female has more than one cub, she often chooses to keep only one alive.

2. The answer is **B**. If a mother hamster feels stressed or threatened, she will assume that she does not have enough food or space for all of her babies to survive inside their small cage.

3. LIONS. In a pride of lions there can be only one alpha male. When a new lion takes over and there are cubs left over from the previous alpha, he will kill them before fathering new children with the females.

4. The answer is **D**. A male bottlenose dolphin looking for a female might pick a random single mother then kill her calf, not wishing to waste his energy taking care of a child that isn't his own. Gangs of male bottlenose dolphins will sometimes team up to target a single female and harass her persistently, forcing her to mate with them. Neither is this sexual aggression limited to members of their own kind. Dolphins have tried to force themselves on human swimmers, a prospect made all the more alarming by the fact that they have prehensile penises.

5. GOATS. We are not the only animals that enjoy non-reproductive sex. The males of at least 80 species and females of around 50 species of primates are frequent masturbators.

6. It's **C**. The use of obliging eels has been witnessed more than once. (Then again, dolphins being dolphins, A, B and D might all be true, too...)

7. The answer is **A**. And the otters are not alone: post-mortem mating has been observed in birds, kangaroos, lizards and frogs. This is often because the prone and still position of a dead female mirrors the body language of accepting intercourse, and presses the right button for the male. Or the wrong one, rather...

8. The answer is **C**. Venturing to the South Pole with the 1910-13 Scott Antarctic Expedition. Levick was shocked by the activities of 'hooligan cocks' that copulated with other males, with females that were injured, with chicks that had tumbled from their nests, and even with dead penguins. Some male also tried to shag the ice until they ejaculated. Levick's findings were so disturbing to post-Edwardian sensibilities that his four-page report 'Sexual Habits of the Adélie Penguin' was omitted from official expedition findings. Far from being deviant, these behaviours were a regular part of penguin life, as reported in a preface to Levick's be-latedly-released report. When a later researcher set out a dead penguin that had been frozen upright, many males found the corpse 'irresistible'. In further, strange field work, the same researcher found that 'just the frozen head of the penguin, with self-adhesive white O's for eye rings, propped upright on wire with a rock for a body, was sufficient stimulus for males to copulate and deposit sperm on the rock.'

9. The answer is **C.** Zoo behaviour is often weird because animals in captivity are far from their natural environment. It's thought that the ritualized sucking and comforting engaged in by the Kutarevo bears has something to do with them being separated from their mothers at an early age. (Doesn't everything?)

10. HYENAS.

11. The answers are **A.** and **D.** Beefed up by a first meal of their own pre-siblings, black lace-weaver spiderlings swiftly grow too large for their mother to care for, so in the ultimate act of parental self-sacrifice, she calls the babies to her by drumming on the web and presses her body down into the gathering crowd. The ravenous spiderlings swarm over their mother's body and eat her alive.

12. The answer is **D.** Rabbit shit contains more protein and vitamins and less fibre than the faeces of other species. (PS For more great rhymes see quiz 21 'Rhymes against Humanity'.)

13. The answer is **D.** The mosquito. To date around 45 billion people have been killed by malaria from the bite of a female. Though encounters with trapdoor spiders and sea snakes often end badly for humans, the numbers of victims are tiny by comparison. You could make a case for fleas, of course, but only if you haven't finished this book...

14. The answer is **B.** One of the Spanish Dancer sea cucumber's other names is the Headless Chicken Monster. As well as being celebrated for the lung/anus party trick, it is prized as a delicacy in certain cuisines.

15. The answer is **C**. Wombats use their poo to mark their territory and the theory goes that dice-shaped dung is best for sitting on top of rocks and logs because it doesn't roll away. Exactly how wombats pass up to a hundred of these cubic stools a night has proved more difficult to work out, if you exclude the possibility that they have square sphincters, which they don't. Wombat intestine doesn't stretch evenly, and when measured around the circumference, some parts give more than others. This allows the intestine to deform in such a way that packs faeces into 2cm-wide cubes rather than the usual sausage shapes. This discovery is of great interest to engineers, because currently there are thought to be only two methods for making cubes: moulding them or cutting them. The wombat's arsehole suggest a third route is possible. Detailed investigation is tricky, however, not least because wombats have an unfortunate tendency to stop pooing when you cut them open.

16. The answer is **B**. The Mongolian marmot. This cuddly member of the squirrel family is susceptible to a lung infection caused by the bacterium *Yersinia pestis,* more commonly known as bubonic plague. The bacterium is then carried by rats and their fleas, passed on to humans – and it's all downhill from there. The 14th-century outbreak in Europe, known as the Black Death, is estimated to have killed 60% of the population, forcing wages higher due the lack of labour, and sparking seismic shifts in everything from the economy to government, religion to art. All in all, the plague has done for well over a billion people, making the marmot actually the second deadliest species after the mosquito.

9 TYRANTS ON TOUR #1 (P. 16)

PART ONE: Everyone except C. King Zog, has been an honoured guest at Buckingham Palace.

A. The Queen greeted Hastings Banda, President of Malawi, at Buckingham Palace in 1985. An Anglophile with a taste for Savile Row suits and Homburg hats, Banda boasted that he fed his opponents to the crocodiles, but he was speaking (at least in part) metaphorically. In 1983 three of his cabinet ministers and a member of parliament died in a mysterious 'car accident'. Several years later it emerged that the victims had had their heads staved in with mallets.

B. In 1873 the Shah of Persia Naser al-Din cut a striking figure on his trip to London with his huge, wax-tipped moustache. It was noted that throughout his stay at the Palace, the Shah repeatedly failed to use the lavatories and went wherever the spirit moved him. Eschewing the formal dinner laid on for him, he allegedly barbecued a pig in his suite and organised a boxing match in the Palace gardens.

C. After being kicked out of Albania in 1939, Albania's autocratic King Zog settled in London's Ritz Hotel before moving to Parmoor House in Buckinghamshire for nearly five years – but he never got an invite to Buckingham Palace.

D. During King Fahd's 1987 visit to London he lost millions of pounds in casinos. He also circumvented the curfew imposed by British gaming laws by hiring his own blackjack and roulette dealers so that he could continue gambling through the night in his hotel suite.

E. When he came to power, Britain sent out a Foreign Office minister, Lord Boyd, to congratulate Idi Amin. Amin requested a signed portrait of the Queen and a royal visit as soon as possible. He assured Boyd that he had already written Her Majesty 'a very nice letter'. In July 1972 Amin got his wish and went to Buckingham Palace to have lunch with the Queen and the Duke of Edinburgh, whom he addressed throughout as 'Mr Philip'.

F. In 1978 Romanian dictator Nicolae Ceausescu and his wife Elena were guests of the Queen. Her Majesty was said to be baffled by the discovery that her guests had brought with them their own bed sheets and a host of minders, including a personal food-taster. Whenever Ceausescu went abroad, he took his own chemist equipped with a portable laboratory to analyse his food – extreme paranoia since he also brought his own cooks.

G. In 1886 Leopold II, King of the Belgians, also known as 'the butcher of the Congo' after killing around 10 million Africans, stayed in the Palace's Belgian Suite, so called because it was first decorated in honour of his predecessor, Victoria's uncle Leopold, first King of the Belgians.

H. A kleptocrat ranked the seventh richest man in the world while his country was among the poorest, Mobutu of Zaire regularly chartered Concorde to pick up his groceries from Paris and Brussels and slept with a bottle of patent medicine by his bedside for 'rheumatism and syphilis'. He turned up in rather more modest fashion for his visit to London in December 1973: the Queen met him at Victoria Station and escorted him back to hers.

I. In 1994 Zimbabwe's Robert Mugabe was entertained at a state banquet and awarded an honorary GCB.

10 GENERALISSIMO KNOWLEDGE (P. 18)

PART 1

1. E. Rafael Trujillo

2. A. Pol Pot

3. C. Idi Amin

4. D. Kim Jong Il

5. H. Mao Zedong

6. F. Jean-Bedel Bokassa

7. G. 'Papa Doc' Duvalier

8. B. Nicolae Ceausescu

PART 2

9. Kim Jong-un

10. Benito Mussolini

11. Stalin

12. Fidel Castro

13. Bashar al-Assad

14. Colonel Gadaffi

PART 3

15. Augusto Pinochet

16. Adolfo Stroessner

17. Enver Hoxha

18. Saddam Hussein

19. Suharto

20. Ferdinand Marcos

11 FANCY A BITE? (P. 22)

PART 1. The answer is D. (And you thought chlorinated chicken sounded bad.)
PART 2: The answer is E. Cats and kittens are considered a delicacy in certain parts of the world, whereas we unknowingly consume extracts from all the other animals in various food additives (see below).

A. Vanilla, strawberry and raspberry flavoured ice creams often contain a bitter, smelly, orange-brown substance called Castoreum. This food flavouring is extracted from the glands of the male or female beaver, which are located near the anus. You will find it described as 'natural flavouring'.

B. Natural Red #4, a.k.a. carmine, is a food colorant produced by boiling female cochineal insect shells in ammonia or a sodium carbonate solution. It takes about 70,000 bugs to produce 1lb of the dye, which is a commonly used ingredient in yogurt, curries and alcoholic drinks.

C. Isinglass is a gelatin-like substance produced from the swim bladder of a fish and added to cask beers and Irish stout to help remove any residue yeast or solid particles in the beer.

D. Gelatine is found in dairy products like yogurts, plus many types of confectionery, jellies and sweets, and may contain horse hoofs and skin.

F. Everything but the oink goes into our food in some form or another. Pigskin is commonly used in sweets and yoghurt.

G. L-Cysteine is an amino acid made from avian feathers and used to prolong shelf life in products such as bread baps, pizza dough, biscuits, pastas and pastries. Most of the hair used to make L-Cysteine comes from birds but some is made from human hair, mostly gathered from the floor of Chinese barbershops and hair salons.

H. Chewing gum contains lanolin, a secretion derived from sheep's wool. It's also found in skincare products. It softens your hands and your chewing gum. Pesto may contain sheep stomach and parmesan cheese contains rennet, a coagulant that helps separate the curds and whey in milk and which is extracted from the innards of dead baby animals, most often lambs.

I. Shellac is derived from the excretions of the Kerria lacca insect, most commonly found in the forests of Thailand, and is widely used as a food colourant or food glaze on confections, chewing gum, fruit and coffee beans.

12 MONUMENTAL **CK UPS (P. 24)

1. The answer is **B**. The Temple of Artemis was destroyed three times – once by a flood, then by arson in 356 BCE and finally by invading Goths in 262 CE. Herostratus was the arsonist responsible for the middle attack, and he claimed, when questioned, that he just wanted his name to be remembered forever. As well as the usual grisly execution, it was ordered that his name be expunged from all records, and never uttered by a living a soul. So that worked, then.

2 The answer is **A**. Unbelievably, Taliban 1.0 envisaged a future where tourists might come and splurge dollars on trips to the idols and… whatever else they imagined might be a crowd-puller in war-ravaged Afghanistan. They revised their strategy as the radical clerics drew up ever more extreme plans against so-called 'un-Islamic' elements.

3. The answer is **B**. Although this rather ran contrary to the Taliban's having previously asked UNESCO for help and funds to protect the Buddhas.

4. The answer is **C**.

5. The answer is **B**. The Goblins of Utah are ancient rock formations of mushroom-shaped boulders perched atop narrow sandstone stalks. Formed over millions of years by a fluke of erosion, there was nothing quite like these rocks to be found anywhere else on Earth. Then in 2013 two boy scout troop leaders decided they were a health and safety risk and decided to topple them. A couple of shoves later, millions of years of history had been obliterated.

6. The answer is **A**.

7. The answer is **B**.

8. The answer is **A**. Good old British derring-do, what? The sacred monument measured 3 metres high and 3 meters wide and stood at the entrance to the Singapore River until 1843 when the British army announced plans to build a fort nearby and blew it up. Only a few fragments were saved, and most of the slab's text was erased forever, leaving the meaning of the script an eternal mystery.

9. The answer is: **IT'S ALL OF THEM**, to a greater or lesser degree. Caesar's accidental burning of a wing of it, during a siege, precipitated a long, slow decline, during which various other bits fell prey to the attacks of emperors and the punitive measures of Christian – and perhaps also Muslim – leaders.

10. The answer is **D**. New Place was where Shakespeare wrote some of his later works, including 'The Tempest' and where he died in 1616. The Rev. Francis soon made himself unpopular with the locals by chopping down a mulberry tree the Shakespeare family had planted. He was also fed up with people leaning over his fence and gawping at his home, so six years after he bought it he decided to just tear the whole thing down. Why destroy the house and not just sell it, you ask? A good question – and one that also vexed the good folk of Stratford-upon-Avon immensely.

13 NEW HEADS ON THE BLOCK (P. 28)

1. The answer is **C**. Pepys watched the hanging in 1664 and paid a shilling to stand on a cart wheel, thus spending an hour 'in great pain' while the victim delayed the inevitable with 'long discourses and prayers,' hoping for a reprieve that didn't come. After the hanging, Pepys returned home, 'all in a sweat,' to dine alone, before eating a second dinner with friends at the Old James tavern. Five years later Pepys also got to see the beheading of King Charles 1 at Whitehall.

2. The answer is **D**. Lord Byron was visiting Rome when he saw three robbers guillotined.

3. The answer is **A**. Thomas Hardy. The hanging inspired his 1891 novel *Tess of the D'Urbervilles*.

4. The answer is **B**. She was apologising to her executioner after accidentally stepping on his foot.

5. The answer is the **1990**s. On 10 July 1992, Anthony Teare was sentenced to death on the Isle of Man, which is a British Crown Dependency and not part of the United Kingdom (where capital punishment was abolished in 1965). On appeal, Teare's sentence was commuted to life with a minumn of 12 years.

6. Anticipating that he would become a major attraction, Haigh bequeathed his clothes to Madame Tussaud's Chamber of Horrors so they could use them to dress his wax figure.

7. He helped to design the device first tested at his own execution – the 'drop gallows'. Brodie was a respected figure in 19th-century Edinburgh. Until that time people condemned to be hanged were pushed from a high platform and left to strangle to death. Brodie helped perfect the trapdoor-and-lever system that became the industry standard. He also lived a double life as a highly skilled cat burglar. His cover was blown when an accomplice turned king's evidence. He fled to Amsterdam but was apprehended, returned to Edinburgh for trial, and condemned to death. On the gallows, Brodie asked if he could inspect the apparatus: after pronouncing it satisfactory, he was dropped to his death.

8. The answer is **D**. A medical to ensure they are fit enough to die.

9. The answer is **A**. Saudi Arabia. Under Sharia law, murder, apostacy, blasphemy, idolatry, homosexuality, sedition, witchcraft, adultery and drug trafficking are capital offences. Saudi Arabian methods of execution include stoning and beheading. The latter is more common, after which the severed head is either sewn back on the body or hung for public display. Stoning is used in cases of adultery. The culprit is buried up to his/her chest or knees in a ditch and stoned to death.

10. CHINA. Although Iran carries out the highest recorded number of executions (508 in 2017) Amnesty International believes thousands of executions and death sentences are being carried out annually in China, where data on capital punishment is a state secret.

14 POT LUCK #1 (P. 30)

1. The answer is **B**. Surveyed in a 2018 poll, 22% of young people born after 2000 said they had not heard of the Holocaust or were unsure whether they'd heard of it. Two-thirds didn't know what Auschwitz was.

2. The answer is **C**. He employed a *praegustator* because he feared Cleopatra might try to poison him. The idea caught on and the *praegustator* assumed an important role in every imperial household. The names of many of them are recorded on their tombstones; the causes of their deaths however are not. Prince Charles does not employ a *praegustator*, but he does have a Travelling Yeoman and someone to warm his biscuits for him.

3. The answer is **A**. Having eaten between 872 and 999 people. He recorded his achievement with a huge pile of stones, adding to it with a new stone every time he ate. According to legend, his warriors would go to the battle and bring back body parts of their victims as titbits for their chief: his favourite snack was the head. He preserved what he couldn't finish in one sitting so he could eat it later.

4. The answer is **B**. A year before he died, Kinsey also circumcised himself with a pocket knife in the bath.

5. The answer is **C**. Until Harrods shut its pet department in 2014, it was also the place to buy panthers, tigers and camels. The playwright Noël Coward had an alligator bought for him for Christmas in 1951 by the Canadian actress Beatrice Lillie. Arguably the most famous purchase was in 1967, when future American president Ronald Reagan phoned to buy a baby elephant called Gertie. Legend has it the shop worker on the other end of the phone said: 'Would that be African or Indian, sir?'

6. The answer is **A** – Guyana. This largely rural country at the north-eastern edge of South America is home to about 740,000 people and its suicide rate is four times higher than the global average. Poverty, alcohol abuse and easy access to deadly pesticides lead to the self-inflicted deaths of more than 44 out of 100,000 Guyanese every year. North Korea is believed to have the second highest. Human rights violations and economic hardship are the main reasons why more than 10,000 North Koreans take their own lives each year, including, allegedly, entire families killing themselves to avoid punishments by the country's regime.

7. The answer is **B**. The blurb for his 2018 biography describes him as 'intriguing, controversial and possibly misunderstood'.

8. The answer is **A**. Described by his Catholic enemies as 'a veteran in evil' with a 'cesspool' for a heart, Topcliffe built a torture chamber in the cellar of his house. One of his victims, Nicholas Owen, who was known for hiding Catholic priests, was found dead in his cell with his bowels hanging out. He suffered from a hernia and Topcliffe had racked him so hard that he burst.

9. The answer is **D**. The dolls were smaller than life-size and could fit easily into a soldier's backpack. Allegedly, Himmler asked Hungarian actress Kathy von Nagy to model for them, but she declined.

10. The answer is **B**. After Pinyan's death several videos circulated around the internet of him and others engaging in receptive anal intercourse with various stallions. He was known locally as 'that fool who took all that horse cock in his ass.'

15 SUFFER THE CHILDREN (P. 32)

1. It's **C**. According to UNICEF, which defines a child soldier as 'any child – boy or girl – under 18 years of age, who is part of any kind of regular or irregular armed force or armed group in any capacity.' Another half a million are believed to be the members of armies not currently engaged in a war.

2. It's **B**. UNICEF's analysis of multi-dimensional child poverty used data on access to education, healthcare, housing, nutrition, sanitation and water from 70 countries, concluding that between March and September 2020, the global total had jumped 15%.

3. It's **D**. World Health Organisation figures state that 10,000 children will die today – one every three seconds.

4. In descending order, it's **A**, Walsall, **E**, Knowsley, **F**, Sandwell (West Midlands), **G**, Barnet, **D**, Greenwich scoring between 30.1 and 28.2%. **B**, Rutland in fact reported England's lowest figure, 13.7%.

5. The answer is **D**. for deprivation.

6. In order, highest to lowest it's Ethiopia, Burkina Faso, Benin, Chad, Mali, Guinea-Bissau, Niger, Burundi, Central African Republic and Côte d'Ivoire.

7. It's **D**. – 15%.

8. The Answer is **C**.

9. The answer is **C**. A clue for the eagle-eyed being the date of the report: Shelter always publish a justifiably damning report during the season of goodwill.

10. The answer is **A DAD**. It is the tenth most popular Christmas list request for children. The request for 'a Mum' was number 23 on the list.

16 DIFFERENT STROKES (P. 34)

1. It's **'WATERBOARDING'** (as it's now known) and it has a pedigree stretching back further than the CIA manual our illustration came from, originating with the Inquisition in **15TH-CENTURY SPAIN**. The 'ordeal by water' was an especially convenient interrogation technique because it needed only a rag or a funnel and a supply of water, leaving no wounds or scars and no bloody mess to clean up. Thanks to the Inquisition's obsession with record keeping, we know that an 'ordinary' ordeal called for the application of five litres of water and an 'extraordinary' one required ten litres.

2. It's **C**. Merciless tickling. It has been used as a torture across the globe since the ancient Chinese and as recently as World War II when Nazis performed it on prisoners with goose feathers, on the soles of feet, between the legs, in the armpits and on other parts of the naked body. In ancient Japan, the authorities used it on people convicted of crimes that were beyond the criminal code.

3. The answer is **D**. Pressing to death was the standard 16th-century method of punishment in Elizabethan England for anyone refusing to enter a plea in court. The victim was stripped, blindfolded and made to lie on a rock roughly the size of a tennis ball. Then a large panel of wood was placed on the victim's chest and gradually loaded with 700-800lb of rocks and stones, until his or her back broke. Within about 15 minutes the victim would be dead, by which time the process had usually succeeded in eliciting a plea. It was still in use in 1726, when a murderer called Burnworth endured a weight of around 450lbs for nearly two hours before he begged to be released; he pleaded, was found guilty, then was hanged.

4. The answer is **C**. The original torture, probably Dutch in origin, consisted on rats in an upturned bucket on the victim's stomach. When hot coals were placed on the bucket, the rats would claw their way through the bowels of the prone human to escape the heat. Orwell's version – a cage-cum-mask applied to his antihero Winston Smith – is gentle by comparison.

5. The answer is **C**. Which is one way to avoid paying an invoice.

6. The answer is **B**. The Breaking Wheel, also known as the Catherine Wheel, comprised a large wooden wagon wheel with several radial spokes. A condemned person was lashed to the device and a club or iron cudgel used to beat their limbs. It was a very slow and painful death: victims might live for four days before finally expiring. The body was usually displayed on the wheel after death.

7. It's **A**. The skull crusher was a German invention but routinely used across Europe during the Spanish Inquisition. The victim's chin was placed over a bottom bar and the head under a upper metal cap. The executioner then turned the screw, gradually compressing the head between the bar and cap.

8. **FALSE**. There's no evidence that the Iron Maiden ever existed.

9. **C**. And that ain't the half of it. The intended victim was trapped between two rowing boats or hollowed-out tree trunks, joined together one on top of the other, with head, hands and feet sticking out. The condemned was force-fed milk and honey until they developed diarrhea. The victim was then left to float on a stagnant pond or exposed to the sun. The combo of honey and faeces attracted swarming insects to eat and breed in exposed flesh, causing gangrene.

10. The answer is **B**.

BONUS QUESTION 11. It's **A**. The most feared instrument at the disposal of the Holy Inquisition, the Pope's Pear/Pear of Anguish was designed to be inserted into various orifices of the human body; a screw-driven mechanism on the interior of the 'pear' allowed it to be expanded as the torturer turned the handle, thus tearing the tender flesh from the inside.

BONUS QUESTION 12. The answer is **THE WINTER'S TALE.** In Shakespeare's play, Autolycus tells the shepherd and his son that because Perdita has fallen in love with the prince, her adoptive brother will be subjected to the following punishment: 'He has a son—who shall be flayed alive; then 'nointed over with honey, set on the head of a wasp's nest; then stand till he be three quarters and a dram dead… then raw as he is, and in the hottest day prognostication proclaims, shall he be set against a brick wall, the sun looking with a southward eye upon him,—where he is to behold him with flies blown to death.' Eek.

17. THE UGLY TRUTH #2 (P. 40)

1. FALSE. Russia actually only ranks 7th, one place behind Britain in the league table of countries listed as the world's hardest drinkers. Belgium has the highest alcohol consumption.

2. TRUE. The odds of you being killed in a plane crash are 11 million to one, but there are a few things your flight attendant won't tell you during take-off. The first three and the last eight minutes of your flight are when 80% of all plane crashes occur. Concentrate on that statistic the next time you're tempted to ignore the flight crew's instructions. Your plane is also basically a large tube full of germs. Planes are flying on ever tighter schedules so there's often no time for cleaning before a flight is turned around for the next group of passengers and harmful bacteria and viruses can live on for days on surfaces. And if the worst happens, pray you're sitting within five rows of an exit. Statistical analyses of plane crashes show that passengers who sit further than five rows away have greatly reduced chances of successfully evacuating a plane during an emergency.

3. FALSE. It almost certainly is. Ever since the 17th-century thinker Thomas Hobbes famously described the lives of humans in their 'natural condition' prior to the development of civil society as 'nasty, brutish, and short', many learned experts have argued that humankind evolved for violence. For example, a 2015 study showed that a buttressed fist – one with the thumb closed against the index and middle fingers – provides a safer way to hit someone with force. Given that none of our primate cousins has the ability to make such a fist, the authors propose that our hands evolved specifically to function as effective weapons.

4. TRUE. But only in very few cases. Our favourite medical standby isn't nearly as effective as you may have been led to believe. Studies have shown that only 2% of adult patients who collapse on the street and receive CPR recover fully and only 18% of elderly people who receive CPR at the hospital survive to be discharged.

5. FALSE. Whatever the old-school NHS Nit Nurses may have said, as they toured schools, poked heads and spread fear across the land, nits don't care what state the hair is in, and they use a special, self-generated glue to stick themselves to it. Nice.

6. FALSE. This fallacy was popularised by the US statesman Thomas Jefferson who said, 'I'm a great believer in luck, and I find the harder I work, the more I have of it.' But a study by Professor Richard Wiseman of the University of Hertfordshire concluded luck had more to do with outlook than effort. Lucky people, he found, were those who spotted opportunities, who believed outcomes would be positive and who viewed failures as setbacks. So anyone can be lucky, if they adopt the right mindset? No – you're much more likely to have that mindset if you come from a privileged background.

7. FALSE. Size, or more to the point, the length of the penis does matter if you hope to become a father. Scientists have found a direct correlation between men with fertility problems and those with small willies. Even a one-centimetre difference significantly decreases fertility prospects.

8. FALSE. The British monarch directly receives £82 million a year, but when other costs are included – helicopter flights, palatial homes, round-the-clock security and so forth – the annual bill for the monarchy is nearer £345m. There is no available data as to whether or not tourists visit the UK because of the royal family. In 2012, the Queen's Jubilee year, which was about a big a celebration of all things royal as you can possibly get, foreign visitor numbers to the UK actually fell. People do visit the UK for its world-class museums, fantastic shopping and unique history, but not necessarily because they might catch a glimpse of Prince Edward. In a list of the most successful tourist attractions in the UK, Windsor Castle, the only royal residence to attract decent numbers of visitors, comes in at no. 24, a long way behind the British Museum, Chester Zoo, Stonehenge and the Roman baths. The most visited palace in Europe is Versailles, so if it was just about the tourist money (which is a funny way of deciding how your country should be run) then Britain would be better off getting rid of the monarchy, as the French did, and opening up all the royal properties to tourists all year round. Although we wouldn't cut off their heads, obviously. We could retrain them as tour guides.

9. TRUE. Some species of penguins gift rocks as part of the mate selection ritual; it's also a practical gift because they add to the nest. But it's hardly the perfect example of true love, according to this quote taken from an article on the BBC's website. 'Penguins are turning to prostitution. But instead of doing it for money, Antarctic dolly-birds are turning tricks to get the rocks off their menfolk. Stones are essential for penguins to build their nests. A shortage has led to the unorthodox tactics.' Dr Fiona Hunter, a researcher in the Zoology Department at Cambridge University, who has spent five years observing the birds' mating patterns elaborates: 'On some occasions the prostitute penguins trick the males. They carry out the elaborate courtship ritual, which usually leads to mating. Having bagged their stone, they then run off.'

10. TRUE. But not for much longer. The NASA rover Curiosity could still fail at any moment when its wheel's drive motors pack in. That's if one of Mars' regular meteor showers doesn't destroy it first.

18. ODD CELEBRITIES OUT (P. 41)

They have all been insulted on the social media forum/bear-baiting arena Twitter by former U.S. President Donald Trump, apart from **B**, who would never insult himself, but whose very existence is a kind of insult.

A Arnold Schwarzenegger – 'did a really bad job as Governor of California and even worse on *The Apprentice*.'

B Some may argue that stable genius Mr Trump is trashing his own reputation, tweet by tweet, but the truth is, the Dayglo Psycho never had a reputation to trash in the first place.

C Meryl Streep – 'one of the most over-rated actresses in Hollywood'.

D Neil Young – 'total hypocrite'.

E Oprah Winfrey – 'very insecure'.

F Robert De Niro – 'a very low IQ individual, has received too many shots to the head by real boxers in movies'.

G Samuel L. Jackson – 'not athletic', 'cheats', 'boring', 'not a fan'.

H Snoop Dogg – 'failing career'.

I Whoopi Goldberg – 'now in total freefall', 'terrible', 'very sad'.

19. ROUGH JUSTICE (P. 42)

1. SIR GEORGE JEFFREYS. Regarded as Britain's most sadistic Lord Chief Justice ever, 'Bloody Jeffreys' passed 331 death sentences and had hundreds more deported to Australia – in the 17th century, arguably a fate worse than hanging

2. It's **C**.

3. The answer is **A**. Judge Roy Bean dispensed justice in Texas for twenty years, presiding from a saloon bar called The Jersey Lily in the town of Langtry. Bean was renowned for his erratic methods, often interrupting trials to serve drinks to the court. Whenever he presided over a marriage ceremony he always finished with the line 'May God have mercy on your soul.'

4. It's **B**. It was guffaws a-go-go during the *Oz* magazine 'School Kids Issue' trial, and not just over Argyle's chat-up lines. At one point, after the Judge had described another morality-corrupting image in the same issue as 'a fake male penis', co-defendant Richard Neville suggested that he, himself, had never yet come across 'a penis that was not male, m'lud.' Later, a lengthy debate occurred as to whether London's Earl's Court area was renowned for its male perverts, Australians, or both. Argyle was somewhat outdone in the comedy stakes by the prosecuting counsel Brian Leary QC, who at one point pressed the psychologist and author Michael Schofield to admit that the Rupert the Bear cartoon had implied under-aged sex. '[Rupert is] a young bear, isn't he?' Leary insisted. 'He goes to school; that's right, isn't it?' 'I do not know whether he goes to school or not,' was Schofield's response. 'I'm sorry, but I'm obviously not as well informed as you are about little bears. I'm a psychologist.'

5. It's **D**.

6. It's **C**. Argyle was a cricket fan and kept a TV set in his robing room to keep in touch with Test match scores. He was similarly forthright in his views on diversity. On the subject of the number of British immigrants in Britain, he noted, 'I don't have the figures, but just go to Bradford', while a black British defendant was told to 'get out and go back to Jamaica'.

7. The answer is **C**. Lord Monboddo's faith in the tail theory remained intact even after he witnessed the births of his own children. He concluded that the crafty midwives had tricked him and destroyed the evidence. Monboddo would frequently interrupt court proceedings at Edinburgh's Court of Sessions by sending notes of enquiry to witnesses who had recently returned from abroad, to ask them if they had seen any foreigners with tails.

8. The answer is **D**. Argyle was in fact a keen chess player and, as his obituary in *The Guardian* (7th January 1999) noted, he spent a considerable amount of his spare time trying to ensure that the people he'd sentenced found work upon release.

9. The answer is **C**. Argyle felt that many crimes were more deserving of a capital penalty than murder, which was often committed in a state of irrational passion.

10. It's **B**. After a public outcry, he realized he'd been a bit harsh and ordered her to be beheaded instead. He was very scared of his second wife, however, and a popular ditty of the time referred to a certain George who had married the dragon instead of slaying it…

11. The answer is **C**. After Argyle announced that his next target was the housebreakers, it was rumoured that habitual thieves had begun prowling the streets equipped with Ordnance Survey maps, to ensure that any houses they burgled would be safely outside the Judge's jurisdiction.

12. It's **D**.

13. The answer is **A**.

14. In each case, one did the crime, the other did the time (or worse). 'The Dreyfus Affair' is one of the most infamous cases of miscarried justice in history. A French army officer of Jewish descent, Alfred Dreyfus (**A**) was found guilty of sharing military secrets with the French and sent to the notorious Devil's Island penal colony as a traitor to his country, but two years later evidence surfaced that another French soldier, Ferdinand Esterhazy (**B**), was responsible. The authorities – anxious to prove that Jews could never be trusted patriots – kept the evidence suppressed until 1899 and it took another seven years for Dreyfus to be finally exonerated. Esterhazy meanwhile fled France and died in exile in the Hertfordshire commuter town of Harpenden, so he got his comeuppance.

Timothy Evans (**D**) went to the gallows in 1950 for the murder of his wife Beryl and their infant daughter, insisting that their upstairs neighbor was responsible. It took another three years, and another six bodies to show up at the address – 10 Rillington Place, in West London – before police took an interest in the landlord, John Reginald Christie (**C**).

19-year-old Derek Bentley (**F**) was hanged in 1953, not for shooting a policeman in the course of burglary, but for being the elder member of the team, and for uttering the ambiguous advice to his 16-year-old accomplice, Christopher Craig (**E**): 'Let him have it, Chris.' Bentley's defence argued that he'd been urging his companion to hand over the gun. The jury felt otherwise.

15. The answer is **D**.

20 AN ARM AND A LEG (P. 49)

Score 5 points for a correct 1st place, 4 points for a correct 2nd place, 3 points for a correct 3rd place, 2 points for a correct 4th place and 1 point for any other correct placing. Score 20 points if you got them all correct from 1- 10.

1. Kidney: $262,000
2. Liver: $157,000
3. Heart: $119,000
4. Small Intestine: $2,519
5. Pair of Eyeballs: $1,550
6. Coronary Artery: $1,525
7. Gallbladder: $1,219
8. Spleen: $510
9. Stomach: $505
10. Shoulder: $500.

The worldwide number of commercial transplants – i.e. those involving payment for the organ – is around 10,000 annually. In most cases the organ is a kidney, illegally sold by a living person. Most countries have laws that prohibit the selling and buying of organs and ban physicians from transplanting organs obtained through payment, and the practice is also banned by the World Health Organisation, but demand for organs massively outstrips supply. For example, in 2016, 100,791 people were waiting for lifesaving kidney transplants in the United States but only 17,107 kidney transplants took place. Meanwhile 4,761 Americans died while waiting for a kidney transplant.

21 RHYMES AGAINST HUMANITY (P. 50)

1. Poem **D** features in *Huckleberry Finn*, but **A, B** and **C** are the authentic works of Julia A. Moore (1847–1920), who, as Twain put it, had 'the touch that makes an intentionally humorous episode pathetic and an intentionally pathetic one funny'. Generally acknowledged as the worst ever American poet, Moore's inspiration usually came from the deaths of neighbours, stories she read in newspapers, anecdotes about heroic Civil War deeds, or her own childhood memories. Her favourite subject matter, tragic and untimely death, caused critics to note that she rattled off poems 'like a Gatling Gun'. Moore's magnum opus was her collection of poems, *The Sweet Singer of Michigan Salutes the Public*, published in 1876. The critics ironically praised the work as a masterpiece: Twain claimed it had kept him laughing for the best part of twenty years. She published no more poetry after her second book, *A Few Words to the Public* in 1878.

2. The last line is '*Her Majesty for two hours showed herself to them.*' (Which conjures up an odd image.) The legendary Scot had a brief and unsuccessful career as an actor until 1877, when a 'divine inspiration' told him to 'Write! Write!' Many of McGonagall's works were dedicated to Queen Victoria, whom he often followed to Balmoral in vain hope of giving his sovereign a recitation of his latest work. Although he never got beyond the palace gates, his persistence paid off when he received a polite note from her private secretary, Lord Biddulph, telling him to clear off and not trouble Her Majesty again. This near brush with royalty went to McGonagall's head and he had a new calling card printed, restyling himself 'William McGonagall – Poet To Her Majesty'.

In the second part of the question, the missing word is **CARBONISED**. McGonagall, like Julia A. Moore, often found inspiration in newspaper reports of grisly deaths.

3. It's **C**. Born in South Carolina during the Civil War, Coogler began writing romantic poetry when he was a schoolboy. His first effort was for a girl called Minnie who went to Galveston and died in a hurricane. Encouraged in his poetic efforts by cruel neighbours, he opened a print shop and put a sign in the window: 'Poems Written While You Wait.' Coogler occasionally prefaced his works with selections of the critical comments he encountered, although they were always less than flattering. He died suddenly aged 36. He posthumously acquired a number of fan clubs across America and since 1975 his name has lived on in the J. Gordon Coogler Award for outstandingly bad journalism.

4. The answer is **B**. The appointment of Alfred Austin (1835-1913) as Poet Laureate by the Prime Minister Lord Salisbury was probably a joke at the expense of the literary establishment. Austin didn't let him down – but he may not deserve all the mud that is flung at him. It was E. F. Benson who really wrote those lines about the Prince of Wales, in parody of Austin's style, and the opening lines of 'The Jameson Raid' are often shortened to 'They rode across the veldt / As fast as they could pelt' – which is worse, although not much worse. Austin had a towering ego and took his appointment as proof that he was officially England's greatest wordsmith. His poems, mostly overblown epics expressing his own reactionary views, were universally panned by the critics but Austin struck a pose of lofty indifference, continuing to churn out rubbish while lambasting his detractors. When it was pointed out to him that his poems were riddled with basic grammatical errors, Austin replied: 'I dare not alter these things. They come to me from above'.

5. It's **D**. Gwyer followed his two great obsessions, poetry and potato selling, with equal enthusiasm, often combining the two, as evidenced by his 1875 volume *Sketches Of The Life of Joseph Gwyer (Potato Salesman) With His Poems (Commended By Royalty)*. A typical Gwyer work was 'Love and Matrimony' in which he points out that the most important thing a man should seek in a bride is an ability to roast <u>POTATOES</u> (the word was always underlined or written in capitals). It should be pointed out that at no time was any of Gwyer's work ever commended by anyone, least of all royalty, but the tuber-obsession earned him a grudging respect. The magazine *Punch* noted of his poem 'The Alexandra Palace, Muswell Hill, Destroyed By Fire': 'We consider this work no small potatoes'.

BONUS QUESTION. 'Dear Mama' would have worked, but Gwyer preferred to be edgy and experimental. The missing word is **DAD-DAD-A**.

6. (i) The answer is **C**. It was fruit that formed the motif of McKittrick Ros' third novel, with a cast including Christopher Currant and the Earl of Grape. (ii) **D**. The others come from Canadian literary critic Northrop Frye, *The Oxford Companion to Irish Literature,* and novelist Barry Pain (who was being ironic).

7. The answer is **A**. The retort to Pain, published in the preface to her second novel, claimed that he was surely only hostile because he loved her.

8. The answer is **B**. Pye specialised in rambling dirges on largely agricultural themes, for example his treatise *The Effect of Music on Animals*. Pye's job was made considerably more difficult when his patron, King George III, became insane during his laureateship. He did his best to avoid or to manfully circumnavigate the subject, a tricky business at the best of times, but especially when it came to the obligatory annual King's Birthday Ode.

9. The answer is **B**. Cheese. His 'Dairy Ode' goes thus:

> The quality is often vile
> Of cheese that is made in April
> Therefore we think for that reason
> You should make it later in the season

McIntyre left Scotland to live in Ontario, Canada in 1841 and it was through his promotion of the local dairy industry that he found his muse. His poetic celebrations of dairy produce include *Lines read at a Dairymaids' Social*, 1887, *Fertile Lands and Mammoth Cheese, Lines Read at a Dairymen's Supper, Father Ranney, the Cheese Pioneer* and *Hints to Cheese Makers*. Many of his poems reached a wide audience when they were printed in the *Toronto Globe* thanks to his political connection to the paper's editor, a fellow Liberal supporter.

10. The line ends with the words **CITY OF TORONTO**.

11. It's **A** – William Wordsworth (1770–1850). Although regarded as one the great poets, he was capable of the odd howler.

12. The answer is Andrew Motion (b. 1952). He became Poet Laureate in 1999 and wrote this 'rap poem' intended to celebrate Prince William's 21st birthday in 2003. According to Motion it was an attempt to show that William was a 'new kind of royal figure'.

22 KILL OR CURE (P. 55)

1. The answer is **B**.

2. Again it's **B**.

3. The answers are **D** and **F** – all the rest were applied to the hapless monarch, whose dying words were, 'You must pardon me, gentlemen, for being for being a most unconscionable time a-dying.' (And not, as is more widely reported 'Let not poor Nellie starve.')

4. The answer is **A**.

5. It's **D**. On 13 December 1799, the 67-year-old former President had a throat infection and was visited by Dr. James Craik, who tried 'two copious bleedings', a cantharides blister, two doses of calomel, and an unspecified injection which 'operated on the lower intestines.' Two more physicians arrived that afternoon to bleed Washington yet again, then made him inhale vinegar in a vapour mixed with steam, followed by more calomel and 'repeated doses of emetic tartar' which produced 'a copious discharge from the bowels'. Between them they drained about

35% of the blood in his body within twelve hours. At this point Washington told his doctors he preferred to die without further intervention, and Thornton's lamb's blood proposals were politely declined.

6. The answer is **B.** Guiteau fired two bullets at the new President: one grazed Garfield's arm and the other lodged itself somewhere inside his body. Over the next eighty days, sixteen doctors were consulted on the President's condition. The first on the scene jabbed a finger into Garfield's open wound then inserted a non-sterile probe to find the bullet, causing so much damage that it misled several other later doctors into believing that this was the path made by the bullet and that the missile had hit Garfield's liver. An army surgeon-general then stuck an unwashed digit into the wound, soon followed by the navy surgeon-general who succeeded in puncturing the President's hitherto-undamaged liver. At which point Alexander Graham Bell was called in, with his latest invention, a metal detector, to help locate the bullet. After several passes with his device Bell announced that he had found it. When the physicians cut Garfield open to remove it they realised that Bell's equipment had in fact located the metal springs in the mattress, while the bullet continued to elude them. By the time Garfield died of a massive heart attack, his doctors had turned a relatively harmless three-inch-deep wound into a twenty-inch-long contaminated gash stretching from his ribs to his groin.

7. C. Bearing in mind the above, the assassin had a point. The President's autopsy determined that the bullet had in fact lodged itself some way from the spine and that Garfield would have survived if everyone had just left him alone.

8. It's **C** – couching. This invasive procedure involved using unsterilized instruments with which the opaque lens was displaced from the front of the eye and shoved underneath it. The immediate results were usually encouraging but the operation was invariably followed by serious infection. Medical historians believe that in Bach's case, the cause of death was also complicated by stroke.

9. The answer is **D**.

10. It's **B**. Dawson also helpfully phoned *The Times* to warn them to hold the front page and expect an important announcement shortly.

23 SICK NOTES (P. 59)

1. **FAKE.** It's just old-fashioned tendonitis, caused by habitually working with our arms and wrists in unnatural positions – e.g. using a keyboard, mouse phone, or game console controller.

2. **REAL.** A report in the *British Medical Journal* found Brexit-induced depression to be a genuine psychiatric illness, although quite how the researchers could distinguish it from anxiety and depression caused by everything else is not obvious.

3. **REAL.** It is the digital version of hypochondria.

4. **FAKE.** A Universty of Florida study published that year found a link, and numerous counsellors, psychotherapists, teachers and users have indicated connections between social media sites and mental unwellness. No researcher has named a condition after a popular app, though, and it's unlikely anyone would dare to.

5. **REAL.** It was added to the Oxford English Dictionary in 2013. A study on FOMO Syndrome defined it as: 'the uneasy and sometimes all-consuming feeling that you're missing out – that your peers are doing, in the know about, or in possession of more or something better than you'. In the study, three-quarters of young adults reported they experienced the phenomenon.

6. **REAL.** It's not cholera, but in a survey nine of ten mobile phone owners claim to have suffered from 'phantom vibration syndrome'.

7. **FAKE.**

8. **REAL.** A condition first described by US doctors, in which a combination of economic, historic, social and cultural factors combine to make life more difficult for people for whom life was already hard. In the UK it is known as a Conservative government.

9. **FAKE**

10. REAL. A joint study by Nottingham Trent University and Thiaga-rajar School of Management proved that you're likely to balance low self-confidence with obsessive attention-seeking and hope that by compulsively detailing the minutiae of your life online you will be part of a larger group, even if it doesn't necessarily exist. Selfitis is also life-threatening. Betwen 2017 and 2019, 69 people died from taking selfies: several fell in rivers and drowned, others were hit by trains and one was trampled by an elephant. The good news? In 2020-21 there was a drastic reduction in selfie fatalities, but more due to covid-related travel restrictions than people acquiring common sense.

24 POT LUCK #2 (P. 60)

1. The answer is **B**.

2. The answer is **D**. Stanley Kubrick's interpretation of Stephen King's haunted-hotel novel did not receive a single Oscar nomination. 'Psycho' fared only slightly better – four nominations, no Oscar.

3. It's **D**. *Deinococcus radiodurans* – 'Conan the bacterium' – is listed as the world's toughest bacterium in the *Guinness Book Of World Records*. It can survive cold, dehydration, vacuum and acid, and is one of the most radiation-resistant organisms known to man.

4. It's **C**. The ancient Greeks thought dead gingers became vampires. After complaints from customers in December 2009, Tesco withdrew a Christmas card that showed a child with red hair sitting on the lap of Santa Claus under the words 'Santa loves all kids. Even ginger ones.'

5. It's **A**.

6. The answer is **D**. Huish, 31, told *The Sun*. 'It wasn't a bet, but I said I'd cut my balls off if we won. I can't have kids now but still want a family. Maybe I'll adopt.'

7. The answer is **D**. 2 million people each year die from work-related accidents as opposed to 650,000 killed in wars. The most dangerous jobs are in mining, agriculture and construction.

8. It's **A** overall, but **B** represents the number of 16-24 year olds who believe it, while **C** and **D** are the proportion of respondents who rely on WhatsApp and YouTube for a fair amount, or a lot of information.

9. The answer is **A**. There were six attempts to kill or harm her, a record she incidentally shares with Tsar Alexander II of Russia, who was finally blown to pieces at the seventh attempt in 1881.

10. It's **C**. His four-month career as chief executioner was marked by several inept hangings, including that of his final customer, 18-year-old Michael McLean at Kirkdale Gaol in Liverpool on 10th March 1884. Binns arrived for work drunk, so the prison governor sent for a local man to assist him. Refusing help, Binns insisted on carrying out the execution alone. After the trapdoor was released, McLean was left choking to death and it took another 13 minutes before his heart stopped.

25. THE REICH STUFF, #1 (P. 62)

1. Adolf Hitler **2.** Adolfo Stroessner **3.** Josef Stalin **4.** Baby Doc Duvalier **5.** Alexander Lukashenko **6.** Saddam Hussein **7.** Robert Mugabe **8.** Jean Bedel Bokassa **9.** Fidel Castro **10.** Kim Il Sung

26 KILLER WORD SEARCH (P. 64)

Ted Bundy, Jeffrey Dahmer, H. H. Holmes, The Mad Butcher (aka Ed Gein), Boston Strangler (Albert de Salvo), Albert Fish, Harold Shipman, Fred West, Yorkshire Ripper (Peter Sutcliffe), Erno Soto

27 MEDICAL MISCELLANY (P. 65)

1. The answer is **B**. It is the rate at which your cells die – literally, the speed of death. The *New Scientist* helpfully expresses it at two millimetres an hour.

2. It's **B**. A study from a group of neuroscientists suggests that people begin experiencing age-related cognitive deterioration in their late 20s. Some aspects of your cognitive skills – for example your ability to make rapid comparisons, remember unrelated information and detect relationships – peak at about the age of 22 and then begin a slow decline starting around age 27.

3. The answer is **C**. This is the point at which your DNA starts to degenerate, which increases the risk of you developing cancer.

4. FALSE. There are currently no available figures on the cost to hospitals of rectal foreign body removal. However a report in *The Sun* in 2017 suggested that around 400 adult patients a year are admitted to A&E in the UK requesting removal of items including wine corks, pens, electric toothbrushes, deodorant cans and 'massagers' with an average cost of £132 – total per annum £52,800.

5. TRUE. By mass and volume, you are more human cells, but at a cellular level, you're more bacteria than person.

6. The answer is **A** – as well as bursting blood vessels in your eyes, a supressed sneeze can, in some rare cases, lead to a brain aneurysm. (Then again, a brain aneurysm can finish you off, without warning, whether you sneeze or not, so why worry?) Yawning can sometimes result in a dislocated jaw and it's possible that if you habitually steer clear of visiting the loo for long periods, the build-up of bacteria might lead to a bladder infection. As for the held-in fart, there have been some rare catastrophic events when people with blocked colons have been unable to pass wind, resulting in sudden rupture, but you'd need to be so unwell for this to occur that it would probably be the least of your worries.

7. TRUE – if you have Auto-Brewery syndrome. A type of yeast in your stomach ferments carbohydrates to produce ethanol, which in turn intoxicates you even without drinking.

8. TRUE. When a body becomes starved for sustenance, cells start eating themselves, a process known as autophagy and a normal part of the cell's life-cycle. It was thought that the brain was largely resistant to autophagy under these conditions but at least one part of the brain appears to self-cannibalize – the hypothalamus, which sits above the brain stem and regulates various functions, including sleep, body temperature, thirst and hunger.

9. FALSE. The odds are ten times higher. One in every 100 people has

Fuchs' Corneal Dystrophy, which often goes unnoticed until it's too late. The gel inside your eyeball fills up the cornea, the pressure builds and your eyeball pops. If this happens to you, blame your parents, because at least one of them passed the gene on.

10. FALSE. The average teaspoon-sized serving may contribute about 3% of your recommended daily intake of zinc, but that's about it, as far as essence of gentleman is concerned. There's a similar quantity of copper in human semen, alongside trace elements of magnesium and calcium, and about a third of the protein you'd obtain from swallowing a single egg white. Calorie-wise, though, pecker-juice does pack something of a punch: the standard 5ml money-shot delivers a count of 3 calories, putting it roughly on a par with extra-strong lager. Devastating to the waistline, then, but only if you drink it by the pint.

BONUS QUESTION: The answer is **B: 3-5**. If you break blood down, there isn't much in it that's good for you apart from a bit of iron, some water and a touch of protein. Human blood is put together in such a way that the body isn't meant to digest, otherwise you'd metabolise your own blood. If you drink more than a pint, you will become violently ill. If a vampire were to drain all of your blood, it would only net them 500 calories, so they'd need at least 3 humans per day to keep going. This is assuming that a vampire requires the same calorific intake as a human being. Of course, if our vampire feasted on uncontrolled diabetics or people with elevated blood glucose levels he (or she) might need fewer humans. Vampires are just bigger mosquitos, if you think about it.

28 ODDLY OUT (P. 67)

All are ground-breaking scientists whose discoveries were overlooked because of sexism, except for I.

A. Lise Meitner. Pioneering physicist and part of the team that discovered nuclear fission (a term she coined). She was overlooked in 1945 when her colleague Otto Hahn was exclusively awarded the Nobel Prize in Chemistry for nuclear fission.

B. Rosalind Franklin. At 33 she made the discovery that would revolutionise biology – that DNA comprised two chains and a phosphate backbone. Crick and Watson 'borrowed' her work and went on to become Nobel-Prize–winning scientists. During her lifetime, Franklin received virtually no recognition in this field.

C. Vera Rubin. The American astronomer made a number of important observations, including confirming that 90% of the universe is made of dark matter. Although she achieved recognition later on, she experienced discouraging sexism and her discoveries were ignored for years. When she told her high school physics professor that she'd been accepted for a scholarship he replied: 'That's great, as long as you stay away from science, it should be OK.'

D. Cecelia Payne. She was the first scientist to assert that stars are primarily made of hydrogen and helium. This conclusion was so radical that she was talked out of presenting it by the senior astronomer with whom she studied. He then stole her idea and published it himself.

E. Chien Shiung Wu. A Chinese immigrant to America, she began her work with the Manhattan Project and the development of the atomic bomb. Her biggest contribution to the world of science was a discovery that overturned a widely accepted law at the time, known as the Principle of Conservation of Parity. Her colleagues stole her idea and won a Nobel Prize for their work.

F. Ida Tacke. Made huge advancements in the fields of chemistry and atomic physics that were ignored until they were later 'discovered' by her male colleagues Carlo Perrier and Emilio Segre.

G. Nettie Stevens. Most textbooks will tell you that Thomas Morgan made established that our sex is determined by our 23rd pair of chromosomes, the X and Y. Morgan claimed that Nettie Stevens was just his lab technician, when in fact she made the discovery working alone.

H. Esther Lederberg. She was the first to solve the problem of reproducing bacterial colonies using a technique known as replica plating. She made the mistake of making her discovery alongside her husband,

Joshua. While they both played equally important roles, Esther's contributions went largely unrecognised, while her husband took home a Nobel Prize. They later divorced.

I.   THE ODD ONE OUT. Maria Salomea Skłowodwska was born in Warsaw, and later became a naturalised French citizen, using both her maiden name and that of her husband, Pierre Curie. If you asked 'who is the most famous woman scientist of all time?' most people would give you her name, although some might not be able to identify her field or her contribution to it. Marie Curie was the first woman to earn a Nobel Prize and the first person ever to earn a second.

29 SOME LIKE IT HOT (P. 68)

1.	E.	Nigel Lawson	2.	D.	Nigel Farage
3.	C.	Vladimir Putin	4.	G.	David Bellamy
5.	H.	Donald trump	6.	A.	Tony Abbot
7.	F.	Ted Cruz	8.	I.	Rush Limbaugh
9.	B.	Nicolas Sarkozy	10.	J.	Sarah Palin

30 TYRANTS ON TOUR #2 (P. 70)

1. B.

2. D. He'd had such a jolly time on his first trip that he'd fully expected to receive a second invitation. When one never appeared, he decided it was no More Mr Nice Guy.

3. D.

4. B. History doesn't record what gifts, if any, Ceaucescu presented to the Queen. Perhaps it was something he'd just nicked off the French President.

5. B. Heartbroken at the thought of his beloved Cara doing a six-month stint in quarantine, Mobutu put her on a plane and sent her to the Embassy of Zaire in Brussels.

31 KILLING FIELDS (P. 72)

1. The answer is **B**.
2. The answer is **C**.
3. The answer is **A**.
4. The Yangzhou Massacre took place in China in May 1645. (Although, China's history being what it is, there was an earlier Yangzhou Massacre in the year 760).
5. It's **C**. The reading out of the Act gave gatherings of more than 12 people who were deemed to be 'riotously, unlawfully and tumultuously' assembled an hour to disperse – or face the death penalty.
6. The answer is **A**.
7. The answer is **D**. The original (and so far, only) Peterloo Massacre was immortalised in Mike Leigh's 154-minute film, 'Peterloo'.
8. The answer is **B**. It was described by an historian as 'the most ferocious and bloody event in the history of industrialised Britain'.
9. It's **A**. The numbers are disputed, but some estimates placed the number of dead at 300.
10. The answer is **B**. On 13 April 1919, the victims were blocked inside the walled Jallianwala Gardens and fired on by Gurkha soldiers under Dyer's command until they ran out of ammunition, killing between 379 and 1,000 protesters and injuring another 1,100 within 10 minutes. It's alleged that Dyer himself aimed at areas where the crowd was thickest, and that he berated any men under his command who fired in the air.

32 ODD ONE ON THE MENU (P. 76)

They are all carcinogenic apart from E.

A. According to a 2012 study in the *American Journal of Clinical Nutrition*, men who drink one can of soda per day are 40% more likely to be diagnosed with prostate cancer. This risk is highest for men over the age of 45.

B. According to the World Health Organisation, hot beverages can increase your risk of getting cancer of the oesophagus.

C. Microwave popcorn contains chemical products, some of which are known for increasing our risk of developing testicular, liver and pancreatic cancers.

D. Levels of organic pollutants are much higher in farmed salmon than in its wild counterpart and eating farmed salmon once a month puts you more at risk of developing cancer.

E. Some types of hard cheese, including Gouda, Edam, Emmenthal and Jarlsberg, can lower your risk of developing cancer because they contain the vitamin K2 that is both antiangiogenic (blood vessel-inhibiting) and kills cancer cells directly. Eating as few as two slices of these hard cheeses a day can lower your risk of lung cancer and prostate cancer.

F. If you consume more than two alcoholic drinks every day you're increasing your risk of contracting different forms of cancer, especially mouth, throat and bowel cancers.

G. According to the WHO, if you eat 3.5 ounces of red meat every day you are 17% more likely to receive a cancer diagnosis.

H. The WHO advises that consuming 50g of processed meat a day – equivalent to just a couple of rashers of bacon – will raise your risk of getting bowel cancer by 18% over a lifetime.

I. Poorly stored peanuts are full of aflatoxin, a substance produced by mould and fungus, which increases your risk of liver cancer.

33 NATION SHALL SING PEACE. . . (P. 77)

1. Algeria **2.** Tunisia **3.** Albania
4. Armenia **5.** Hungary **6.** Italy
7. Turkey **8.** Vietnam **9.** France **10.** Mexico

BONUS QUESTIONS

1. A. Britain's 'God Save the Queen' is an old tune that became popular in its current form in 1745 when London was preparing to defend itself and its Hanoverian rulers from a Jacobite rebellion. The sixth verse goes:

Lord grant that Marshal Wade
May by thy mighty aid
Victory bring.
May he sedition hush,
And like a torrent rush,
Rebellious Scots to crush
God save the King!

Not the best way to persuade the Scots to stay in the Union...

2. All of them. The tune's origins are unknown, but various composers including Purcell and Dowland have been mentioned. There's a competing theory that the melody was French, and originally used for a hymn to celebrate Louis XIV's recovery from an operation on his piles.

34. OR NOT TO BE (P. 80)

1. The answer is **B.** Tolstoy's widow was prevented from being with her husband by the crowds of acolytes and reporters.

2. The answer is **D.** In a suicide note to her husband, she explained that voices in her head had told her to drown herself.

3. It's **C.** Iceland. The country, not the supermarket chain. Larkin enjoyed shocking his readers, as in his most-quoted line, 'They fuck you up, your mum and dad'. He may have had a point about his dad, who kept a statue of Hitler on his mantelpiece. And he might have agreed with those who answered D. Wellington was the Shropshire town where Phil had his first librarian job. He called it 'this hole of toads' turds' and described his job as 'handing out tripey novels to morons'.

4. It's **D.** Poe suffered from bouts of depression and sporadic manic episodes. The precise cause of his death remains unclear, but alcohol abuse was probably involved. Equally uncertain is the exact location of the tavern, which might be why the owners of the 'Horse' claim it happened there, but haven't added any cheesy Poe references to the pub's current name.

5. The answer is **C**. But it didn't happen. After Williams died in a hotel bedroom in 1983, having choked to death on the plastic cap of a nasal spray, his brother Walter had his remains buried alongside their mother, in Missouri. Tennessee Williams grappled with depression and addiction issues throughout his career. One thing that was guaranteed to put him in a bad mood was any mention of the 1958 film version of his 'Cat On a Hot Tin Roof', which he loathed. Before a showing in Florida he harangued a crowd of cinema-goers lined up outside the theatre, shouting, 'This movie will set the industry back fifty years. Go home.'

6. It's **H**. Increasingly depressed and paranoid, Hemingway shot himself in the head on 2nd July 1961.

7. The answer is **A**. Boilermakers are composed of a shot glass of bourbon dropped into a glass of beer.

8. The answer is **C**.

9. It's **B**. Although she was a former fashion model, signed to the Hart Agency of Boston.

10. A IS TRUE. B, C AND D ARE FALSE. Plath died in February 1963, a month after her only novel, *The Bell Jar* was first published in the UK – a semi-autobiographical account of her declining state of mental health, various suicide attempts, and her time in a mental institution. It would be another four years before her own name was attached to the work, and it wasn't until 1971 that the book would be published in Plath's native USA.

35. KILLER WORD SEARCH #2 (P. 83)

TUBERCULOSIS. GONORRHOEA. PNEUMONIA. MENINGITIS. RABIES. MUMPS. CHOLERA. SALMONELLOSIS. GASTROENTERITIS. TYPHOID. SHIGELLOSIS.

36. DEAD CHICK LIT (P. 84)

1. Lavinia – 'Titus Andronicus'
2. Cordelia – 'King Lear'
3. Desdemona – 'Othello'
4. Ophelia – 'Hamlet'

5. Anna Karenina – *Anna Karenina*
6. Cio-Cio-San – 'Madam Butterfly'
7. Bertha Mason – *Jane Eyre*
8. Catherine Earnshaw – *Wuthering Heights*
9. Nancy – *Oliver Twist*
10. Charlotte Haze – *Lolita*

37. IT'S BEHIND YOU! (P. 86)

1. **B: MR. PUNCH.** Since his first mention in Pepys' diary in the 1600s, this stick-wielding xenophobic misogynist has miraculously survived political correctness into the 21st century, although some of his routines, such as the one where a hangman gets hanged, have not.

2. **G: PINOCCHIO.** According to the original serialised children's book upon which the Disney film was based.

3. **I: SLEEPING BEAUTY.** In the original, she is unconscious when the king comes across her, and he decides to take advantage. On the plus side, she gets to marry the man who violated her, and they all live happily ever after. Here's the last line of the story: 'Lucky people, so 'tis said, are blessed by fortune whilst in bed.'

4. **D: RAPUNZEL.** In the 1812 original, a prince impregnates Rapunzel after the two spend days together living in 'joy and pleasure.' He then scarpers, leaving her, a single mum, stuck up a tower-block (kind of).

5. **H: THE FROG PRINCE.** In another, slightly more violent version the princess decapitates the frog.

6. **E: CINDERELLA.** In the original version recorded by the Brothers Grimm, the stepsisters ensure that the glass slipper fits by amputating parts of their own feet; the blood pooling around their shoes gives them away.

7. **F: LITTLE RED RIDING HOOD.** In most versions, the woodsman cuts Red and her grandmother out of the wolf's belly, finding them none the worse for being eaten alive. During the Third Reich, the Nazis adopted the tale for propaganda purposes. They claimed that Little Red

Riding Hood symbolised the German people suffering at the hands of the Jewish wolf. Also that Cinderella's Aryan purity distinguished her from her mongrel stepsisters.

8. J: THE LITTLE MERMAID. Hans Christian Andersen's original mermaids were soulless creatures destined to dissolve into sea foam when they died, whereas humans were promised a beautiful afterlife. Terrified of her abysmal fate, the little mermaid wanted nothing more than a human soul, but as her grandmother explained to her, the only way a mermaid can grow a soul is to wed a man who loves her more than anything. If the man won't marry her, she dies.

9. A: SNOW WHITE. In the 1812 version the heroine is just seven years old when the huntsman takes her into the forest with orders to bring back her liver and lungs, which the evil Queen intends to eat. In another version, the Queen asks for a bottle of her daughter's blood, stoppered with her toe. Other Grimms' Tales yet to be interpreted by Disney include *The Juniper Tree*, in which a woman decapitates her stepson as he bends down to get an apple, then cooks him in a stew and serves it to her husband, who enjoys it so much he asks for seconds. Then there's *The Jew in the Brambles* whose protagonist happily torments a Jew by forcing him to dance in a thicket of thorns, and *The Robber Bridegroom* in which some bandits drag a maiden into their underground hideout, force her to drink wine until her heart bursts, rip off her clothes and then hack her body into pieces.

10. C: PETER PAN has been interpreted as Barrie's own psychodrama, a consolation for the lack of affection his mum gave him as a child. We know Peter Pan doesn't want to grow up, but what the Disney version doesn't mention is the length to which he's prepared to go to fight it. In Barrie's works, Pan kills the Lost Boys to keep them from ageing.

BONUS QUESTIONS
1. The answer is **E**.
2. The answer is **C**.

ANSWERS | ROUNDS 37-39

38. PURPLE PASSAGES (P. 89)

Passages 1, 3, 6, 9, 10, 11 and 12 hit the literary g-spot, the rest merely made the shortlist. (Not that size matters, of course.)

1. **G** Melvyn Bragg, 1993 *A Time To Dance* (winner)
2. **K** Robert Seethaler, 2012 *The Tobacconist* (shortlist)
3. **D** Norman Mailer, 2007 *The Castle in the Forest* (winner)
4. **A** Dominic Smith, 2019 *The Electric Hotel* (shortlist)
5. **E** Wilbur Smith, 2017 *War Cry* (shortlist)
6. **B** Ben Okri, 2014 *The Age of Magic* (winner)
7. **B** Ben Okri, 2014 *The Age of Magic* (shortlist)
8. **H** Neil Griffiths, 2017 *As A God Might Be* (shortlist)
9. **F** Morrissey, 2015 *The List of the Lost* (winner)
10. **J** Didier Decoin, 2019 *The Office of Gardens and Ponds* (co-winner)
11. **C** Christopher Bollen, 2014 *The Destroyers* (winner)
12. **L** James Frey, 2018, *Katerina* (winner)

39. IT'S ALRIGHT MA, I'M ONLY DYING (P. 93)

Score one point for each correct blank filled in.

1. Give **SORROW** words; the grief that does not speak knits up the o-er wrought **HEART** and bids it break.
2. When sorrows come, they come not single **SPIES**, but in **BATTALIONS**.
3. A grief without a pang, void **DARK** and drear
A stifled, drowsy, unimpassioned **GRIEF**
Which finds no natural outlet, no relief
In word, or sigh, or **TEAR**
4. I have experienc'd
The worst, the World can wreak on me – the worst
That can make Life indifferent, yet disturb
With whisper'd Discontents the dying **PRAYER**
I have beheld the whole of all, wherein
My Heart had any interest in this **LIFE**,
To be disrent and torn from off my Hopes

That **NOTHING** now is left. Why then live on?

5. Nothing begins, and nothing ends,

That is not paid with **MOAN**;

For we are born in others' **PAIN**,

And perish in our own.

6. I sit in one of the dives

On Fifty-second Street

Uncertain and **AFRAID**

As the clever hopes expire

Of a low dishonest **DECADE**

7. Preacher was a-talkin', there's a sermon he gave

He said every man's conscience is vile and depraved

You cannot depend on it to be your **GUIDE**

When it's you who must keep it **SATISFIED**

8. Don't turn away, in **SILENCE**

Your confusion

My illusion

Worn like a mask of **SELF-HATE**

9. If you are the dealer, I'm out of the game

If you are the **HEALER**, it means I'm broken and lame

If thine is the glory then mine must be the **SHAME**

You want it darker

We kill the **FLAME**

10. Oh, oh, oh

I just can't **SLEEP** tonight

Knowing that things ain't right

It's **IN** the **PAPERS**, it's **ON** the **TV**, it's **EVERYWHERE** I go.

Oh, oh, **OH**.

40. THICK AS OLD BOOTS #1 (P. 95)

1. PATCHES

2. THE THREE OF THEM

3. **THEY SCORE GOALS**
4. They were **UNDER PRESSURE**
5. **HIMSELF**
6. **OUTNUMBERED**
7. **C. NOT TO WIN IS GUTTERING**
8. **FALSE**

(But he did once describe Justin Fashanu as 'a black Frank Bruno')

9. **TRUE**
10. **PRO-ME**
11. **CONFIDENT**
12. **INCONSISTENT**
13. **FALSE**
14. **TRUE**

(Not that it matters much, but it was a cricket ball)

15. **TRUE**
16. **SMALLER THAN**
17. **FALSE**
18. **FALSE**
19. **THERE'S NONE BETTER**
20. **TRUE**

41. SETTLING SCORES (P. 98)

1. Richard Wagner
2. Gioachino Rossini
3. Pyotr Ilyich Tchaikovsky
4. Hector Berlioz
5. Frederic Chopin
6. Giacomo Puccini
7. Camille Saint-Saëns
8. Richard Strauss
9. Sir Thomas Beecham
10. Igor Stravinsky

42. TEN DRUMMERS NOT DRUMMING (P. 100)

1. Al Jackson. Reports conflict on whether the culprit was a burglar or his estranged wife, who had already shot him in the chest a few months earlier. He decided not to press charges, but he was in the process of divorcing her.

2. Keith Moon of The Who.

3. John Bonham, drummer in Led Zeppelin. At the coroner's inquest it emerged that in the 24 hours before he died, Bonham had drunk forty measures of vodka.

4. Dennis Wilson, founding member of The Beach Boys.

5. Razzle was a passenger in a car driven by Motley Crue lead singer, Vince Neil, who lost control of the vehicle. Razzle was pronounced dead on arrival at hospital, aged 24. Motley Crue would title their 2003 and 2005 sets 'Music to Crash Your Car To': Vols. 1 and 2. Touching.

6. TRUE. The 38-year old drummer suffered a heart attack caused by a severe allergic reaction to the pesticide he was using on his garden.

7. Cozy Powell, drummer with Jeff Beck and Rainbow, amongst others.

8. Buddy Miles – he died 13 years later of congestive heart failure. According to friends, 'he turned off his defibrillator and was ready for heaven.'

9. Tommy Ramone of The Ramones.

10. Dominic Joseph 'DJ' Fontana. He drummed on more than 450 Elvis songs, including Hound Dog and Jailhouse Rock.

43. CRIMINAL RECORDS (P. 101)

1. William Shatner. From Captain Kirk's 1967 debut LP 'The Transformed Man', possibly the most derided cover version in the history of recorded music. Quite an achievement considering that he also covered 'Space Oddity'.

2. Duran Duran. Some middle-class art-school lads from Birmingham singing about getting shot and the police being slow to respond on account of them being, erm, black.

3. Take That. As any long-suffering Nirvana fan will attest, the song has been used and abused by just about every artist looking to build his or her street cred, including Miley Cyrus, Paul Anka, Limp Bizkit and Michael Bublé.

4. **Madonna.** *Rolling Stone* noted, 'Madonna got the new millennium off to a rather shitty start.' Her mate Rupert Everett put her up to it.

5. **Hilary Duff.** She reportedly covered a song she'd never heard of (and played it live) because her manager was a fan of The Who. 'Godawful', said *New Musical Express*.

6. **Susan Boyle.** To be fair, her version of a Stones song about a drugs overdose went down very well in the US. 'Time to take Susan Boyle seriously,' reckoned the *LA Times*.

7. **Sean Connery.** On the plus side, he doesn't attempt to sing, but when he coughs it sounds just like bagpipes.

8. **Justin Bieber.** A live set staple of one of the world's most reviled popstars.

9. **Ronan Keating.** His version was responsible for 7 million downloads on Spotify. He changed the line. 'You cheap, lousy faggot' to 'you're cheap and you're haggard' in case he offended anyone. It didn't work, Ronan.

10. **Kanye West.** His regrettable decision to take on Queen's master-piece at Glastonbury was made worse by him forgetting the words.

44. POT LUCK #3 (P. 102)

1. **B.**

2 **A.** After trying out various representations of masculinity in their advertisements, including athletes, gunsmiths and sea captains, Marlboro went for rugged cowboy iconography. Five actors who appeared in Marlboro ads subsequently died of smoking-related diseases, including David McLean, the best known 'Marlboro man', who expired from respiratory failure due to chronic obstructive pulmonary disease in 1995. Ahead of its time, MAD magazine dreamt up the 'Marble Row' campaign in the 1960s, spoofing the fag ads with tombstone-shaped packets, and showing the Wild West broncos saddled up, but cowboy-less in an overgrown graveyard.

3. A. Hudson tolerated his role as royal pet for many years with good grace but the joke wore thin, and he let it be known that he would no longer take insults about his height. When offence was given and taken in 1644, he challenged his detractor to a duel. Hudson chose pistols on horseback and planted a musket-ball through the man's forehead.

4. A. They concluded that his skull was 'just like Napoleon's' and they had seen 'nothing like it since Frederick the Great'. This contradicted a medical report written when he was on trial in 1923, describing the Führer's features thus: 'bad race, mongrel, low receding forehead, ugly nose, broad cheekbones, small eyes and dark hair.'

5. D. The buttons on their uniforms disintegrated when the temperature dropped to -30°C.

6. C.

7. A. This classic has been the number one funeral song for several years. Disappointingly, most dead people request Sinatra's version, not the definitive Sid Vicious cover. Monty Python's 'Always Look On The Bright Side Of Life' is still in the top 10, the leading pop choice for the over-50s, followed by Led Zeppelin's 'Stairway To Heaven'.

8. A. Nostradamus' prediction was:

Earthshaking fire from the centre of the Earth
Will cause tremors around the New City.
Two great rocks will war for a long time,
Then Arethusa will redden a new river.

On the morning of September 11, 2001, the two towers (two great rocks) of the World Trade Centre in New York City (New City) collapsed after al-Qaeda terrorists crashed hijacked passenger planes into the buildings. The bit about 'fire from the centre of the Earth' doesn't seem to link with anything pertaining to 9/11, though if you asked a hardcore Nostra-theorist, they might say the 'fire from the centre of the earth' referred to the burning jet fuel. Our advice is, don't ask.

9. A.

10. D. Ivan went on to ruthlessly exterminate potential rivals for power, including members of his own family. He died playing chess.

45. TOP TRUMP TWEETS (P. 104)

1. B
2. C
3. B
4. D
5. D
6. D
7. A
8. D

46. AND THE WINNER ISN'T... (P. 107)

1. How Green Is My Valley. The absurdity of Citizen Kane's loss became clearer over the decades; Welles film is now widely acclaimed as one of the best films of all time.

2. The Greatest Show on Earth. The Academy wanted to reward Cecil B. DeMille for his 40-year career, so they chose this bloated, gaudy circus epic over the infinitely superior, critically acclaimed, definitive and popular western classic, 'High Noon'.

3. The Sound of Music. The mid-'60s were a grim time for Hollywood, as reflected by this beige Nuns n' Nazis flick. 'Except for Julie Andrews…the cast is generally stiff or mawkish. In the case of Christopher Plummer, it is both.' *New York Times*

4. Rocky. A great film, if you're 12 years old.

5. Ordinary People. Not a terrible movie, but better than Scorsese's masterpiece about the madness of boxer Jake LaMotta, featuring that amazing performance from Robert De Niro? 'The Shining' wasn't even nominated.

6. Dances With Wolves. A three-hour movie that felt more like ten, it

had more nominations than any other film that year, but 'Goodfellas' is remembered as the classic.

7. Forrest Gump. 'Movies are like a box of chocolates. You never know what you are going to get. Forrest Gump is a chocolate that will surely make you gag' theodysseyonline.com.

8. Titanic. The biggest box office hit in history and winner of 11 Oscars was also voted worst film ever by viewers of BBC One's 'Film 2003'. Among the comments received were: 'My father fell asleep after 20 minutes. He was lucky. It was only his snoring that kept me awake.' Another said. 'It sank. There. I've saved you three hours of your life.'

9. Shakespeare In Love. As we now know, Harvey Weinstein has a lot to answer for. A 'deeply silly piece of fluff', according to *Esquire*.

10. The King's Speech. 'Yet another Harvey Weinstein-produced historical picture about a brilliant white guy.' *Time*.

47. THE UGLY TRUTH #3 (P. 109)

1. FALSE. Pythagoras' vegetarianism was motivated by his belief that it was the only way to ensure you weren't eating your grandmother or another relative, whose soul could have migrated (for example) to your neighbour's pig. He met his own death passionately defending a bean field.

2. FALSE. His final prediction was the rise of wealthy superhumans. His fear was that genetic engineering was likely to create a new species of elite humans who could destroy the rest of civilisation.

3. TRUE. Money trumps genes. Researchers have found genetic endowments are distributed almost equally among children in low-income and high-income families. Success is not. The least-gifted children of high-income parents graduate from college at higher rates than the most-gifted children of low-income parents.

4. TRUE. It is 22 times more likely that an American gun owner will accidentally or deliberately shoot themselves.

5. TRUE. Westlife have had 14 Number Ones; the Stones, 8.

6. TRUE.

7. TRUE. Men are killed by lightning at an alarmingly high rate compared to women. In a survey conducted by the American National Weather Service, between the years of 2006 and 2016 men accounted for 80 percent of all lightning-related deaths. The study concludes that men are much more likely to die from lightning because they are unwilling to be inconvenienced by the weather. Most women, meanwhile, understand that when you see lightning you should probably go indoors until it passes.

8. TRUE. It might be why we haven't done something about it sooner.

9. FALSE. It's one a fortnight.

10. TRUE.

48. WORDS FAILED HIM (P. 110)

1. **D - MARK TWAIN**
2. **F -THACKERAY**
3. **H - OSCAR WILDE**
4. **I - W.H. AUDEN**
5. **E -VIRGINIA WOOLF**
6. **C - PERCY WYNDHAM LEWIS**
7. **A - SAMUEL JOHNSON**
8. **J - CARLYLE**
9. **B - KINGSLEY AMIS**
10. **G -GERMAINE GREER**

49. THE WISDOM OF CROWDS (P. 112)

PART I

1. TRUE. 51% or 160 million Americans believe that JFK was not killed by a lone assassin, Lee Harvey Oswald, according to the results of a conducted by Public Policy Polling. The usual suspects include Vice-President Lyndon B. Johnson, the KGB, Fidel Castro, Woody Harrelson's dad, secret service agent George Hickey, the CIA, Carlos Marcello, Joe DiMaggio and UFO researchers.

2. FALSE. But this theory is gaining traction thanks to American conspiracy broadcaster Alex Jones, who has for several years been warning his viewers that their government is turning people gay by putting chemicals in their juice boxes, water bottles and potato chip bags. 'The reason there are so many gay people now is because it's a chemical warfare operation,' Jones said in June 2010. 'I have the government documents where they said they're going to encourage homosexuality with chemicals so people don't have children.'

3. TRUE. It may be big in the USA, but let's be proud, this popular theory originated with former British TV sports presenter David Icke, aka 'the Special One', whose football career was cruelly cut short at the age of 21 when he retired suffering from arthritis after brief spells between the sticks with Coventry City and Hereford United. He became a sports presenter with the BBC but lost his job in 1991, after surprising his employers by announcing he was the Son of God at a press conference at Gatwick Airport. Accompanied by his spiritual advisor, a Canadian lady called Mari Shawsun, or 'Daughter of God,' and his wife Pamela, a.k.a Spirit of the Angel of God, Icke predicted the Second Coming. Wearing his trademark turquoise shell suit, he went on to make a series of TV chat show appearances, during which he foresaw sundry environmental disasters including the disappearances of Cuba, the Isle of Arran and the White Cliffs of Dover. He revealed that he always knew he was 'special' because of his ability to locate parking spaces in central London. Icke became reclusive in the 1990s but re-emerged on the university lecture circuit as a conspiracy theorist, his chief concern being that the world was being run by reptilian extra-terrestrials who suck human blood, and that Hillary Clinton, the Duke of Edinburgh and the Queen of England were shape-changing reptiles from an ancient cold-blooded family line. The former Sky Blues 'keeper has since however recanted his claim to be the Messiah, explaining that he was 'mad' at the time.

4. TRUE. According to a YouGov poll in 2013, 33% say it was at least 'probably true' that Princess Diana was assassinated, while 25% also believe that MI6 was involved. Another 25% believe that Diana was pregnant with Dodi al Fayed's child at the time of her death. 19% believe that her driver Henri Paul was in the pay of a national security service, while 16% think that the SAS was involved or that Diana's seatbelt was sabotaged (14%).

5. FALSE. The number is much higher. Some 28% (88 million) of Americans believe in the Illuminati, supposed overlords controlling the world's affairs, operating secretly as they seek to establish a New World Order. For Christ's sake don't tell the Lizard People.

6. TRUE. According to some polls, up to 30% of Americans believe that the US government was behind the 9/11 attacks. Another 28% believe Saddam Hussein was somehow involved.

7. TRUE. The poll was conducted by Public Policy Polling, the only American polling organisation that correctly predicted the 2016 presidential election. PPP has a reputation for asking the difficult questions of the day. e.g. in 2011 they asked voters if they thought Barack Obama would be taken up by The Rapture to Heaven: 19% thought that he would, 44% thought that he would not, 37% were not sure.

8. FALSE. It's 54% of Russians, just ahead of 49% of South Africans and 45% of French people..

9. TRUE. According to a survey by the Anti-Defamation League of more than 53,000 people in over 100 countries.

10. TRUE. To a certain kind of fan, almost every line of the song 'I Am The Walrus' relates to Paul's death, and in that sense they are fulfilling its creator's wishes. According to Lennon's friend Pete Shotton, John intended to write a song with nonsensical imagery to confound people who looked for significance in every Beatle lyric. After recalling a song they used to sing as children, John strung together the silliest imagery he could think of. Shotton recalls that after writing the song, John said, 'Let the fuckers work that one out, Pete.' Half a century later, they're still at it.

11. TRUE

12. TRUE

13. FALSE The true figure is double.

14. TRUE In the 2021 study, a further 42% felt tighter gun controls would make no difference to the number of mass shootings, and 34% felt they would have no impact on gun crime either.

15. TRUE Some 8% of respondents opposed any change in the legal status of the drug.

PART II

A.	Roswell	**21%**
B.	TV Mind Control	**15%**
C.	Fluoride	**9%**
D.	CIA invented crack	**14%**
E.	Moon landings	**7%**
F.	Contrails	**5%**

BEATLES MINI-ROUND

A, B, C AND E are all regularly peddled by the sort of people who also believe that Marlboro packets convey Ku Klux Klan symbolism and that the kids' tv series 'Rainbow' was all about doing 'shrooms. No wacky rumour emerges in a vacuum, though, and since this one began in earnest in the USA in the last months of the 1960s, various sociologists and psychoanalysts have wondered whether the era's assorted assassinations, White House scandals and cover-ups might have played their part. You might be suffering from paranoia, man, but that doesn't mean they're not out to get you. **D** is completely made-up by us and **F** is half made-up: there *is* a theory about playing 'Strawberry Fields' backwards, in order to hear John Lennon apparently intoning the words 'I buried Paul'. Or perhaps he is saying, 'You are buggering up your stylus, lar.'

50. GLASS HALF EMPTY #1 (P. 115)

1. **B - ALAN BENNETT**
2. **A - SIMONE DE BEAUVOIR**
3. **A - FRIEDRICH NIETZSCHE**
4. **A - DOROTHY PARKER**
5. **B - OGDEN NASH**
6. **D - OSCAR WILDE.** This was Wilde's character Lord Henry in *The Picture of Dorian Gray*. His words in full are: 'The reason we all like to think so well of others is that we are all afraid for ourselves. The basis of optimism is sheer terror. We think that we are generous because we credit our neighbour with the possession of those virtues that are likely to be a benefit to us. We praise the banker that we may overdraw our account, and find good qualities in the highwayman in the hope that he may spare our pockets.'
7. **B - GEORGE CARLIN**
8. **C - WILLIAM HAZLITT**
9. **A - QUENTIN CRISP**
10. **D - ALEXANDER POPE**

51. ODD ONE OFF THE WALL (P. 117)

All have been deemed by English Heritage to be unworthy of a blue plaque, except for F, David Bowie, who has three for himself, and another one commemorating the fictitious backing band for his fictitious stage persona.

A. VLADIMIR NABOKOV, novelist. The writer of *Lolita* was turned down because his stays in London were not regarded as significant enough in his life to warrant commemoration. J.R.R. Tolkien has five blue plaques, including one on a hotel in Birmingham where he stayed the night.

B. DAME THORA HIRD. The actress and entertainer won three BAFTAs, but can't have a blue plaque to commemorate her because it's 'too soon after her death to know how she will be regarded by future generations.'

C. RONALD COLMAN, Hollywood star. The Richmond-born actor was a romantic lead in films including 'The Prisoner Of Zenda' and 'A Double Life', which won him an Oscar.

D. ALBERT TROTT, cricketer. The Australian was well known for the exceptionally rare feat of having struck a ball over the pavilion end of Lord's cricket ground. He had the odd distinction of representing both his homeland and his adopted England and played at county level for Middlesex. He shot himself in Willesden while suffering mental illness.

E. PHILIPPA FAWCETT, mathematical and educational reformer. Daughter of the suffragist Millicent Fawcett, she later lectured in mathematics and was director of education at London County Council.

F. DAVID BOWIE. The musician has three blue plaques: one outside the former home of Trident Studios in London, where he recorded the albums Hunky Dory and The Rise and Fall of Ziggy Stardust, one in Maidstone, Kent where he regularly played with an early band, and one on Hull station in honour of Ziggy Stardust's backing band, The Spiders from Mars.

G. EVA GORE-BOOTH, poet and women's rights campaigner. Born into the aristocracy, she turned her back on her privileged upbringing and dedicated her life to trade unionism and women's rights in the workplace.

H. ISADORA DUNCAN. In her heyday she was the world's most famous dancer, and known as 'the mother of modern dance'. Born in America, she performed and stayed in London many times from 1900 until her freakish death in 1927, strangled when her scarf caught in the spokes of a car wheel.

I. SIR NEVILLE CARDUS, cricket writer. Considered by many to be greatest ever writer on his sport, Cardus' florid style is said to have blazed a trail in the industry. He was also a renowned music critic.

52. BEYOND BELIEF (P. 118)

1. **FALSE.** It was Denis Diderot (who did briefly consider becoming a priest.)
2. **THEIR CONVICTIONS**
3. **EPICURUS**
4. 'Science flies you to the **MOON**. Religion flies you into **BUILDINGS**.'
5. **STEVEN WEINBERG**
6. **B. GOD**. Dawkins is also once quoted as saying: 'Science is interesting, and if you don't agree you can fuck off.' He later insisted he was only quoting a former editor of *New Scientist* magazine, but he didn't say which one.
7. **POETRY**
8. **THE BIBLE**
9. **FROM MURDERING THE RICH**
10. **WOODY ALLEN**

53. BLOOD ON THE TRACKS (P. 120)

1. Teen Angel – Mark Dinning
2. Tell Laura I Love Her – Ray Peterson
3. Ebony Eyes – The Everly Brothers
4. Terry – Twinkle. Led Zeppelin guitarist Jimmy Page was a session musician on this track.
5. Last Kiss – J. Frank Wilson and The Cavaliers (1964) / Pearl Jam

(1999). Tastefully based on the actual news story of the deaths of 16-year-old lovers Jeanette Clark and J.L. Hancock. It was a stroke of luck for songwriter Wayne Cochran, who lived nearby and just happened at the time to be working on a song about a road accident.

6. Leader of the Pack – Shangri-Las

7. Laurie (Strange Things Happen) – Dickie Lee

8. Ode to Billie Joe – Bobby Gentry

9. Honey – Bobby Goldsboro. In the 1970s this received more airplay than was strictly necessary when BBC DJ Tony Blackburn had an on-air lapse while going through a sticky patch with his wife Tessa and played the song on loop. It was voted by users of CNN.com as the worst single ever; the Beach Boys once considered releasing a version, but thought better of it.

10. Seasons In The Sun – Terry Jacks (1974) / Westlife (1999). Originally recorded as Le Moribund (The Dying Man) by Belgian singer-songwriter Jacques Brel. The B-side of the Terry Jacks single was the little known Put the Bone In, in which a woman in a butcher shop begs the butcher to 'put the bone in' for her because 'her doggy had been hit by a car.'

54. THE REICH STUFF #2 (P. 122)

1. A

2. B

3. FALSE

4. TRUE

5. TRUE

6. D

7. TRUE

8. C

9. B

10. A. But he could walk at the age of three weeks and speak at eight weeks, so he was still a pretty bright lad.

55 FLY ME TO THE MOON (P. 124)

1. **C, F** and **J** were made up.
2. **TRUE**
3. **TRUE.** (Which might, perhaps, encourage some flight crew to ignore that leaky pipe or rattling door, so that the flight takes off on time and they get their wages...)
5. **TRUE.** About one in every 108,500 cruise ship passengers will snuff it on board. Mostly just because they're old, and old people like cruises.

56. CORGI REGISTERED (P. 125)

1. **REAL.** At the time of writing the Warden of the Swans is biologist Christopher Perrins, an Emeritus Fellow at Oxford University who has held the position since 1993. The British monarch owns all of the un-marked mute swans in the UK but only chooses to exercise ownership rights on certain stretches of the Thames. It is the Warden's job to conduct the annual census of swans on the river, a process called swan upping. Not to be confused with swan tupping, which could get you banned from a 47-mile stretch of the Thames from Sunbury to Abingdon.

2. **FAKE.** Now redundant, the job title Chocolate Maker to the Queen originated with Queen Marie Antoinette who brought her personal chocolate maker to Versailles in 1770 to create such recipes as 'choco-late mixed with orchid bulb for strength', 'chocolate with orange blos-som to calm the nerves', and 'chocolate with sweet almond milk to aid the digestion'.

3. **FAKE.** There hasn't been a Keeper of the Lions in the Tower since the mid-1800s. The lions were not, as one might suspect, used to intim-idate prisoners; the Tower of London was also a zoo for around 600 years.

4. **REAL.** A position with no set responsibilities, the title Master of the Queen's Music is given to a prominent musician for a period of ten years – currently, composer Judith Weir, appointed in 2014. Though the position does not formally require it, she can compose

music for royal or state occasions if the mood takes her. Ms Weir introduced a special arrangement of the UK national anthem, 'God Save the Queen' during Richard III's re-interment in March, 2015.

5. REAL. The senior Astronomer Royal is required to 'be available for consultation on scientific matters for as long as the holder remains a professional astronomer', according to the British Monarchy's official website.

6. REAL. A permanent position since Queen Victoria created it in 1843, Piper to the Sovereign is tasked with playing bagpipes every weekday at 9am for 15 minutes under the Queen's window when she is in residence at Buckingham Palace, Windsor Castle, the Palace of Holyroodhouse or Balmoral Castle.

7. REAL. Being in charge of royal barges has been a proper job since 1215. It is mostly ceremonial but was no doubt a lot more stressful in the 18th century when the sovereign regularly travelled down the Thames by barge.

8. REAL. Obviously. Those thousands of pictures won't survey themselves. Former job-holders include disgraced Soviet agent Anthony Blunt.

9. FAKE. There was once a Necessary Woman to the Corridor and Entrance Hall, but the position is now redundant.

10. FAKE. Now redundant, the role originally involved assisting the king with bodily functions and washing, the stool in question being a 'close stool' i.e. a commode. The lucky job-holder was trusted to get up close and personal to the monarch, and so in theory was let in on many secrets and thus regarded with fear and admiration by the rest of the court. The job was not without risks. In 1536 Henry VIII had his Groom of the Stool, Henry Norris, executed because he was thought to be sleeping with Anne Boleyn. The office lapsed under Elizabeth I. Strictly speaking, the last Groom of the Stool was probably Sir Michael Stanhope, who served Edward VI. He was hanged for 'felony' before Edward's death and it's not clear if his role was taken by anyone else. Under the Stuarts, the office became 'Groom of the Stole', with its implications of dressing the monarch rather than helping him on the lavatory. In 1750 a Groom of the Stole could earn around £1,200 a year, roughly equivalent to £180,000 today. The last Groom of the Stole was James Hamilton, 2nd Duke of Abercorn (1838–1913) who served the Prince of Wales, but the job became redundant when the latter became King Edward VII.

57. END NOTES (P. 126)

1. **A.** George Sanders
2. **B.** Pete Ham's band Badfinger signed with a new label and procured a new manager, Stan Polley, but soon discovered that through dubious contractual obligations to Polley, they were completely broke. Ham, despondent due to having just bought a new house and his girlfriend being pregnant, hanged himself in his garage.
3. **D – HUNTER S. THOMPSON**
4. **C – TONY HANCOCK**
5. **C – SID VICIOUS**
6. **27.** A typical pattern, worldwide: fewer than half of all suicides leave a note, and while most suicides are male, the majority of note-leavers are female.
7. **D – VINCENT VAN GOGH**
8. **C.**
9. **B.**
10. **D.**

58. POT LUCK #4 (P. 128)

1. **A.** Puppy water was considered very good for removing wrinkles, tightening and lightening the skin and eradicating blemishes. It supposedly worked best when blended with 'a pint of fasting spittle', i.e. saliva collected from a person or persons who had not eaten for several days. It has also been alleged that Welsh miners had extraordinarily soft and unblemished complexions due to their habit of washing their faces with the still-warm contents of the chamber-pot before heading off to their shifts.

2. A. The Queen Mary was converted into a troop ship for the duration of World War II, and is said to be haunted by the ship's cook, a man so unpopular with his kitchen staff (or the soldiers eating his food) that he was stuffed in the walk-in oven and roasted alive.

3. D. In the interests of racial purity. Churchill also believed in a racial hierarchy with white Protestants at the top, just above white Catholics. He wasn't fond of Indians: 'a beastly people with a beastly religion.'

4. C. According to legend, Anaxarchus made light of his punishment.

5. B. A colleague noted: 'He was trying to convey a point that guns kill. It's not up to us to question God's motives.'

6. A. The word *comprachicos* – Spanish for 'child buyers' – was coined by Victor Hugo. Dwarfs were so highly prized as servants and entertainers in royal households that the population of 'natural' dwarfs was exhausted, so techniques were developed to manufacture them. In China, children were placed in large vases to constrict the growing body. With no room to extend up or down, the children expanded outwards to fill the vase until it cracked open, thus producing new dwarves.

7. B. The 3'9" actress made her first film in 1999 and has since appeared in at least 65 more, including 'Mechanical Elf', 'Little Fuckers' and 'Slop Shots 4'. Reviewing her career in *Bizarre* magazine, she reflected: 'Once I did a film with a guy who had a penis of nearly a foot and a half and it scared me. That is like a six-foot-tall woman being impaled on a three-foot traffic cone.'

8. A. Rev. Baker was then killed and eaten, along with seven followers.

9. A - 3; B - 4; C - 2; D - 1

10. C.

59. GLASS HALF EMPTY #2 (P. 130)

1. A - KAFKA

2. A - CARROT

3. C - TOAD (The remainder of the line being: 'so as to be sure not to encounter anything more unpleasant all day.')

4 B - **SCHOPENHAUER** *The Wisdom of Life* is packed with advice on how to disappoint yourself before life gets a chance to do it for you. His general view is that you'd be mad to expect happiness from a relationship. Not coincidentally, he spent nearly 30 years living alone with only a series of poodles for company.

5. A - **OSCAR WILDE**

6. FALSE It was Leonard Cohen's favourite bard, Canadian-Romanian poet, Irving Layton.

7. A - **ROBERT LOUIS STEVENSON**

8. B - **JANE AUSTEN**

9. C - **TRAGEDY**

10. D - **WILLIAM HAZLITT**

60. DOPE AND GLORY (P. 133)

1. B. He also paid the judges to declare him winner of a race in which he'd crashed and not completed.

2. C. Of 32 starters in the marathon, held over a hilly course in the middle of a hot afternoon, only 14 made it to the finish, and Lorz came in first. When accused, he made no attempt to deny that he'd ridden just under half the course in a car, but claimed it was all a practical joke. His lifetime ban was later rescinded. Meanwhile, Thomas Hicks, the American handed the gold medal after Lorz's disqualification, was fuelled by a cocktail of strychnine sulphate (a common rat poison) and brandy. At the end of the race, he had to be carried off the track and might have died in the St Louis stadium had he not been immediately treated by several doctors.

3. A. The so-called 'Black Sox' scandal erupted when eight members of the Chicago baseball team were charged with accepting $100,000 from gamblers to throw the 1919 World Series against the Cincinnati Reds. A grand jury convened to investigate the case and several of the accused, including 'Shoeless' Joe Jackson, confessed. A young boy is said to have called out to Jackson as he left the hearing, 'Say it ain't so,

Joe'. The phrase went on to become one of the most famous in American porting history, although Jackson later claimed the incident never happened. In June 1921, just before the jury trial began, the players' testimony mysteriously disappeared and they were acquitted due to lack of evidence. Neverthless, eight players – Jackson, Eddie Cicotte, Claude 'Lefty' Williams, Buck Weaver, Arnold 'Chick' Gandil, Fred McMullin, Charles 'Swede' Risberg and Oscar 'Happy' Felsch – were banned from baseball for life. Almost worse than all of the above, Kevin Costner starred in a film about it, in which mysterious voices tell a cash-strapped farmer to turn one of his fields into a baseball ground, which is then inhabited by the ghosts of 'Shoeless' and his team-mates.

4. TRUE. Subsequently the record Klobukowska helped set when winning the Olympic gold in the 4 x 100 metres relay in 1964 was struck from the record books and she was banned from performing in female athletic events. None of which prevented her from giving birth to a healthy baby boy a few years later.

5. D. He exited the Games in disgrace, denounced as 'Dishonestchenko' and 'Boris the Cheat'. The most bewildering aspect of his deception was that he was the hot favourite to win the gold anyway.

6. Canadian sprinter Ben Johnson was stripped of the 100m gold medal after testing positive for anabolic steroids. As six of the eight finalists ended up failing drugs tests, it is assumed to have been 'the dirtiest race in history' but given the inefficiency of the dope-testing system, and the to-ing and fro-ing over what constitutes a banned substance and a banned level of a substance, that may not be fair.

7. D.

8. C.

9. Because a month earlier, at the US championships, figure skater Nancy Kerrigan had been attacked with a telescopic baton, sustaining injuries that put her out of the competition and allowed rival Tonya Harding to win. A high-profile investigation followed, during which Harding's bodyguard and ex-husband were charged over the assault.

Both Kerrigan and Harding competed in the event, which took place in Norway, as part of the U.S. team.

10. D – **BITING.**

61. POT LUCK #5 (P. 136)

1. A. In 1558 he had his tomb erected in a chapel and made his servants march in procession while Charles followed behind dressed in a shroud. When the service began and the hymns struck up, the emperor jumped into his coffin and joined the prayers.

2. D. 1.6 billion people live in places where they have access to water, but they can't afford it.

3. B – **THE PICKLED HEAD OF A YOUNG GIRL.**

4. A

5. A

6. C. Among his more *outré* theories were that Italians were 'half ape' and Aryans were better at singing because 'the shape of the Nordic gum allows a superior movement of the tongue'.

7. C

8. A. CHERRY. Chocolate is the least popular. Edible lingerie was invented in the 1970s by Chicago entrepreneurs David Sanderson and Lee Brady. The prototype was fashioned from an edible film originally used to wrap frozen turkeys, and it was liquorice flavoured.

9. C. According to tests, it's more like one in five, or 20% of office coffee cups that come with an extra shot of shit.

10. IT'S D. No one has, as yet, come up with a term for being turned on by the late Baroness Thatcher. But that doesn't mean it isn't an illness…

62. PET PROJECTS (P. 139)

They all form part of national dishes apart from A. The Koala species has survived more than 70,000 years of hungry human habitation on the Australian continent because they taste foul. Incidentally, they also have a big chlamydia problem.

B. Tunisia/Morocco. Saharan Bedouins love gerbil couscous. Many other cultures throughout the world will happily dine on small rodents.

C. France. The Brits may be squeamish about snacking on Black Beauty, but the French can't get enough horse flesh. According to French chef Martin Leman it is 'delicious, like rich beef'.

D. China. A parrot-smuggling racket discovered on the India-Nepal border in 2016 was attributed to the demand for parrot by Chinese gourmets. They were also popular with certain Roman emperors as an alternative to flamingo tongues.

E. Bengal/Bangladesh. Although illegal, tortoise is still very popular in Bengal. Cooks put them live into boiling water; this slow, painful death facilitates the separation of the flesh from the hard shell.

F. Hawaii. In Hawaii, broiled puppy meat is prepared by flattening out the entire eviscerated animal and broiling it over hot coals. The traditional Hawaiian accompaniment for dog is sweet potatoes. In Asia, butchers 'improve' the flavour of dog meat by hanging or beating the dog to death. In Germany, dog meat has been eaten in every major crisis at least since the time of Frederick the Great; the Germans call it 'blockade mutton'.

G. Switzerland. Although chiefly famous for their chocolate and cheese, the Swiss also eat a number of cats (estimates vary from a couple of hundred to the – probably far-fetched – 250,000) every year.

H. Cameroon. In Cameroon, 80% of the meat consumed is killed in the wild and known as bushmeat. The nation's favoured dishes are chimpanzee and gorilla because of their succulent and tender flesh.

I. Peru. Thousands of guinea pigs are eaten every year in the United States. They arrive from Peru as whole, frozen, hairless rodents in plastic bags and are served in restaurants for $17 a plate. The guinea pig is splayed down the middle like a lobster and served with a front leg and a back, an eye, an ear and a nostril. According to activists, guinea pigs are great for the environment because they represent a low-impact meat alternative to carbon-costly beef.

63. HEIL HONEY, I'M HOME (P. 140)

1. WALT DISNEY. His animator Art Babbitt claimed that in the 1930s Disney also attended meetings of the German American Bund, a pro-Nazi organisation.

2. HENRY FORD. Hitler created the special award for foreigners so that no regular German medal would be 'defiled'. It was also quite a bit cheaper than the gold cigarette cases that he usually gave to overseas visitors. The car manufacturer reciprocated by expressing admiration for Hitler, and in the *Dearborn Independent*, a local newspaper he owned, published a number of anti-Semitic writings later collected and published as a four-volume set entitled 'The International Jew'.

3. CHARLES LINDBERGH. The first man successfully to fly an airplane across the Atlantic made frequent trips to Nazi Germany prior to 1942 and was very vocal about his fondness for eugenics. The famed aviator also liked to hang out with anti-Semitic automobile pioneer Henry Ford. The American car-maker cheerfully noted in 1940, 'When Charles comes out here, we only talk about the Jews.'

4. HUGO BOSS. The German designer obliged with a natty black uniform, set off with a silver death's-head hat badge. By 1938 the Hugo Boss label was working exclusively for the German military machine and using slave labour to meet the high demand.

5. COCO CHANEL. According to her most recent biographer Hal Vaughn, she was a high-ranking Nazi agent during the Second World War and was active in several spy and recruitment missions. She took as a lover the young German officer Baron Hans Gunther von Dincklage, allowing her to pass freely in restricted areas. When questioned on her relationship with the boyish Baron, she told Cecil Beaton: 'Really, sir, a woman of my age cannot be expected to look at his passport if she has a chance of a lover.'

6. POPE BENEDICT XVI. 14-year-old Joseph Ratzinger, aka 'God's Rottweiler', joined the Hitler Youth in 1941, after membership became compulsory in 1941.

7. UNITY and **DIANA** Mitford were fervent fascist fangirls. Famous for her adulation of and friendship with Adolf Hitler, **UNITY SHOT HERSELF IN THE HEAD DAYS AFTER BRITAIN DECLARED WAR ON GERMANY** (she survived but died of meningitis in 1948). Married to British fascist leader Sir Oswald Mosley, **DIANA WAS INTERNED IN HOLLOWAY PRISON DURING THE SECOND WORLD WAR**. She never renounced her belief in fascism.

8. TRUE.

9. FALSE. Wodehouse was interned by the Nazis as an enemy alien when war broke out, and before being quartered in Paris, he was taken to Berlin to record a series of broadcasts, aimed at the USA – which had not yet joined the war. He later claimed that the upbeat tone of his broadcasts was down to 'stiff upper lip' and cheerfulness under pressure, and MI5 concluded that the radio broadcasts had not been definably pro-Nazi. However, a later review of the case in 1946 recommended that Wodehouse be prosecuted if he returned to Britain – and he never did.

10. MICHAEL JACKSON. After the King of Pop's death in June 2009, *US Weekly* questioned his 'Nazi obsession' amid reports that Jackson was fascinated by 'master race' experiments and collected Nazi paraphernalia.

64. TITANIC SUNK, NO LIVES LOST (P. 141)

1. TRUE. Dockyard worker James Dobbins died at 12:13 pm on 31 May 1911, the very moment the ship was launched, fatally injured by a collapsing timber support.

2. FALSE. Third-class passengers had just two baths. Even so, Titanic's cattle-class was superior to that on most boats of the time.

3. TRUE(ISH). The Titanic was only ever promoted as 'practically unsinkable'.

4. FALSE. Marconi was invited to sail, but declined because his son Giulio was ill.

5. FALSE. Smith was appointed, not on account of his ability to captain a very big ship, but his skills at socialising with the first-class passengers. A lifeboat drill was scheduled for the day before the collision with the iceberg, but for reasons unknown Captain Smith cancelled it.

ANSWERS | ROUNDS 64-65

6. FALSE. Survivors reported that the last song they heard was 'Songe d'Automne'. As no members of the band survived, it's unlikely this will ever be corroborated.

7. TRUE. Two Pomeranians and a Pekingese survived; nine other less fortunate dogs drowned.

8. FALSE. The entire crew was fired after the ship sank. The widows of drowned crewmen were forced to rely on charity or remarry quickly in order to survive.

9. TRUE. Two days after the Titanic sank, the Mackay-Bennett sailed from Halifax, Nova Scotia, to retrieve bodies from the Atlantic. The bodies of first-class passengers were returned in coffins, second- and third-class passengers got canvas bags, while mere crewmen were delivered on stretchers.

10. FALSE. Although 328 bodies were recovered, 119 were too badly damaged to bring home and received a sea burial.

BONUS QUESTION: Stoke Council blocked it, and Smith's statue stands 40-odd miles away from his hometown in Beacon Park, Lichfield – the nearest place prepared to accept a monument to the disgraced captain.

65. HOMO DISAPPOINTUS (P. 142)

1. D - HORACE WALPOLE
2. B - QUENTIN CRISP
3. E - ROBERT FROST
4. J - ROBERT LOUIS STEVENSON
5. G - HENRY MILLER
6. A - OSCAR WILDE
7. H - ERNEST HEMINGWAY
8. I - GROUCHO MARX
9. C - VOLTAIRE
10. F - HOMER SIMPSON

66. IDLE WORSHIP (P. 144)

1. **B. 20**
2. **C. 23%**
3. **B.**
4. **A.**
5. **D.**
6. **A.**
7. **2.** And Joyce did all his writing in bed. But to be fair, the pioneer of stream-of-consciousness prose holds the record for literature's longest sentence. Molly Bloom's soliloquy in *Ulysses* weighs in at a whopping 3,687 words. Two them of a day and you'll have a novel in a fortnight.
8. **B** and **D**
9. **Adolf Hitler.** After his 2pm appearance, he would eat lunch and then go for a walk. After dinner, he would watch a movie and then go to bed. As the war became more desperate, he started working longer hours, but by then it was too late.
10. **C.** The young man's lawyer admitted that his client had some issues around motivation.

67. SLIPPED DISCS (P. 147)

1. 'I'll Be Home' – Pat Boone. It was the best-selling single of 1956 in the UK.
2. 'The Carnival Is Over' – The Seekers
3. 'Knock Three Times' – Dawn
4. 'Long Haired Lover from Liverpool' – Little Jimmy Osmond
5. 'Gonna Make You A Star' – David Essex
6. 'I Don't Want to Talk About It' / 'First Cut is the Deepest' – Rod Stewart. Legend has it that the charts were deliberately rigged to keep the Pistols off the No.1 spot in Her Majesty's Silver Jubilee year.
7. 'Shaddap You Face' – Joe Dolce Music Theatre
8. 'The Look Of Love' – Madonna
9. 'I Believe' / 'Up On The Roof' – Robson and Jerome.

10. 'Unchained Melody'/'White Cliffs of Dover' – Robson and Jerome. It spent seven weeks at No. 1 and went on to become the best-selling single of 1995.

68. ONLY WHEN I LAUGH. . . (P. 150)

1. B. According to legend, the old woman had commissioned a painting of Aphrodite but insisted on sitting as the model.

2. A - **WATCHING IT TRY TO EAT FIGS.**

3. D. Continuing the chortle-rich, animals-eating-figs theme, the jester apparently told King Martin that on his way over to the castle, he'd seen a donkey hanging by its tail from a tree, as if someone was punishing it for eating figs.

4. The soothsayer predicted the death of Calchas. Ironic, huh?

5. D.

6. The Scottish royalist died laughing on hearing the news that King Charles II had been restored to the English throne.

7. C. The killer punchline to 'Spend more time with my grandma' being, 'Er, well, she died.'

8. A. The episode in question featured a kilt-clad Scotsman performing Kung-Fu to the sound of bagpipes.

9. B. The footage is still viewable on the site, although there is a warning beforehand.

10. C. 'A Fish Called Wanda'. Bentzen's heart rate was later calculated at between 250-500 beats per minute, causing cardiac arrest. The official verdict on his cause of death was 'mirth'.

69. MEET YOUR HEROES (P. 153)

1. D - **PERCY GRAINGER.** Grainger's dying wish was that his skeleton should go on display in the Grainger Museum, a request quietly ignored by the trustees.

2. A - **ERIC GILL.** The best known British artist and sculptor of the 1930's was dubbed 'the married monk' because of his choice of work wear, a habit and a girdle of chastity of the order of Saint Dominic. So it caused something of a furore in the Catholic church when, forty years after his death, Gill's diaries revealed a colourful, not to say, nausea-inducing sex life, chronicled with perverse precision across forty volumes, including incest with his sister, the abuse of his own daughters and details of sex sessions with the family dog. His name lives on in the world's favourite typeface, Gill Sans.

3. C - FRANZ KAFKA. His favourite top shelf material was girl-on-girl action and bestiality, according to Kafka expert Dr. James Hawes. But there are no signs of an interest in beetles.

4. C - GANDHI. In his seventies, much to the surprise of Mrs Gandhi, the skinny pacifist decided to 'test' his celibacy. Gandhi's virgin-sandwich attracted public attention in 1947 when it emerged that the master was bunking nightly with his 19-year-old great niece, Manu. Gandhi's entourage explained that the naked sleepovers were partly tests of purity for both participants, and partly an effort to stay warm in the winter.

5. A - D.H. LAWRENCE – although on occasion all the others also expressed eugenicist ideas.

6. C - ENID BLYTON

7. A - ROALD DAHL

8. D - ALBERT EINSTEIN

9. It's **D.**

10. B - IDRIS ELBA. If the Hackney-born actor does have the odd 'problematic' thought, he's wise enough not to stick it on Twitter or tell a journalist.

70. POT LUCK #6 (P. 155)

1. **A.**
2. **D - 60%**
3. **D - NAPOLEON BONAPARTE**
4. **A.**
5. **B.**

6. A. According to the advertising copy, his Holiness carried a hip flask of Vin Mariani, a wine laced with cocaine, under his robes at all times. With Papal blessing, the surprisingly addictive beverage sold better than anyone could have guessed and Leo XIII went on to become the oldest pope in history. Vin Mariani's success allegedly inspired one John S. Pemberton to invent another energy-boosting tipple called Coca-Cola.

7. C.

8. C. Despite his deteriorating condition, Scott continued to record his fate in grim detail to the bitter end of his badly-organised and failed expedition. He was unsympathetic with colleagues who did not share his stoicism. When one of them complained that his 'blackish, rotten-looking nose' seemed likely to 'drop off' Scott wrote, 'to my surprise, he shows signs of losing heart over it'. Although none of the expedition made it home, a lot of their samples did, including some Emperor Penguin eggs. Not a total disaster then.

9. B. For reasons not entirely clear, the most popular time to top yourself is on a Monday or Tuesday afternoon in spring. The most common methods of suicide in the UK are by hanging, strangulation and suffocation, followed by poisoning. Hans Klaus from Kiel, Germany, was the world's least successful suicide. He failed in 28 attempts on his own life, including ten slashed wrists, four poisonings, two hangings, stabbing, gassing, drowning and drug overdosing. He finally gave up after throwing himself out of a 4th-floor window and landing on a passer-by.

10. D.

71. CURSE THE WORLD (P. 159)

1. A. TRUE   B. TRUE   C. FALSE   D. TRUE   E. FALSE
    F. TRUE   G. TRUE   H. FALSE   I. TRUE   J. FALSE
2. B
3. C

4. **B**

5. **A**

6. **A**

7. **A MANDARIN**. Based on an old currency, where 1,000 was the lowest unit, so to be 250 was a bit like being 'not the full shilling'.
   B ARABIC.
   C SERBIA.
   D GREECE. The act of breaking wind onto someone's testicles is probably depicted on an old vase, somewhere.
   E PORTUGAL. If you comb monkeys, then you are one yourself, apparently, in Portugal.

72. HOPE I DIE BEFORE I GET OLD (P. 161)

1. Robert Johnson, Blues Legend – death by strychnine poisoning.
2. Brian Jones, original Rolling Stone – death by drowning.
3. Jimmy Hendrix, guitar maestro – death by asphyxiation.
4. Janis Joplin, singer – heroin overdose.
5. Ron 'Pigpen' McKernan, founding member of the Grateful Dead – gastro-intestinal haemorrhage.
6. Amy Winehouse, singer – alcohol poisoning.
7. Richey Edwards, lyricist and guitarist of The Manic Street Preachers – missing since 1995, presumed officially dead in 2008,
8. Kurt Cobain, grunge rocker – self-inflicted gunshot wound
9. Pete Ham, leader of Badfinger –suicide by hanging
10. Jim Morrison, The Doors' frontman – heart failure

Incidentally, the notion that musicians have a higher frequency of death at 27 doesn't stand up to statistical scrutiny. In a population of dead musos spanning seven decades from 1950 to 2010 for which an accurate age of death can be identified, 1.3% died aged 27, while 1.2% died age 26 and 1.4% died age 28. The highest frequency of musician deaths occurs at 56 (2.2%). Amongg the greats who gasped gasped their last at this age include Charlie Mingus, Rick James, Eddie Rabbitt, Mimi

Farina, Johnny Ramone, Chris LeDoux, Vandy 'Smokey' Hampton, and Charles 'Baby' Tate and Tammy Wynette.

73. PRE-TWITTER TROLLS (P. 162)

1. **C.**
2. Elizabeth I
3. **D.**
4. Suet dumpling
5. **TRUE**
6. A – Lucifer; B – arse; C – Babylonian; D – Macedonian; E – fucker; F – swineherd; G – pig; H – thief; I – catamite; J – fool / Underworld; K – idiot / Serpent / dick; L – snout; M – arse; N – cur; O – Screw / mother.
7. **D.**
8. **A.**
9. **C** - Abraham Lincoln.
10. A. **TRUE**   B. **TRUE**   C. **FALSE**   D. **TRUE**   E. **TRUE**
    F. **FALSE**   G. **TRUE**   H. **FALSE**   I. **TRUE**   J. **FALSE**   K. **TRUE**

74. COME TOGETHER (P. 166)

1. **FALSE** on two counts. Onan was unjustly made the founder of Onanism (a.k.a. wanking) by Victorian prudes. A custom called the 'levirate' (still practised in parts of East Africa and S.E. Asia) obliges a man to conceive children with his dead brother's wife, if said dead brother has died without an heir. Onan didn't fancy that kind of fatherhood so he, er, pulled out. The Israelite and later Jewish religion forbade all forms of seed-spilling, but that had more to do with taboos about bodily fluids.
2. **C.**
3 **D** is **FALSE**. The medical profession has yet to record a case of semen-induced ocular sepsis. Oddly, the prostate cancer/pecker-pulling index depends entirely on your age. A study in the *British Journal Urology* concluded that the relationship was not causal in young men: it was merely that young men who masturbated a lot had higher levels

of testosterone and were thus more likely to develop prostate cancer. In men over 50, however, a quick hand-shandy might have active, cancer-preventing benefits, in ridding the prostate of hormone-heavy fluids which could turn nasty.

4. natural / what / real / artificial
Other Lust Control hits include 'Condom Nation', 'Mad At The Girls' and 'You Make Me Puke'. (Form an orderly queue, ladies.)

5. B.

6. The Beatles. Paul McCartney told *GQ* magazine that he and his fellow mop-topped Mersey music makers had indulged in what we'd call en masse masturbating and what he called 'early bonding sessions'. He added that it didn't happen often and they 'didn't think much of' these episodes at the time. 'We were all just in these chairs, and the lights were out, and somebody started masturbating, so we all did.'

7. F.

8. B. He would shortly be admitted to a psychiatric institution.

9. D. 58%. (suggesting that young American women are either more inhibited or just less open when they're asked personal questions)

10. B.

75. LOVE IS... (P. 169)

1. A. A grave mental disease.
2. bad marriage
3. coldest end
4. C. Marriage.
5. A. Oscar Wilde.
6. dirty / trick / continuation
7. D. Robin Williams.
8. 'a new wife, or a new car'
9. options
10. herpes

76. THE TRUTH IS OUT THERE (P. 171)

1. C. Around 116 million Americans believe global warming is a myth.

2. FALSE. The actual figure is much higher. 20% of Americans believe that a UFO crashed at Roswell, New Mexico, in 1947, and that the US government covered it up. Another 32% are 'not sure' whether it happened or not.

3. D. Market research agency Atomik Research found that 52% of those surveyed thought the Apollo 11 Moon landing – one of the most well-documented and defining moments of our species' history – was an elaborate hoax.

4. B. 73% of 25-34 year olds believed the moon landing was faked.

5. C. 64% of Britons claimed dinosaurs never existed.

6. B. (To be fair, the Hot Chocolate song is pretty persuasive.)

7. A –MORE (23%); **B** – LESS (32%), **C** – LESS (40%); **D** – LESS (42%).

8. B IS FALSE. THE REST ARE ALL TRUE. The NHS finally abandoned homeopathy in 2017. A bit late, given that the 'like cures like' principle stretches back not just to medieval times (when, for example, a croaky frog on the tongue was a remedy for a sore throat) but even to ancient Greece, where it was believed that gold, being yellow, cured jaundice. Anthropologists like E.E. Evans-Pritchard, who worked among the Azande people of South Sudan and Central Africa, noted that the same principle was at work in the magic used to curse people, or bless them with special powers. (Which, guess what, also DID NOT WORK.)

9. A. Psychic dentistry – including turning silver fillings into gold ones and straightening crooked teeth (and later proved to be a pile of utter mouthwash).

10. D.

11. B.

77. ART INTERRUPTED (P. 173)

1. A.

2. A. TRUE   B. TRUE   C. FALSE   D. TRUE

3. HIS BODY. Stolen by phrenologists, Haydn's head was not reunited with his body until 1954.

4. BEETHOVEN'S 10TH.

5. D. Schubert died from the combined effects of tertiary syphilis and mercury poisoning.

6. D.

7. A. It was a throat infection.

8. B. President Franklin Delano Roosevelt. On 12 April 1945, her second day of painting the president, artist Elizabeth Shoumatoff was filling in the outlines of his face and shoulders when he experienced a severe head pain and collapsed. He died three hours later in his bed. As a result, the painting was never finished. It remains on display in the Little White House, a testament to the vagaries of fate.

9. C.

10. A.

78. AND ANOTHER THING. . . (P. 176)

1. H. Ibsen's nurse had just assured a visitor that the playwright was feeling a bit better.

2. A. Marx was berating an attendant who asked if he had any last words.

3. B. According to an alternative version, Whitman said to his nurse: 'Warry, shift!'

4. C.

5. I.

6. E. O'Neill was born in a Broadway hotel room and was 65, broke and depressed when he shuffled off the mortal coil in Suite 401 of the Shelton Hotel in Boston.

7. F. According to another version, Nostradamus said: 'You will not find me alive at sunrise.' Either way, it was his last and possibly only accurate prediction. Unless you count the time he foresaw Twitter: 'A flock of blue starlings, covering the world, giving voice to the mad and the wicked.'

8. D. Though this long-accepted version is disputed. According to the *Oxford Dictionary of Quotations* it's what some people heard him say, though others heard 'Oh my country! How I love my country!' or 'Oh, my country! How I leave my country!' or 'My country! Oh, my country!' A mistake easily made.

9. J.

10. G. Possibly apocryphal. Pancho Villa died in a hail of bullets, so it seems unlikely that he was able to say much at all (or, if he did, that anyone nearby heard what it was).

79. POT LUCK (P. 178)

1. D. Leopold had been injured when his horse fell on him during a jousting tournament. Despite the homespun amputation, he died.

2. D.

3. B. When Shakur grew tired of the joke, he had Valerian skinned and stuffed with straw and manure instead.

4. C.

5. B.

6. B. The girls were dancing near an open fire, when their dresses caught fire. Both girls died from their burns, Mary first, Emily a couple of weeks later.

7. C. Elizabeth (aka 'Mrs') Gaskell was not the highest-earning female novelist of the time (that was George Eliot, probably because everyone thought she was a man) but she lived comfortably, travelled extensively, and had enough money to purchase a handsome pile in Hampshire without her husband's knowledge. Recognition for Melville's greatest work *Moby Dick* didn't begin until 30 years after his death, so he worked as a customs inspector for 19 years and died broke and largely unknown. Poe died destitute days after being found wandering the streets drunk, rambling incoherently and wearing clothes that weren't his. Paine died a penniless drunk in Manhattan, where only half a dozen people turned up for his funeral.

8. B - P.J. O'ROURKE. To be fair, he is just as underwhelmed by the French: 'A smallish, monkey-looking bunch and not dressed any better, on average, than the citizens of Baltimore.'

9. The answer is **C - OIL OF BADGER.** Toenails and pubic hair were used to treat a hernia. Goose turds were for jaundice or skin ailments (take two turds, dissolve in white wine, strain and drink two hours before meals). The hands of corpses were a cure for just about everything. Sick people would be brought to a house where a dead person was laid out so that the hand could be laid on them.

10. The answer is **C.** The late theoretical physicist may not have predicted a *Day of the Triffids* style apocalypse, but he didn't see much to look forward to. He proposed several doomsday scenarios. One is that Earth will become so overpopulated that our energy consumption will make the planet glow red-hot. (The good news is that it probably won't happen for another 600 years.) Hawking also warned that robots could soon take over the world; if people can design computer viruses, it follows that someone will also design artificial intelligence that replicates itself, producing new forms of life that will outperform humans. He also believed that we're hard-wired to kill ourselves with weapons of mass destruction: 'I fear evolution has inbuilt greed and aggression to the human genome. There is no sign of conflict lessening.'

80. APOCALYPSE NOW AND THEN (P. 180)

1. TRUE. Ever since 1975, the cult's followers have been predicting that the world will end 'shortly'. Although the JW's massive investment in building huge media facilities in Essex suggests that they don't believe the end to be all that nigh. And/or if it is, then The Rapture is deffo going to start in Chelmsford.

2 . D. Many of Martin's followers quit their jobs and sold their belongings in anticipation of the end. They gathered at Martin's home on Christmas Eve, 1955, singing Christmas carols while they waited to be saved by aliens in flying saucers. At 4:45 a.m. on Christmas Day, however, Martin announced that God had been so impressed by their actions that he would no longer destroy the Earth.

3. The Reverend Sun Myung Moon was the founder of the Unification Church, whose followers are colloquially known as Moonies.

4. D. Gayce's track record as both a prophet and a healer was erratic and he was obliged to keep his day job selling photographic supplies. He did have one major success, however, just before the 1929 Wall Street Crash, when he advised a client against investing in the stock market because he saw 'a downward movement of long duration'. Cayce's followers claim he also foresaw World Wars I and II, the independence of India, the state of Israel and the assassination of President Kennedy. They keep his memory alive from their base at his former home in Virginia.

5. The answer is **A.** though they're all genuine Nostradamian chunterings. Whatever it was, it didn't happen – unless it was an extremely cryptic way of saying that Posh and Becks were going to get married in an Irish castle on a pair of massive thrones.

6. B. Weinland subsequently issued a new end-of-the-world warning for June 2019, which… well, work it out.

7 C - KAISER WILHELM. During World War II, invading Japanese soldiers told the cult-following inhabitants of Karkar Island: 'We are the people you have been expecting'. Also in the South Pacific, Prince Philip has since 1974 been regarded as a living god in a handful of villages on the island of Tanna, in Vanuatu. Victor Hugo, meanwhile, is one of a number of 'saints' in the Cao Dai religion, followed in Vietnam.

8. A. It's not at all clear whether the Mayans also made any predictions about the future. If they had, they probably weren't very good at it, having apparently neglected to foresee the collapse of their own civilisation in the 9th century, and the arrival of the Spanish in the 16th.

9. C. Although, if Rasputin had made prediction **B**, he might have gained more soothsaying cred, as Michael Kalashnikov, inventor of the world-renowned assault rifle, died on 23 December 2013.

10. The missing word is **STEEL**.

11. The answer is **B** - **THE COLD WAR.** The magazine's point was that the fight against global communism was diverting national resources.

12. The missing word is **RIDICULOUS**.

13. THE INTERNET

14. APPLE.

81. SPEAKING ILL OF THE DEAD (P. 185)

1. Sorry but the answer is **PISS**. At least it rhymes.

2. GEORGE VI, her son. Even by the parenting standards of the Royal Family, she was uncommunicative with her children.

3. D - **PIMP.**

4. Truman Capote

5. B.

6. Elvis.

7. Michael Jackson

8. B - **JILL BENNETT.**

9. C - **ENTERTAINMENT** .

10. D.

82. POT LUCK (P. 188)

1. A. In America the creation of Mother's Day is credited to Anna Jarvis, who, following the tragic death of her own mother, wanted to honour the important role she'd played. She campaigned tirelessly to have the day officially recognised as a holiday, but regretted it as soon as shops started using it to pressure people into buying stuff. Jarvis singled out greetings cards as the thing she hated most about the phenomenon, describing them as 'meaning nothing except that you are too lazy to write to the woman who has done more for you than anyone in the world.' Jarvis spent the last few years of her life opposing the day she invented. She died penniless and alone while others made billions exploiting the memory of her dead mother to flog tat.

2. D. Eight million tons of plastic end up in our oceans each year. If that doesn't shock you then this statistic might: the number of microplastic molecules in the ocean surpasses the number of stars in the Milky Way.

3. A - EVERY 40 SECONDS.

4. A -THE NORTHERN LINE.

5. PART 1. Spring

5. PART 2. In first place is King's Cross, followed by Mile End and Tooting Bec.

6. B. The *Oxford English Dictionary* also lists deipnodiplomatic, which means 'inviting people round to dinner in order to patch up an argument.' They are both from the Ancient Greek *deipnon* – dinner. A deipnosophist is 'somebody who talks wisely over dinner' (aka someone you'd be advised to think carefully about before inviting).

7. A, B and **C** were all declared extinct in 2020, along with the Aragua robber frog, the Chiriqui harlequin frog, the Piñango stubfoot toad, the Simeulue Hill mynas bird, 17 different types of freshwater fish from a single lake in the Philippines, 32 of the orchid species native to Bangladesh and 65 North American plants. On the plus side, **D**, the European bison is one of several species whose risk factor was downgraded in 2020.

8. C. The term itself was coined in 1897 by a French psychologist, Theodule Ribot, who used it to refer to an 'insensibility... to pleasure alone', as distinct from analgesia, insensibility to pain.

9. B - BLOOD. Much of it goes to the UK. Should we be worried? Yes, because the blood is taken from paid donors, who are more likely to lie about their health than volunteers. Many of the donors are immigrants from Mexico. Mexican blood isn't the problem, it's the targeting of the most desperate donors and the risks that go with that.

10. A. The oldest sex dolls were probably made in the 17th century by lonely sailors on long journeys. The human sex drive seems to snap up anything that can be prostituted to suit its own purposes: the dildo is likely to have been invented a good 15,000 years before the wheel.

ANSWERS | ROUND 83

83. ODD ONE DOWN IN ONE (P. 190)

They all drank their own urine apart from E (Mike Nichols), who drank someone else's.

A – Bear Grylls. The survival expert has often drunk his own pee on his own tv show 'Man vs. Wild'.

B – Hippocrates. The Greek physician believed urine boosted the body's immune system.

C – Jim Morrison. The Doors' frontman drank his own pee while on an LSD-induced spiritual quest in the Mojave Desert.

D – Keith Richards drank his pee in the 1970s as part of a failed detox cure. (It's possible that the widdle of a diehard rocker like Keef contained quite a quantity of alcohol and drugs, rendering rehab futile.)

E – Mike Nichols, film director. In 1991 Nichols unwittingly drank urine after upsetting crew members on the set of *Regarding Henry*. According to actor John Leguizamo, Nichols made a habit of complaining that his cappuccino 'tasted like piss' during shooting, so they exacted revenge by urinating into the director's personal espresso machine. Leguizamo claimed that the unsuspecting director drank the brew, then commented, 'Now that's a cup of coffee.'

F – Sarah Miles. The British actress enjoyed a drop of the amber nectar for over thirty years. 'It tastes like good beer,' she told *The Independent* in 1998. 'You take it mid-flow every evening and morning. You just swig it down. It tastes fine.'

G – Steve McQueen. In the last stages of cancer, he lived on a diet off boiled alligator skin and apricot pits washed down with urine, as prescribed by his Mexican doctors. The flaw with such an approach, of course, is that if you get better, you can't know if it was down to the poached reptile, the pits or the piss.

H – John Lennon. All he was saying is give piss a chance. When Lennon was shot dead in 1980, his killer Mark Chapman was holding a copy of the book *The Catcher in the Rye* by…

I - J. D. Salinger, who also drank his own wee.

84. THICK AS OLD BOOTS PART II (P. 191)

1. **SCORE GOALS**
2. Tell the **DIFFERENCE** between the **TWO SIDES**
3. **SEE** it **ALL OVER** their **FACES**
4. **NO HIGHER PRAISE** than **THAT**
5. **IT IS LOST**
6. David Beckham was unsure into which religion his son should be... *christened.*
7. **I NEVER WILL**
8. Apparently, living in Italy was like living in a foreign country. (Ian himself denies having said anything so silly.)
9. That's the **ONLY WAY**
10. a **PIECE** of **PAPER, SAYING YOU WANT** to **LEAVE**
11. **MY RIGHT SOCK**
12. **ABOUT SEVEN**
13. **WON THE LEAGUE**
14. **GETTING OUT OF BED, AT THE END OF THE DAY**
15. Stuart was lucky enough to glimpse the **CARROT** at the end of the tunnel.
16. **AT THE TIME**
17. **BARCELONA**
18. **HE LOST US THE MATCH**
19. **VICE-VERSA**
20. The **FIRST 90** minutes

85. THE LAW'S AN ASS (P. 193)

1. **TRUE.** The 1313 Statute Forbidding Bearing of Armour is still current.
2. **FALSE.** The Treason Felony Act 1848 makes it an offence to do anything with the intention of deposing the monarch, but placing a stamp upside down does not quite fulfil this criterion. According to the Royal Mail, it is perfectly acceptable to stick any stamp on upside-down.

3. FALSE. The Tudor monarchs passed 'sumptuary laws' restricting what adornments people could make to their houses, or wear on their persons. Their purpose was basically to stop anyone displaying more bling than the King. For example, non-monarchs were prohibited from appearing at court wearing shirts with 'outrageous double ruffs', or hose of 'monstrous and outrageous greatness'. These laws were repealed by James I, who was quite fond of the odd monstrous and outrageous hose.

4. TRUE. This is an offence under the Salmon Act 1986.

5. TRUE. This is an offence under Transport for London Railway Byelaws.

6. FALSE. It has also been suggested that the Town Police Clauses Act 1847 contains a provision which allows a pregnant woman to relieve herself anywhere she likes, including in a policeman's helmet, but this is not so. Sadly.

7. TRUE. This is an offence under the Metropolitan Police Act 1839. Other offences covered include slaughtering cattle in the street, singing profane or obscene songs in the street; and wilfully and wantonly disturbing people by ringing their doorbells or knocking at their door.

8. FALSE. The Chelsea and Kilmainham Hospitals Act 1826 prohibited fraudulent claims to pensions that belonged to Chelsea Pensioners, but it was repealed in 2008.

9. FALSE. The Madhouses Act 1774 made it an offence to keep 'more than one Lunatick' without a licence for a madhouse but it has been repealed so you can keep as many as you like.

10. TRUE. According to the Licensing Act 1872, 'every person found drunk... on any licensed premises, shall be liable to a penalty'. It is also an offence under the Metropolitan Police Act 1839 for the keeper of a public house to permit drunkenness or disorderly conduct on the premises. Furthermore, under the Licensing Act 2003, it is an offence to sell alcohol to a person who is drunk. And to a Police Officer in uniform. Toughest penalties of all, of presumably, if you serve alcohol to a Police Officer in uniform who is also drunk.

86. WHEN IN ROME (P. 194)

1. TRUE. It is considered that the bowl limits oxygen flow and can cause the fish to go blind.

2. TRUE. The state of Victoria has a host of restrictions on loud noises, especially during certain times of day.

3. TRUE. A hand shandy will earn you a maximum 32 months in prison (where, presumably, you won't have much to do all day except lie on your bed, and…).

4. TRUE.

5. FALSE. The use of ketchup is, however, restricted in French schools, along with the very Gallic vinaigrette dressing and mayonnaise.

6. TRUE. In 2017, Pakistan banned people from celebrating Valentine's Day, because it is not a Muslim tradition and it focuses on love that isn't directed towards God.

7. FALSE. The maximum number of times a man may beat his wife in Arkansas is once a month.

8. TRUE. Sweeps have had protected status since medieval times but the laws were bolstered under the Third Reich, whose jurists clearly thought it might be handy to have a load of people licensed to peer down other people's chimneys.

9. TRUE. Since 2010, Iran has enforced a strict 'no mullet' policy. Other banned Western hairstyles include ponytails and 'long, gelled hair for men'. Sounds fair enough, really.

10. TRUE. Tibetan Buddhist monks may not be reincarnated without permission from the Chinese government. The State Religious Affairs Order No.4 was passed in 2007. Difficult to enforce, you might think.

87. WHO YOU GONNA CALL? (P. 195)

1. TRUE. A recording of the New Year's Day conversation was posted on Twitter by the North West Ambulance Service. The operator asks the man, 'Is the patient breathing?' to which he replies, 'OK, please, I'm just ringing because my partner has cheated on me.'

2. TRUE. The operator replied: 'This is the ambulance service, we can't advise you about eggs I'm afraid.'

3. TRUE. The call was made to Greater Manchester Police.

4. FALSE. (Could happen, though…)

5. TRUE. The 999 call was made to West Midlands Ambulance Service.

6. FALSE.

7. TRUE. West Midlands Ambulance Service also received a call from a man who 'couldn't walk after too much dancing'.

8. TRUE. The call was made to London Metropolitan Police in 2018.

9. TRUE.

10. TRUE.

11. FALSE.

12. TRUE.

13. TRUE.

14. TRUE.

15. TRUE.

88. FIGHTING MAD (P. 196)

1. TRUE. In October 1925 the shooting became a rallying cry for the Greeks, who invaded Bulgaria and occupied several villages. They were about to shell the city of Petrich when the League of Nations intervened. An international committee negotiated a ceasefire, but not before the misunderstanding had resulted in 50 deaths.

2. TRUE. In 1738 British mariner Robert Jenkins went to the House of Commons to show off a chunk of severed, decomposing ear he claimed that a Spanish coastguard officer had forcibly detached from his head seven years earlier. His stirring testimony caused the British to declare war on Spain; thus began the 'War of Jenkins' Ear'. In fact Jenkins' missing appendage merely served as a convenient catalyst for a conflict that had been simmering for ages between the two countries. The spat merged with the more expansive War of the Austrian Succession, which didn't end until 1748.

3. TRUE. In 1828 during a military coup a mob destroyed large parts of Mexico City. One of the victims of the rioting was a French pastry chef called Remontel, whose small café was trashed. Mexican officials ignored his complaints, so Remontel petitioned the French government for compensation. Ten years later it came to the attention of King Louis-Philippe, who was already furious that Mexico had failed to repay millions in loans and now demanded a further 600,000 pesos to compensate the pastry chef for his losses. When the Mexicans refused, Louis-Philippe declared war. In October 1838, his French fleet blockaded the Mexican city of Veracruz and began shelling the San Juan de Ulua citadel. A few minor land battles followed, killing up to 250 soldiers. Fighting ended in March 1839 when the Mexicans agreed to pay for the damaged café.

4. TRUE. In the mid-18th century, Britain couldn't get enough of those lovely new Chinese silks and varieties of tea, but China didn't really fancy anything the British Empire had to offer in exchange. The East India Company came up with the ideal solution – drugs. Sell loads of Indian opium to China, get the Chinese people addicted to it, and let the money roll in. China banned the opium trade in 1838, which struck Britain as being unsportsmanlike, so they went to war. This drug-dealing dispute is known as the First Opium War, because Britain tried to do it all over again fourteen years later.

5. TRUE. In 1325 tensions between the Italian city-states of Bologna and Modena were high. Modena's soldiers snuck into Bologna, stole an oak bucket from the main city well and filled it with loot. Bologna demanded the return of said bucket and when Modena refused, they declared war. Bologna lost the war and the bucket remains in Modena.

6. TRUE. The July 1970 match, between El Salvador and Honduras, was really a Franz Ferdinand moment – the final straw in a much longer story of building tensions. Poverty and land-grabs, fat-cat fruit growers and the migrations/expulsions of desperate peasants brought the beef between the two Central American countries to a point where only a bunch of irremediable fuckwits would suggest they ought to play a two-match World Cup qualifier against each other. But that's FIFA for you.

7. FALSE.

8. TRUE. Chariot racing wasn't for kicks, it was serious business, closely tied to Imperial politics. The Nika Riots of 532 AD occurred when supporters of two rival chariot teams started fighting. In the ensuing riot, half the city of Constantinople was destroyed, and an attempted coup resulted in thousands being massacred by the Imperial army

9. FALSE.

10. FALSE. In *Gulliver's Travels*, the eponymous hero gets entangled in a holy war over which end to open a hard-boiled egg. 'It is computed that eleven thousand persons have at several times suffered death rather than submit to break their eggs at the smaller end [...] Neither are any wars so furious and bloody, or of so long continuance as those occasioned by difference in opinion, especially if it be in things indifferent.'

89. DEATH BY IRONY (P. 197)

1. D. On 17 February 1673 the French dramatist collapsed on stage playing the title role of his play 'La Malade Imaginaire' (The Imaginary Invalid). He died a few hours after the play ended.

2. B.

3. C. The mordant actor died on Christmas Day 1946. He once told a reporter: 'Sleigh bells give me double nausea.'

4. A. Treves was widely known for his friendship with Joseph Merrick, dubbed the Elephant Man for his severe deformities. Despite his specialism Treves was unable to save his youngest daughter, who died from a perforated appendix in 1900.

5. B.

6. B. New Orleans Recreation Department was so proud that there had been no drownings that season at the city's swimming pools, they threw a huge poolside party. Moody's lifeless body wasn't discovered at the bottom of the pool until the party started winding down.

7. A.

8. C.

9. B. Her last role was in the film 'To Be Or Not To Be'.

10. D.

90. YOU'RE BARD (P. 200)

The genuine Shakespeare quotes are:

2. 'Henry IV Part I'

6. 'King Lear'

9. 'Troilus and Cressida

10. 'Coriolanus'

13. 'Henry IV Part I'

16. 'The Taming of the Shrew'

18. 'The Taming of the Shrew'

20. 'Macbeth'

21. 'Henry IV Part II'

23. 'Henry IV Part I'

91. EVIL, INC. (P. 202)

1. They sold the dodgy original elsewhere. At least 100,000 units of Factor VIII, a medicine to induce blood clotting, made their way to Asia and Argentina after Bayer stopped selling it in America.

2. SIEMENS. The company funded the Nazi Party during the 1930s and supported Hitler's regime once the war broke out. They had more than 400 factories operating throughout Germany by late 1944, many of which used Jewish labour.

3. C. It was the Czech Republic, in 2000.

4. D.

5. B.

6. C. The US company Purdue Pharma produces OxyContin, which at the time of writing was in part responsible for opioid addiction disorders among 2.4 million Americans. In 2006 Purdue Pharma pleaded guilty to marketing OxyContin 'with the intent to defraud or mislead'. At the time, the company paid a $600m fine – widely seen as a slap on the wrist for the Sackler family, whose wealth exceeds that of famed American dynasties such as the Rockefellers.

7. LIBOR. The financial scandal involving the fixing of interest rates on trillions of dollars' worth of financial products is a fiendishly complicated business, but in essence. according to one American commentator, it 'made Bernie Madoff look like a Girl Scout'.

8. B - BP. The Gulf of Mexico oil spill or Deepwater Horizon oil spill was the biggest of its type in the petroleum industry's history. In April 2010 a spill from a seafloor oil gusher lead to an explosion of BP's oil rig, Deepwater Horizon. The accident killed 11 men working on the rig and resulted in an oil spill that continued for over three months. An estimated 53,000 barrels were flowing into the Gulf of Mexico every day, killing over 82,000 birds, 25,900 marine mammals, 6,000 sea turtles and tens of thousands of fish, among others.

9. PART I. On 3 December 1984 around 45 tons of the gas methyl isocyanate escaped from an insecticide plant owned by the American firm Union Carbide. The gas drifted over the densely populated neighbourhoods around the plant, killing thousands of people and creating a panic as tens of thousands of others attempted to flee Bhopal. The final death toll was estimated at between 15,000 and 20,000. Half a million survivors suffered respiratory problems, eye irritation or blindness and other problems resulting from exposure to the toxic gas. Many were awarded compensation of a few hundred dollars. Substandard operating and safety procedures at the understaffed plant were the cause of the catastrophe.

9. PART II. *The Independent* made this claim exactly 30 years after Union Carbine had made its settlement, on 14 February 1989.

10. D.

92. TRUE OR FALSE? (P. 204)

1. TRUE. Bad eating habits accounted for a fifth of all deaths world-wide in 2017 and almost 70% of coronary heart disease-related deaths.

2. TRUE. In the early days of the drug Pergonal (whose name was derived from the Italian per gonadi, from the gonads), it took one nun ten days to collect sufficient urine for one dose of the treatment. In the mid-1980s, by which time widdle shipments of 70,000 litres were required to meet demand, the manufacturers Serono finally worked out how to synthesise the hormones, putting the nuns out of a job. A nephew of Pope Pius XII was an influential Serono board member, and the Vatican owned a 25% share in the company, although the impetus to create a mass market fertility drug came from Vienna-born Israeli medical student named Bruno Ludenfeld, whose interest was in part stimulated by the need to replace the six million lives lost in the Holocaust.

3. TRUE.

4. FALSE. Less than one tenth of the US annual military spend would solve world hunger. The UN reports that it would cost $30 billion to solve world hunger. Trump's 2018 military budget was $469 billion.

5. FALSE. 80% of the world lives on less than $10 (£8) per day.

6. TRUE.

7. FALSE. According to the World Resources Institute, 100 species die each day due to tropical deforestation.

8. TRUE. When plants are harmed, they release organic compounds called green leaf volatiles (GLVs). Besides emitting a unique odour, GLVs help form new cells to heal wounds faster, prevent bacterial infection and fungal growth – like an antibiotic – and produce compounds to prevent further damage.

9. FALSE. Britain's drug-death figure for 2020 was 3,284, highest in Europe, and five times higher than runner-up Turkey.

10. TRUE. Although that number might have just gone up a bit.

93. EGRETS, I'VE HAD A FEW (P. 205)

K is the red herring. **D** - the Japanese Sea Lion – is the most recent to become extinct; the last recorded sighting was in 1974. The sea lions were hunted in vast numbers for their skins to make leather, for their bones to be used in traditional medicines, for their fat to make oil for lamps, and even for their whiskers to make brushes and pipe cleaners. The naval battles of the Second World War decimated the last remaining colonies.

The other species, in order of extinction with the most recent first are:

F. Tasmanian tiger – the last known specimen died in Hobart Zoo in 1936. It was already rare or extinct on the Australian mainland before the arrival of British colonists, but a handful survived on the island state to the south of the Australian mainland. Hunting, disease, human settlers and their dogs soon ensured that they were completely wiped out.

J. Bubal hartebeest – the last known, a female, died in Paris in 1923. Despite its Biblical pedigree, this magnificent beast was no match for French hunters, who systematically wiped out the species for meat and sport.

E. Carolina Parakeet – the last known specimen died in Cincinnati Zoo in 1918. Killed in large numbers by farmers as pests, their feathers were also in demand as decorations in ladies' hats.

G. Passenger Pigeon – the last bird, a female named Martha who was being held in captivity at the Cincinnati Zoo, died in 1914. Considered a plentiful source of cheap meat, the birds were hunted on an industrial scale. In the 1870s up to 50,000 birds were killed every day over a period of five months. The last surviving flock of 250,000 birds was wiped out by one group of hunters in a single day in 1896.

C. Quagga – extinct in the wild by 1878, the last captive specimen died in Amsterdam in 1883. Valuable for their meat and hides, quaggas were heavily hunted after the Dutch settlers arrived in South Africa and found that they competed for forage with their domesticated animals.

H. Falklands Islands wolf – the last one was killed in 1876. The species became trapped on the islands during the last Ice Age when the bridge connecting them to the South American mainland melted. When the Falklands were settled by humans in the 1760s, the wolves were seen as a threat to livestock and were hunted. With no trees or forests on the island in which to hide, their fate was sealed very quickly.

I. Atlas Bear – the last one was reported to have been killed by hunters in 1870. Their demise was lengthy, traceable all the way back to the Roman Empire when the bears were hunted for sport or captured to battle gladiators or to execute criminals in a gruesome spectacle known as *damnatio ad bestias*. Numbers continued to decline through the Middle Ages when great swathes of forest in northern Africa were felled for timber.

B. Great Auk – the last were killed in 1844. The birds were highly prized for their down which was used as a stuffing for pillows and mattresses. Reportedly, the last pair were strangled to death in their nest by a pair of Icelandic hunters, while a third man stamped on the single egg that the female had been incubating.

A. Dodo – the last confirmed sighting was in 1662. Dodos were wiped out within just a few decades of the first recorded mention of the flightless bird in 1598. Up until that point the Dodo had led a charmed life with no predatory mammals, reptiles, or even large insects on its island habitat, and consequently no need to evolve natural defences. Innately trusting, they would waddle up to armed settlers, unaware that these strange visitors intended to kill them for fun.

BONUS ROUND

1. B.

2. C. At least we tried.

3. A. They dubbed it *walghvodel* – 'disgusting bird' – because of the toughness of its flesh.

4. C. The pets of the Dutch settlers weren't as choosy as their owners.

94. A PEST CALLED PEOPLE (P. 208)

1. CATS IN NEW ZEALAND. Dogs will rip your throat out, then eat your corpse. Snakes will asphyxiate you then escape and eat any mammal it finds. Pet parrots perpetuate a trade that destroys ecosystems and hamsters give you dangerous zoonotic diseases. But if you want to completely trash your ecosystem, get a cat. They are particularly damaging on islands that are home to species found nowhere else on earth – e.g. New Zealand, where birds and mammals evolved in the absence of cat-size predators. They nest on the ground and have no defences against an invasive species that plays with and then decapitates its victims. The first cats arrived there with early European explorers in 1769, helping control unwanted rats aboard voyaging vessels. Within 50 years, a huge feral cat population was established, dining on local wildlife. Since then cats have been responsible for the extinction of six endemic bird species and over 70 localised subspecies, as well as depleting New Zealand's populations of bird and lizard species.

2. CANE TOADS IN AUSTRALIA. Often cited as the example *par excellence* of an introduced species gone horribly wrong. Before 1935, Australia didn't have a single toad; today, around 1.5 billion of them have made Australia their home. Cane toads eat just about anything that they can fit in their big fat mouths - which is quite a lot, because they can grow to over 30 cm in length.

3. STARLINGS IN NORTH AMERICA. In 1890 Eugene Schieffelin, scion of a prosperous pharmaceutical enterprise and a noted bird enthusiast, liberated 60 starlings in New York's Central Park in the hope they would breed. Due to Schieffelin's other passion – William Shakespeare – it's often claimed that he released the starlings as part of a mission to introduce all the avian species mentioned in the Bard's works to the New World. This is tosh, but he deserves some stick, because the US is now home to an estimated 200 million European starlings, a particular problem at airports where the 'feathered bullets', as they're called, flock in great numbers. In 1960 they caused the most deadly bird strike in US aviation history, when the birds flew into the engines of a plane taking off from Boston and it crashed into the harbour, killing 62 people on board. Starlings also cost US agriculture about $1bn (£595m) annually by damaging crops and causing milk production to drop by stealing the grain being fed to cows.

4. GREY SQUIRRELS IN GREAT BRITAIN. Imported from North America in the 1870s as fashionable additions to English country estates, the grey squirrel is now the main threat to the survival of the native red population. Much bigger than red squirrels and capable of storing up to four times more fat, greys are better at surviving tough winter conditions. Rivalry between the species isn't the only problem. Greys are carriers of the Squirrel pox virus, against which the reds have no defence. Today more than 3.5m of the invasive rodents live in Britain. Luckily HRH Prince Charles has a cunning plan to reduce the numbers of these American interlopers by concealing oral contraceptives inside Nutella hidden around the country's forests.

5. JAPANESE KNOTWEED IN BRITAIN. The thug of the plant world arrived in the 1840s, brought from Japan by the famous German Philip von Siebold. It was cultivated in England as an exotic ornamental perennial. Its handsome foliage and popularity with bees meant that it quickly found favour with gardeners. By the early 1900s the influential English botanist Gertrude Jekyll was praising its 'quick growing ways'; something of an understatement. In the right conditions the plant can grow upwards of a foot per day and is capable of undermining building foundations, roads, walls, bridges, railways and flood defence structures. In Britain, estate agents, mortgage lenders and insurers flee from this pleasant-looking plant like rats from an inferno, as its mere presence can render a multi-million-pound property valueless.

PART TWO

7. C. Pig blood and human blood rank high among the favourite delicacies of rabies-carrying Brazilian vampire bats. More pigs = more vampire bats = more humans contracting rabies.

8. A.

9. B. There's some good in everyone. Even cane toads.

PART THREE: JUNKIE MONKEYS

10. A. Ming the clam had lived for 507 years – making him and her (clams are both genders) the world's oldest animal, until researchers opened him and her up to verify this, accidentally killing them in the process

11. B. Every year in the UK alone around 65 million prescriptions for antidepressants pass through the human body into sewage-treatment systems or waterways, thereby entering the digestive systems of wild birds. This is even having an effect on population levels, since male starlings are less attracted to, and show more aggression towards females who are hooked on anti-depressants.

12 B. Neonicotinoids are a highly controversial group of chemicals that have recently been the target of a near-total EU ban but they are still key ingredients of the most widely used pesticides in the world. Once fed with food containing these pesticides, bees keep coming back for more, in behaviour that looks remarkably like a human developing a fondness for tobacco...

95. THE ICE-PICK MAN COMETH (P. 211)

1. D.

2. B.

3. B.

4. C.

96. BRING OUT YOUR DEAD (P. 213)

1. B. Later historians have arrived at the same conclusion, and suspect it was smallpox or measles.

2. A. The Plague of Justinian killed an estimated 25 million people, almost 13% of the world's population. Later historians suggest that the poor harvests led to increased numbers of people moving around, in search of work and food, and thus aided the spread of the plague.

3. B.

4. A.

5. C.

6. Ethiopia, New Caledonia and Laos. And since there were reports of plague from nearby Egypt, Australia, Thailand and Burma, those three countries were very lucky.

7. C.

8. B. They were all volunteers – incentivised by the fact that the prison was already in the grips of a plague outbreak – and a number of those in the control group died. Haffkine also tested the vaccine on himself beforehand – and his discovery saved up to 4 million lives.

9. C.

97. COVIDIOCY (P. 216)

1. C
2. F
3. J
4. D
5. B
6. H
7. I
8. G
9. E
10. A

98. POP BITCHES (P. 218)

1. D.
2. JAMES BLUNT
3. C.
4. C.
5. A.

6. **B.**

7. **D.**

8. **'STRANGLE HIM.'**

9. **D.**

10. **B.** (**A** was Noel's comment on Kaiser Chiefs and **D** was his broadside against NME journalists.)

99. MIND THE GAP (P. 220)

1. The answer is **B.** The 42 richest people in the world hold about as much wealth as the poorest half of the world, or 3.7 billion people.

2. **SWITZERLAND**, with each adult worth, on average, £413,000 ($513,000), has the richest. The poorest are in **SOUTH SUDAN**, with GDP per capita at $246.

3. According to the World Bank, **SOUTH AFRICA** is the world's most unequal country for income distribution. The top 1% of South Africans own 70.9%% of the nation's wealth while the bottom 60% of South Africans collectively control only 7% of the country's assets (according to 2018 figures). **UKRAINE** is currently the country with the most equal distribution of wealth, closely followed by Slovenia and the Czech Republic.

4. The answer is **ITALY.** The home of Dante and co. is the top scorer in the reading difficulty stakes, with a rate of 27.9%, closely followed by Spain at 27.7%, and then France at 21.7. Finland has the lowest rate – 10.6%, followed by the Slovak Republic at 11.7.

5. **ICELAND** came top, joint with Norway. **SOMALIA**, was bottom, joint with the Central African Republic.

6. **B.** So that's 4140 doctors for a population of 41 million.

7. **ANY TWO WILL DO**, as they all have a GDP lower than Jeff's estimated £84.5 billion ($105 billion) personal price tag. Yes, it's a points giveaway! Just as well because Amazon won't be giving you any freebies.

8. 11,612. (Two points for 12,000, one point for 11,000.) To give you some context, the USA as a whole has one billionaire for every 559,000 citizens.

ANSWERS | ROUND 99

9. $82,200 (£66,161). 5 points for $82k; 3 points for $83k; 1 point for $81k or $84k.

10. D. At a value of £89.1 billion ($110.8 bn) in July 2018, Google would be the 16th largest economy in the world after Mexico (£98.4 bn /$1223.3 bn) and just ahead of Indonesia (£82 bn/$102 bn).

ANSWERS TO BACK COVER QUESTIONS

1. At what age does the human brain start to deteriorate?

At 27. A recent study of mental agility in 2,000 healthy people aged between 18 and 60 concluded that the first measurable signs of decline in areas like processing speed and visual puzzle-solving appeared in the late twenties. However, the researchers also found that other areas of brain function, such as vocabulary, improved with age. So even if you can't find the milk aisle in your local supermarket, you will be able to vent your frustration on a passing employee with gratifying eloquence.

2. How many press-ups does it take to burn off one Creme Egg?

A lot. To be more specific, a person weighing 70 kg would need to do around 300 press-ups in 15 minutes to burn off a single egg.

3. When will the sun go out?

In 5 billion years. Not a minute too soon.